COP 4

Benyo, Richard.

The Masters of the marathon.

Atheneum, 1983

242 p. : ill. ;

1.Marathon runnin 2.Runners(Sports)

The Masters of the Marathon

The Masters of the Marathon

RICHARD BENYO

EXECUTIVE EDITOR, *Runner's World*

INTRODUCTION BY ERICH SEGAL

Atheneum

New York   1983

LIBRARY OF CONGRESS CATALOGING IN PUBLICATION DATA

Benyo, Richard.
  Masters of the marathon.

1. Marathon running—History.   2. Runners
(Sports)—Biography.   I. Title.
GV1065.B46   1983   796.4'26 [B]   82-73028
ISBN 0-689-11340-4

Published simultaneously in Canada by McClelland and Stewart Ltd.
Composed by American–Stratford Graphic Services Inc.,
    Brattleboro, Vermont
Manufactured by Fairfield Graphics, Fairfield, Pennsylvania
Designed by Mary Cregan
First Edition

FOR DREW,
who knows what it takes to get there—
and what it takes to get back.

Contents

Introduction by Erich Segal   ix

1. THE MARATHON—*How it All Began*   3
2. SPIRIDON LOUES: *Pheidippides Junior*   15
3. CLARENCE DeMAR: *Against the Odds*   29
4. JOHNNY KELLEY (THE ELDER):
   The Mayor of Boston   53
5. JIM PETERS: *Time Tripper*   63
6. EMIL ZATOPEK: *Triple Play*   79
7. JOHNNY KELLEY (THE YOUNGER):
   Constant Companion   97
8. ABEBE BIKILA: *The Tragedy of Excellence*   119
9. DEREK CLAYTON: *Mister 2:08*   129
10. FRANK SHORTER: *Distant Drums*   143
11. BILL RODGERS: *Everybody's Brother*   163
12. WALDEMAR CIERPINSKI: *The Shadow Mask*   177
13. TOSHIHIKO SEKO: *Ninji Runner*   191
14. GRETE WAITZ: *The Reluctant Mother*   201
15. ALBERTO SALAZAR: *The Eternal Rookie*   221
   Suggestions for Further Reading   241

Introduction

Marathon madness is a totally modern phenomenon. In Greek antiquity (to which everyone loves to hark to give a classy patina to their athletic endeavors) Pheidippides was literally a nobody. The real superstars were men like Koroibus, Phyallos and Astylos.

Don't panic if these names are unfamiliar—they were all sprinters. For to the Greeks this was the only event that really counted. In fact, they actually despised distance runners. Two epigrams from the *Greek Anthology* will demonstrate:

> *He was such a plodding runner that he finished eighth*
> *—in a field of seven!*
> *The man was such a slowpoke that the janitor*
> *locked him in the stadium—he thought he was a statue!*

Pheidippides, as Rich Benyo indicates, had the social status of a telegram. If they'd thought much of his achievements, the Greeks would have at least left him an epigram or two.

Why, one may well ask, did they think so little of us distance men? To begin with, because we *were* so little—nay, scrawny. Bill Rodgers is cute, make no mistake, but he's not the stuff of which Greek statues are made. Sprinters on the other hand, look really good on pedestals. Also, one of the basic tenets of Greek wisdom—and it was carved on the temple at Delphi, where games second only to those at Olympia were held—was: nothing in excess. The first recorded Olympics had as its only event the 200-meter sprint. It was not till half a century later that the 400 was added to the schedule—and yet another quarter-century until the final running contest, a "grueling" 4,800 meters was deemed worthy of a spot on the Olympic program. Anything longer was regarded as . . . excessive.

One may also ask why, in this supersonic automobilized age, there should suddenly be a mania for distance running. Why, for example, do more people now run the New York marathon than used to watch it? Some years ago I offered the following theory: There has been an outbreak of what I would call the Pheidippides Complex, a psychic condition based on the myth that the first marathon runner actually dropped dead when he finished. Physical fitness buffs—and here again we differ from the Greeks, who never exercised a muscle that wasn't visible to the naked eye—are obsessed with their cardiovascular condition. Dr. Tom Bassler has gone so far as to claim that anyone who completes the marathon distance has immunized himself from heart attack. This remains unproven, but I venture it is taken as gospel by every jogger in the world. Thus to run 26 miles—officially—is to cheat death, out-Pheidippides Pheidippides.

I have also come to think that this accounts for the irrational abuse heaped on runners-in-training by drivers in passing. Wouldn't you hate sitting opposite Ponce de León if you were drinking water and he, his new-found Youth Juice (a form of ERG, no doubt)?

I also note that among marathoners the focus seems to have shifted from achieving some magic time (in my Boston heydey it was breaking three hours), to simply finishing. Again, the Pheidippides Complex. Death can be whipped, even at 4:49.

Benyo quotes Frank Shorter as saying that marathon-mania didn't reach fever pitch till after the '76 Olympics, and he may well be right. The distance certainly wasn't in vogue when I wrote *The Games* in 1967. This 20th-Century-Fox epic (based loosely on Hugh Atkinson's novel) told the tale of four marathoners from disparate corners of the earth: a Limey, an aborigine, a Commie, and a preppie—all striving for Olympic gold. Even the fact that Ryan O'Neal played the preppie couldn't save this cinematic entry from dying at Heartbreak Hill. Indeed, during the shooting, when I told Ryan that I actually had run a whole marathon (not just 200 yards for the camera), he remarked politely, "you must be an animal." It was, I think, meant as a compliment. Indeed, nowadays Ryan and Farrah run religiously.

Which is another point: Distance running is co-ed. Long before the female harrier won the right to compete against the opposite sex, we were already experiencing the rare joy of running *with* them. *Pace* Christopher Marlowe:

Come jog with me and be my love
And we shall make our pulses move
Why bother acting Casanovic?
Love's more healthy when aerobic.

But the *embourgeoisement* of distance running, and even its commercialization by the track-shoe makers, clothing magnates, etc., do not diminish its unique beauty. And the proliferation of four-hour marathoners does not reduce the crescent admiration for those supermen like Salazar who are fast (very fast) approaching the two-hour mark.

Rich Benyo has here chronicled the best and the fleetest. To his vivid account I dare add but one facet, one bit of certain knowledge that may add to our understanding of these unique men and women speeding at the very frontier of human capability.

Once upon a time, long long ago, I was working out with a legendary marathoner, indeed one of the stars chronicled in this book (no, not Shorter—I've dined out enough on him—but another member of the pantheon). A big championship was drawing nigh, and this star was the favorite. He was tapering, which explains why I had enough breath to converse. After a few miles I asked him the obvious:

"How do you think you'll do next week?"

"I don't know," he replied, and without false humility (we were alone in the woods) added, "I just hope I'll finish."

I was astounded. "Are you serious?"

"Hey," he answered gently (with a perceptible tinge of fear that nearly made me shiver), "every time I get out there, I'm always scared I won't go all the way."

I will never forget that moment of candor—and humanity. Because suddenly I realized that there is a bond that links the 4:15 marathoner with the "god" who finishes more than two hours earlier. They share a common enemy that frightens them and makes them brothers under the sweatbands.

ERICH SEGAL

The Masters of the Marathon

1.

THE MARATHON:
How It All Began

In an age when it is difficult to persuade most people to travel a block on their own two feet instead of in an automobile, it is a profound irony that tens of thousands of otherwise sane people are running marathons. Traveling 26 miles, 385 yards in an automobile can be deadly dull, but the distance seems to lure many people when you pin numbers on their chests and place the race in the context of a challenge—it is a way of making a definitive statement *for* individual achievement and *against* collective inertia.

Sociologists are having a field day analyzing the incredible growth of interest in marathon running in the United States during the late 1970s. Their interest is piqued further by the fact that what started as an American peculiarity has now spread to Europe, Australia, New Zealand, South Africa, and Japan.

Most people running the marathon have only a vague idea of its origin. When pressed, they will cite the popular legend of Pheidippides, the Greek soldier who ran from the Plains of Marathon to the city of Athens, gasped out the news of the unexpected Athenian victory over the Persians, and expired.

Most people accepted that legend much as parishioners accept legends of the saints, perhaps because legends are usually pretty clear-cut and inspirational and therefore easier to remember than the truth.

Actually, the "marathon" was invented by a Frenchman in 1894, and, although there really was a Greek named Pheidip-

3

pides, it is highly unlikely that he ran forty kilometers from Marathon to Athens just to drop dead at the front gates of his city. The year was 490 B.C., and the Greek city-states were being beaten into submission by Darius the Great of Persia (much later to be renamed Iran). Darius picked Athens as Persia's victim as a lesson to the rest of the Greek city-states because Athens was offering aid to city-states in Asia in revolt against the Persian Empire.

The plan Darius conceived was a brilliant one. He would make a show of landing nearly thirty thousand troops on the Plains of Marathon, lure the Athenian army out to do battle in the open, and then land another force behind the city to take it while its army was occupied.

Battles in those days were cumbersome affairs. Landing thirty thousand men takes a great deal of time, so the Athenians had plenty of time to bring their ten thousand troops up to face the Persians across less than a mile of open space. The Athenian army was composed of about nine thousand hoplites together with an additional one thousand hoplites from nearby Plataea. Hoplites were the heavy infantry of the period.

Realizing their plight, the Athenians sent Pheidippides, one of their *hemerodromoi,* or "all-day runners," to lobby for aid at Sparta. Sparta was some one hundred and forty miles of bad road away. The *hemerodromoi* were trained to run great distances, carrying messages between cities and between different flanks of armies in battle.

We have Pheidippides' name as the messenger sent to Sparta from the historian Herodotus: ". . . first, before they left the city, the generals sent off to Sparta a herald, one Pheidippides, who was by birth an Athenian, and by profession and practice a trained runner. . . . He reached Sparta on the very next day after quitting the city of Athens."

Now it seems phenomenal that Pheidippides could run one hundred and forty miles in one day. But what Herodotus says is that Pheidippides left Athens one day (probably first thing in the morning) and arrived in Sparta the very next day (before sundown?). That means he was underway about thirty-six hours. For a trained runner, the feat is not inconceivable. In 1981, at the famed Western States 100, which is a 100-mile footrace through the Sierra Mountains from Squaw Valley to Auburn in California, the co-winners (one of them over forty years of age and with a full-time job) completed the race, at that high altitude, in just over sixteen hours. Pheidippides' trip to Sparta is, therefore, quite within reason.

Once at Sparta, however, Pheidippides encountered a problem. The Spartans were willing to send help, but, because of their religious beliefs, they could not leave for battle until the next full moon. That was five days away. Pheidippides therefore returned to Marathon and rejoined the army.

Things quickly began to happen. The Greek general, Miltiades, gave the command to charge. This the Persians, who felt themselves sufficiently strong to decide when the battle should take place, had not expected. The ten thousand Greek hoplites charged across the plain. Although heavily armored, they moved swiftly, for part of their physical training was to run four-hundred-yard sprints in full armor. By the time the Persians organized their deadly archers, the Athenians were among them, hewing and hacking. In a relatively short battle, the Persians lost 6,400 men and quickly withdrew. The Greeks lost a mere 192.

Word of victory was sent to the anxious citizens of Athens. It is almost certain that the messenger, probably another *hemerodromos,* made it safely. A trip of just over twenty miles was virtually a Sunday stroll to the *hemerodromoi.*

In his 1967 book, *Greek Realities,* Finley Hooper of Wayne State University put the legend into its proper perspective:

A story about a young man who ran from Marathon to Athens and shouted "Nike" ("Victory") before falling dead first appeared in the literature about 600 years after the battle. This is of course the basis for the Marathon run in the Olympic Games. The story does not appear in the writings of Herodotus, however, and this argues against its truth, for Herodotus liked a good story and it is unlikely that he would have missed this one.

The legend of the dead messenger was further enhanced by the English Romantic poet Robert Browning in his 1879 poem "Pheidippides":

So, when Persia was dust, all cried "To Akropolis!
Run, Pheidippides, one race more! the meed is thy due!
'Athens is saved, thank Pan,' go shout!" He flung down his shield,
Ran like fire once more: and the space 'twixt the Fennel-field
And Athens was stubble again, a field which a fire runs through,
Till in he broke: "Rejoice, we conquer!" Like wind through clay,
Joy in his blood bursting his heart, he died—the bliss!

The legend was so enticing that, as plans began to be formed
in the early 1890s to revive the Olympic Games, a Frenchman
named Michel Breal offered a silver cup as a prize for the winner
of a special race that would be run to celebrate the victory at
Marathon and Pheidippides' legendary run.

The Greeks were not the only people in history who used a
specialized long-distance runner to carry their messages. The
long-distance runner has been—and still is—in evidence in many
societies, in many cultures, in diverse parts of the world.

In Hawaii, there was a caste of hard-working runners known
as the *kykini,* or king's messengers. In Tibet, there is a sect of
monks who travel great distances, at great altitude, by running;
they use a form of self-hypnosis to endure the arduous journeys.
And in northern Mexico, near the border of the United States,
dwell the Tarahumara Indians. Though they are a destitute people to whom a scrawny chicken cooked in a pot and shared by a
dozen family members is like a Thanksgiving Day feast, a people
whose mortality rate is one of the highest in the world, the Tarahumara engage in casual running games that would put to
shame—and force into early retirement—any world-class
marathoner.

Amidst some of the most rugged and desolate landscape this
side of the moon, their ritual for passage to manhood requires a
boy to run one hundred miles between sun-up and sundown.
Moreover, the Tarahumara frequently play a game in which they
kick a wooden ball around the countryside. While one team tries
to keep the wooden ball moving, the other team tries to take it
away and move it somewhere else. These far-ranging games can
cover two hundred miles in two days.

The distance that captivates one person's imagination repels another. The 26-mile, 385-yard marathon distance is, to some degree, quite arbitrary. As a result, there is much heated discussion as to why it has become almost sacrosanct while distances such as 20 miles or 100 kilometers (62 miles) are not run with such reverence.

The 20-miler, it seems, is too short to offer maximum challenge, whereas the 50-miler or the 100-kilometer race is so long that the factor of speed almost becomes secondary to strategy and pacing.

There are various theories as to why the 26-mile, 385-yard distance is perfect as a challenge. One is grounded in anthropology. In man's prehuman stage of evolution, his hunting territory was marked by a ten-mile radius, so that on a typical day he could scour the territory up to that distance from home and comfortably return in the same day, a twenty-mile trip in all. This out-and-back twenty-mile journey was supposedly imprinted on the human genes after many thousands of generations, and the body reacts even today to those genes, signaling when it is taxed beyond twenty miles. Hence the tremendous effort required to get through the final 10 kilometers of a marathon.

The physiological explanation is much more direct. After about eighteen miles of effort, the human body has expended its ready stores of glycogen, a substance that comes from carbohydrates and is stored in the body to provide fuel to the working muscles. When the readily available supply of glycogen is exhausted, the body must turn to the "hidden" supplies in the liver and muscles, thus depleting emergency stores and putting great pressure on the muscles to perform on their own with little cooperation from the rest of the body systems. While not a great deal of energy is required to free readily available glycogen for muscle use, freeing liver and muscle glycogen requires huge amounts of extra effort on the part of the body. It is this depletion of glycogen stores that accounts for those tremendous struggles in the latter stages of a marathon when the mind tries to force an exhausted body onward. Physiologically, the body is running on empty. And, for some, that is where the challenge lies—pushing the body well beyond its natural limits.

Actually, the ten-mile radius theory is merely conjecture. Whether or not such a trait could be imprinted on the genes of all nationalities, races, and cultures and both sexes around the world, just because some long-ago tribe functioned that way, is highly arguable. The glycogen theory, on the other hand, has a great deal of scientific basis. Even so, a well-trained runner can push the threshold of glycogen depletion back beyond the eighteen-mile mark through selected workouts and through certain dietary practices that increase glycogen stores.

The magic of the 26-mile, 385-yard distance and the challenge it offers seems to have a much simpler basis: extreme distance, backed by the legend of Pheidippides. As such, it represents that almost superhuman level where a brilliant meshing of speed and endurance is demanded if one is to do it well. And, of course, it has its own identity: *Marathon.*

The 26-mile, 385-yard distance has become the official length of the marathon, whether or not it is the distance from Marathon to Athens. Today it has a certain sanction the world over. The distance seems long even if driven in a car. At the speed limit of 55 mph, barring any traffic signals, it takes almost a half hour to cover. It seems so long by car, in fact, that many marathoners refuse to drive the course before they run it lest it become too formidable psychologically.

No other specific distance is given its own name. Some race promoters call their 10-kilometer events "mini-marathons," but that is a misnomer, because there is no such thing as a "mini-marathon"—either the race is a marathon or it isn't. On the other hand, distances beyond the marathon are merely lumped into one catch-all word: ultramarathons. In them, the course can vary from 30 miles to distances measured in days, the longest being six-day races. The name is in any case based upon *marathon,* a term everyone grasps without additional explanation.

An advantage of the marathon over other long-distance races historically was that, although running events beyond five miles were not publicized, the marathon managed to sneak into the press—perhaps only as an abnormality, it still made the papers. And they spelled its name correctly.

In the Olympic Games, the marathon has always been something of an abnormality, an appendix. It was not certain, really, if it would remain in the Olympics following its inclusion in the first modern Olympics in 1896. In 1896, it was actually treated as a special event, with its own separate prize.

Other running events in the Olympic Games are all contested on the track—except for a brief period when cross-country was included. The marathon, which ranges far and wide over the countryside before ending in the Olympic stadium, is usually held as the final event of the games.

The marathon is a difficult event for the media to cover, and, to those not deeply interested in the strategies and subtleties of the sport, it is a very boring event to watch. The exception is the finish, with its human drama of the winner valiantly moving across the finish line while his body is screaming for surcease. There are almost never races "to the wire" in a marathon; all the moves that have allowed the winner to break the tape are executed miles back with strategic surges, judicious pacing, and training that began many months before.

In the early days of the modern Olympics, the most media coverage one expected of the marathon was a photo of the winner breasting the tape, often looking like an escapee from a death camp. No spectator could imagine what type of person would want to run such mind-boggling distances. There was sympathy between the spectators and the marathoners, but no feeling of identity.

In the United States—which has been known for embracing abnormalities as a way of life—marathoning has long existed, certainly. Many of the spectators who had gone to Athens for the 1896 Olympic Games were from the Boston area, and they returned home fired by the drama of the marathon. Within a short time they had put together their own marathon, and, although it started in a small way and stayed small for years, its persistence eventually made it a sporting tradition. Although few people could identify with the crazy runners who gathered in Boston in April for their 26-mile run, the Boston Marathon became an annual fixture in the sports pages of newspapers across the country.

A sports-page reader who in April opened his newspaper and saw the picture of a small knot of men in their underwear running through the streets and along public roads on their way to Boston would snicker and laugh to himself as he sipped his coffee. Subconsciously he probably felt a little twinge of delight. Spring was here because all those nuts in Boston were running themselves silly again. The news of the Boston Marathon was comparable in importance to the heralding of the seasons, and served much the same purpose as the Punxsutawney (Pennsylvania) groundhog, whose shadow would indicate whether or not we were going to have another six weeks of winter before spring broke. Ironically, the Boston marathoners often relied on the groundhog to learn whether that year's Boston Marathon was going to be a hot one or not.

To virtually all Americans, the marathon was something that belonged only in the Olympic Games and (in America) indigenous to Boston. And that was it. The marathon had nothing to do with them.

Until 1972.

There were three Olympic Games in the 1960s, and in each of them the marathon was won by an Ethiopian: Abebe Bikila won in 1960 and 1964, and Mamo Wolde won in 1968. The African nations then were producing some very gifted distance runners, and their talents reached all the way down to the 1500-meter race, which Kenya's Kipchoge Keino won in 1968, setting an Olympic record in the process.

The marathon had not been won by an American since the controversial race in 1908, when British officials had helped a dazed Dorando Pietri across the finish line, thereby depriving him of the gold, which was then awarded to John J. Hayes, an American. Another American, Thomas J. Hicks, had won the gold in the marathon in the 1904 Olympic Games. Sixty-four years was quite a drought for the United States team.

There were changes in the wind, however.

Americans were becoming more fitness-conscious. During John F. Kennedy's relatively short administration, an awareness of fitness was awakened, symbolized by JFK's fifty-mile walks. In 1968 another milestone was reached in the growing involvement of Americans in a fitness movement. An Air Force doctor, Kenneth Cooper, published *Aerobics,* which set out a fitness-points program with jogging as its backbone. Thousands of

Americans began jogging regularly, following Ken Cooper's program of moderate but regular exercise.

Then, in 1972, at the Munich Olympics—an Olympics marked by dark politics, bloodshed, and death when Palestinian terrorists stormed the Olympic Village and took Israeli athletes hostage, later killing eleven of them—an irrevocable movement began. For the first time in history, an Olympic Marathon was being covered from start to finish, live and in color, by American television.

That marathon was won by an American, Frank Shorter, a graduate of Yale who until a year or so before had shown very little interest in the race—who, in fact, used to throw good-natured taunts at one of his professors, Erich Segal, when he encountered him at the Yale track running twenty-mile workouts in preparation for his perennial trip to the Boston Marathon.

Shorter's precise, very controlled, fluid stride as he made his way through the streets of Munich also made its way into the living rooms of millions of Americans. The impact of an American victory was further buttressed by Shorter's teammate, Kenny Moore, who took fourth place.

Suddenly there developed an awareness that the arcane marathon was accessible to mere American distance runners: the race was not reserved for dimly apprehended foreign athletes. The number of marathons in America increased, as did the number of participants. At first it was only a ripple. But a ripple that was merely a hint of what was to come.

Shorter's accomplishment cannot be minimized on the level of individual sports achievement. Neither should it be minimized as a catalyst for what would become one of the most unique phenomenons in sport. His victory at Munich had symbolic meaning for an America poised at the starting line. So much so that, if you were to ask some young runners "who invented the marathon?", they'd answer: "Frank Shorter."

Four years later in 1976, there was a real consciousness in America of what the event entailed. That year the Boston Marathon found it necessary to set qualification times for admission because the field threatened to outgrow the fragile two-lane country roads on which it started (and at which point it was most jammed). Frank Shorter, Billy Rodgers (American record holder at 2:09:55), and the lanky Seattle runner, Don Kardong, went to the Montreal Olympics as the U.S. marathon team.

In a bit of unfortunate prophecy, Shorter confided to TV commentator and former teacher Erich Segal before the race that, if it rained, he'd lose. Shorter likes relatively warm, even hot, marathons. Montreal provided humid and damp weather with a bit of a drizzle, and, although he was in excellent condition, Shorter was beaten by East German Waldemar Cierpinski. Shorter took second place, with Kardong fourth—another good American showing. The event again served to catapult interest in the marathon to new peaks.

As though the Olympic Marathon were not enough, the New York City Road Runners Club, which had been holding a club marathon each October within the confines of Central Park, decided that the Bicentennial was a good excuse to move the marathon into the streets of the city. The club formulated a course that began on Staten Island, wound through all five boroughs, and ended amid the flaming fall foliage of Central Park at the door of Tavern on the Green, a popular restaurant.

Thousands signed up for the chance to run through the streets of New York City in their underwear. As though to make up for his dismal showing at the Olympic Marathon, Bill Rodgers promptly laid claim to the New York City Marathon crown (he would win it four years in a row, 1976–79) and began one of the most impressive—and consistent—road racing careers ever seen.

Whereas previously the only place to read about road racing (and especially about marathoning) was in the pages of the long-distance runner's bible, *Runner's World,* the media now began to take notice of marathoning and of the running boom. Once the momentum was established, the media that had ignored running began to smother it with attention.

From then on, in America marathoning would be the media's superstar. A sport where very private people made very private attempts at excellence would become an arena in which meandering thousands would create and fulfill their private dreams in public drama.

*   *   *

There is a theory in the world at large that when a trend begins in America—whether it is hoola-hoops, Frisbees, surfing, or rock 'n' roll—it will eventually be embraced like a cute puppy by the rest of the world. Marathoning has been no exception. In recent years, the sport has become a passion of people in virtually every major nation in the world.

Marty Post, who keeps statistics for *Runner's World* with an in-house computer, could not dispense with the services of this sophisticated tool; without it the magazine would have to hire an entire monastery to keep track of marathoning's growth. Until 1977, when he stepped down as the magazine's editor in order to pursue a writing career, Joe Henderson kept all marathoning statistics (for the entire world) on a pile of 3x5-inch cards that were cross-referenced by name, performance for that year, site of performance, age, and state or country of residence.

The transition from Joe Henderson's file cards to Marty Post's computer is perhaps the most vivid indication of the sport's growth. Here is a sampling of statistics:

	1977	1978	1979	1980	1981	1982
Marathons in US	235	291	325	337	350	390
US marathoners	40,000	55,000	75,000	90,000	100,000	112,000
Sub-3:00 US males	5,500	7,300	10,500	13,000	15,000	9,600
Sub-3:00 US females	29	53	126	190	300	265
Boston entries	3,000	4,800	7,866	5,400*	7,000	6,780
NYC entries	5,200	9,316	11,000	15,000	16,000	15,906

* *Decrease due to institution of more stringent qualification requirements following 1979 Boston Marathon.*

For once, numbers speak louder—and better—than words.

Behind the numbers are thousands and thousands of runners, faithfully putting in their thirty, forty, fifty and more miles a week, initially going the distance, then bettering their times. The faces in the crowd are individuals who, in most cases, have arranged to step out of the march of their daily lives to become *athletes,* participants in a great challenge.

But beyond those merely faithful and dedicated, there is in the marathon a special place—at the front of the pack—where the air is rare and the performances and consistency often stagger the imagination. Here are the runners who awe the scientists, and who serve as guinea pigs for the new breed of sports-medicine doctors. Routinely they run faster and better than anyone else in the world. Occasionally, they run even beyond themselves, either setting records that astound the public, or pulling themselves together on a certain day in history, against the best marathoners in the world, to overcome the distance *and* the competition.

There are ready phrases for these people: the cream of the crop, the cutting edge, the best of the lot. They are the people who, from the event's inception in 1896 until today, may be considered the Masters of the Marathon.

This book is about those rare and special people.

2.

SPIRIDON LOUES:
Pheidippides Junior

The first modern Olympics at Athens in 1896, it would be safe to say, was a resounding success because of the invention of the marathon—and because of the victory of the home team in that event.

The 1896 games themselves had not been brought into being without a struggle. Baron Pierre de Coubertin—the Frenchman who thought up the idea of an Olympic revival—was often frustrated by the negative responses of leaders from many nations who should have supported him, and his idea was almost stolen from him at the moment of its realization.

The Baron had dedicated his life—and his health and his fortunes—to the idea of promoting peace between nations through friendly competition, pulling meanwhile his native France up by its athletic bootstraps by encouraging what he called "muscular Christianity." De Coubertin was inspired by the British practice of heavily promoting sports in schools and universities and by the exuberant affinity of American schoolboys for team sports.

The Baron's persistence overcame obstacles that would have deterred anyone with more common sense. As the nineteenth century drew to a close, he had convinced Greece (as the cradle of Olympic competition) to host the first of the modern Olympic Games. He had hoped to use Mount Olympus, but the site proved unsuitable to modern requirements and Athens was chosen instead. As the enthusiasm among the Greeks increased and they developed plans for the games, they began to ignore de

Coubertin, going so far as to try to disassociate him from the very concept of a modern Olympics. They envisioned it as a wholly Greek enterprise with no share of the glory going to a Frenchman. Ultimately the problem was resolved amicably and the Greeks turned their attention from making de Coubertin persona non grata to trying to raise the money needed to construct a suitable stadium and other facilities.

Commemorative stamps were commissioned and a public appeal was instigated. Together, the schemes raised only $165,000. Crown Prince Constantine, resorting to an exalted form of begging, then appealed to George Averoff, a shipping magnate and famed philanthropist whose largesse had been directed toward Greek educational systems. Averoff obviously liked the idea, because he agreed to finance the restoration of the Panathenaic Stadium, then over twenty-two hundred years old and in pitiful condition. The stadium, which seated seventy thousand, ultimately set Averoff back some $386,000. But between de Coubertin, the Greek royal family, and George Averoff, the modern Olympic Games finally began to take shape.

Despite the tenor of world politics at that time, with outright antagonism shown toward the games by some nations, benign disregard by others, and begrudging support by a handful, the event began to acquire an identity. Perhaps it is overly cynical to characterize it as such, but Olympiad I was the first and last innocent Olympics. There was about the games of 1896, despite political strife, a certain naive enthusiasm for the Olympic ideal. The Greek royal family was very enthusiastic about the games and throughout was intimately involved in bringing about their success. The organizers, although they lacked a model, attempted to be as fair and equitable as they could despite their obviously passionate partisanism. The crowds (and there were huge crowds) were, of course, partisan but were just as likely to burst into wild cheering for an American as for a Greek, if the performance was outstanding. And the athletes! They were a mixture of members of national teams and complete amateurs from college teams. Because this was the first Olympiad, nations who participated did not have selection processes by which they could pick their teams. Many teams came on their own nickel. James B. Connolly, a Bostonian attending Harvard, heard about the games and, being adept at the jumping events, wanted to enter. When he applied for a leave of absence from Harvard, Harvard turned him down, so Connolly dropped out of school, paid his own way to Greece, and only returned to Harvard many years later as a guest speaker after he had developed a reputation for his novels and stories of sea adventures.

Thus it was with a certain naiveté that the Greek rulers, the officials, the spectators, and the athletes began arriving in Athens to put de Coubertin's idea and ideals to the test.

Although we are first and foremost interested in the marathon, it is valuable to follow the competition at Athens in April of 1896, leading up to the starting gun at 2:00 P.M. on the tenth day of that month in order to get an appreciation of the atmosphere into which Spiridon Loues stumbled nearly three hours and twenty-four miles later.

A total of 311 athletes took part in the games, representing thirteen countries. Several of those countries (Australia, Bulgaria, Chile, Sweden, and Switzerland) had only one athlete entered. Greece had 230. The United States, according to some accounts, had 14 athletes; according to others, 13. In any case, the team that entered from the United States was not considered to be the cream of the crop. The powerful New York Athletic Club, which had a large percentage of the country's best athletes in track and field, voted to ignore the games. The team that left New York on March 20, aboard the *Fulda*, was composed of four Princeton men (Robert Garrett, shot-putter; Francis Lane, sprinter; Albert Tyler, pole-vaulter; and Herbert Jamison, miler), five members of the Boston Athletic Association (Tom Burke, sprinter; Thomas Curtis, hurdler; Ellery Clark, jumper; Welles Hoyt, pole-vaulter; and Arthur Blake, distance runner), and, going along as individuals, James Connolly (the outlaw Harvard undergrad), swimmer Gardner Williams, and two brothers, John and Sumner Paine, experts with revolvers.

The trip took the team past the Azores to Naples, where they boarded a train to cross Italy. They boarded another boat to get from Brindisi to Patras and then boarded yet another train to cross Greece. They arrived in Athens the day before the competition was to begin.

The Greeks were in a righteous frenzy of goodwill. Thomas Curtis wrote about the experience some years later: "We were met with a procession, with bands blaring before and behind, and were marched on foot for what seemed miles to the Hotel de Ville. Here speech after speech was made in Greek, presumably very flattering to us, but of course entirely unintelligible. We were given large bumpers of the white-resin wine of Greece and told by our advisors that it would be a gross breach of etiquette if we did not drain these off in response to the various toasts. As soon as this ceremony was over, we were again placed at the head of a procession and marched to our hotel. I could not help feeling that so much marching, combined with several noggins of resinous wine, would tell on us in the contests the following day."

Curtis's fears of doing badly were doubled when he entered his hotel and the proprietor inquired as to his specialty. When Curtis told him he was a hurdler, the proprietor went into gales of laughter. After he recovered, the proprietor told Curtis he felt it was the height of folly for a man to travel five thousand miles to take part in a senseless contest. Why, only that afternoon the Greek hurdler had gone through a practice session with a time that was absolutely unbeatable. This wasn't quite what the weary Curtis needed to hear, but he asked the proprietor what the time had been. The proprietor whispered to Curtis that the Greek champion had run nineteen and four-fifths seconds. Accepting the proprietor's condolences and his best wishes for Curtis to take second place, the American retired to his room. Curtis was used to running the 100-meter high hurdles in eighteen seconds flat.

The next day, April 6, was the 75th anniversary of Greek independence from Turkey, so the occasion was doubly important when, at 3:00 P.M., King George and Queen Olga arrived with Crown Prince Constantine, Prince George, Prince Nicholas, and Baron de Coubertin. After settling themselves, King George rose and announced: "I hereby proclaim the opening of the First International Olympic Games in Athens."

Although throughout Olympic history various sports have been contested (some of them only once), the showcase has always been track and field. So it was at Athens.

The first events were the three heats of the 100 meters. Although the only current American national champion entered was Tom Burke (in the quarter-mile), Americans took all three heats: Lane, then Curtis, then Burke.

In his 1975 book *History of the Olympics,* Dick Schaap relates a curious incident between Curtis and a Frenchman during the second heat that perhaps better than any other puts the upcoming marathon event in its proper perspective:

> Before his heat, Curtis noticed that one of his rivals, a short, stocky Frenchman, was wearing white kid gloves. "Why the gloves?" Curtis asked.
>
> "Aha," said the Frenchman, "zat is because I run before ze Keeng!"
>
> After the Frenchman failed to place before the King, Curtis asked him what events he had entered. "Ze *cent* meter and ze Marathon," said the Frenchman.
>
> The combination struck Curtis as a curious one. "How do you train for such different events?" the American asked.
>
> The Frenchman smiled. "One day I run a leetle way, vairy quick," he explained. "Ze next day, I run a long way, vairy slow."

The first final of the games was the hop, step, and jump, and the first Olympic champion in modern times was the Harvard outlaw, James B. Connolly, who handily won the event before fifty thousand spectators inside the stadium and an equal number sitting on the hillsides looking down on the activities.

Next came the discus which, with the marathon, was being contested in international competition for the first time in history. The event was supposedly a foregone conclusion, with the Greek champion, Paraskevopoulos, scheduled to win easily. After all, he had centuries of tradition on his side, and the discus was an event regularly contested in Greece. After seeing the other athletes warming up and preparing for their events, the Greeks were ready to concede the track and field contests to the British and the Americans, but they knew they were guaranteed a victory from Paraskevopoulos.

Bob Garrett of Princeton had been practicing at home with a discus he had had a friend make for him according to what he thought were the proper dimensions. When he arrived at the stadium, he found to his surprise that the real discus was much lighter and easier to handle than the crude object he'd been practicing with. He let go a throw that once and for all put Paraskevopoulos into the showers.

In the days that followed, Tom Burke won the finals of the 100-meter dash and the 400-meter run. Tom Curtis took the hurdles. W.T. Hoyt took the pole-vault. Ellery Clark won the jumps, both broad and high. Garrett repeated his discus success in the shot put. The only athlete who had been able to best the Americans in track and field was E.H. Flack of Australia, who was now living in England and competing for Great Britain. He handily won the 800-meter run and the 1500-meter race.

The Greeks were taking all of this in good spirits. Whenever one of the contingent from the Boston Athletic Association did well in an event, his teammates would let loose with a rousing cheer of "B! A! A! Rah! Rah! Rah!" The enthusiasm of the Americans matched that of the Greeks for the entire affair, and every time the Bostonians cheered, the Greeks cheered the Bostonians. In fact, the king repeatedly asked the Bostonians to repeat their cheer.

Yet underneath the goodwill of the Greeks was a rising disappointment in their performances. With more athletes competing than all the other countries combined, the only events they had won were the individual titles in rifle-shooting, fencing, and gymnastics. The ancient Olympics had been a Greek tradition, and that tradition was built on track and field, and even the expected Greek shoo-ins had been ousted. The Greeks were desperate for something to salve their pride.

Everything was going to hinge on the marathon, the event created by a Frenchman, inspired by a Greek legend created by an Englishman, but taken to heart by the Greeks with a devout passion.

The first Olympic Marathon is traditionally thought of as the first marathon ever run. In actuality, it was the third. Greece was also the home of the first two marathons.

Soon as the Greeks heard that a long-distance race would be included in the Olympic Games to commemorate their victory against the Persians at Marathon, they became excited beyond belief. Naturally they felt it a matter of pride that a Greek should win the event. Thus they immediately set about searching villages and cities alike for anyone capable of making a good showing.

The first marathon trial was held as part of the Pan-Hellenic Sport Celebration (the Greek national championships), and was open only to members of sporting clubs signed up to compete. The race was held on March 10, over the course that ran from the bridge at Marathon to the new Olympic stadium in Athens. A dozen club members took part. First place was taken by Harilaos Vasilakos in 3:18:00, second by Spiridon Belokas in 3:31:00, and third by Dimitrios Deliyannis in 3:33:00. Two weeks later, on the twenty-fourth of the month, an open race was conducted over the same course. This time there were thirty-eight entrants, and they were apparently a hardier group than the club runners, because their times were significantly better, a tribute to the Greeks' unabashed search for running talent wherever they could find it.

The winner of the open trials, a man listed only as Lavrentis, ran the course in 3:11:27; second place was taken by Ioannis Vrettos in 3:12:30, third by Eleftherios Papasimeon in 3:13:37, fourth by Elias Kafetzis in 3:15:50, and fifth by Spiridon (listed in some accounts as Spyros) Loues (Louis or Louys), a shepherd and water hauler, in 3:18:27.

On Sunday, April 10, as the sixteen Olympic competitors lined up on the far side of the bridge in Marathon before a crowd of several hundred, there were a dozen Greek runners and four foreigners. Spectators filled the Panathenaic Stadium to watch several finals while allowing the tension of the marathon to build to a frenzy as news was brought from messengers on horseback of the progress of the runners. The official Greek historian for the event summed up nicely what was riding on this contest:

"If only the Cup of Marathon would be gained by a child of the soil!" was the ardent wish of every Greek. All kinds of rewards were promised to the victorious champion, should he be a Greek. Some hotelkeepers had pledged themselves to give him board and lodging free of expense—some for a fixed term of years, some for his whole lifetime. Tailors, barbers, hatters offered their services for nothing.

Professionalism was already creeping into the Olympics, this time on the side of national pride.

Spiridon Loues, the fifth-place finisher in the open marathon trials, had been urged to enter the event by his former commanding officer in the Greek First Infantry Regiment, a Colonel Papadiamantopolous, who was a member of the Olympic Organizing Committee—and, incidentally, the man who fired the starting gun on that historic April 10. Papadiamantopolous recalled the frail-looking little soldier as having shown great spunk on forced marches. Loues was twenty-five years old, a classic dark-haired Greek with a fashionable and impressive mustache. He spent the two nights before the race on his knees praying. On the day before the race he fasted.

Before Colonel Papadiamantopolous fires his starting gun, while the seventy-thousand-seat stadium fills and the surrounding hills and roadsides crowd with spectators, let's pause a moment to examine the field—especially the four hardy foreigners who will attempt to defraud Greece of its finest moment in its own event in its own Olympic Games.

Three of the four invaders had placed first, second, and third three days previously in the 1,500 meters, but none of them had any previous experience at distances approaching the marathon. These three were:

Edwin Flack of Australia, running for Great Britain, who had alone broken the American stranglehold on track and field events by taking the 1,500 meters and winning the 800 meters the day before the marathon. After his win in the 800, in fact, Flack had not stayed around for the victory ceremony but had departed for Marathon where the long-distance competitors were to spend the night. At the time of the competition, he held the Australian record for the mile with a respectable time of 4:44, set in 1893.

Arthur Blake of the USA was runner-up in the 1,500 meters, and probably as close to being a distance runner as any of the trio.

Albin Lermusiaux of France, who finished third in the 1,500 meters, was the other entrant. He had little if any experience in long-distance running.

Of the foreigners, Gyula Kellner of Hungary was perhaps the

best qualified to shake the confidence of the Greeks. He had run a 40-kilometer time trial in three hours in Budapest to qualify to come to the Olympic Games, specifically to run the marathon. Forty kilometers is about 24.4 miles; his time for that distance made him theoretically the fastest man in the field at the marathon distance.

(An aside. Italy did not take part in the first Olympic Games. Had they done so, it is likely that the outcome of the marathon would have been different, because the Italians were then enjoying a distance-running craze, with most of the events contested at 50 kilometers—well beyond the Athens marathon distance.)

Now back to the bridge at Marathon. Watches of the officials, not to mention those of several hundred spectators and the medical personnel manning the "meat wagons" that will trail the field, are being consulted. The sixteen runners alternately paw the ground with their shoes, shake the tightness out of their arms, and glance nervously across the bridge, imagining what lies ahead of them on the road to Athens. Spiridon Loues does very little beyond look quietly down the road. He is ready. Colonel Papadiamantopolous raises his revolver solemnly, glances at the runners, and very professionally squeezes off the shot that is still being heard 'round the world hundreds of times each year.

The field was off in a rush, all running according to their adrenaline levels instead of according to their common sense. Within a few hundred yards, however, common sense took over and the pace settled in.

Perhaps out of naiveté, never having run the distance before, the Frenchman Lermusiaux took a commanding lead, completely dominating the first half of the race. His pace had an effect on the field, for some of the starters dropped out and were picked up and treated by the meat wagons. The starter, Papadiamantopolous, had gone to horse and was leapfrogging ahead so that he would be able to give a report to the king when the leader got within striking distance of the stadium.

Along the roadside, Greeks from villages miles away lined the course, pressing drinks of wine and pieces of food into the hands of any runner who felt the need for nourishment. At the halfway point, the order was Lermusiaux, Flack the Australian, and Blake of the United States. It looked like another bleak day for the host country, but that did not dampen the enthusiasm of the crowds. A tradition twenty-three centuries old was being revived.

When Lermusiaux ran through Karvati, the city in which an arch of triumph had been erected specifically for this event, he was so far in advance of the field and looked so confident that the townspeople pushed through the police line and placed a victory wreath upon his head. Such confidence by the spectators did nothing to dampen Lermusiaux's pace, and this was to be his undoing.

Outside Karvati, the course climbed uphill. The order was still Lermusiaux, Flack, Blake, followed by Hungary's Killner, Lavrentis of Greece, and the diminutive Spiridon Loues. As they ran through the village of Pikermi, Loues sipped some wine and kept on at his dogged pace, commenting to spectators that he would make his way to the front in his own good time. The hills and the distance got to the American, Blake, at twenty-three kilometers (23-K), and he dropped out. Flack was now closing on Lermusiaux, and Harilaos Vasilakos, the winner of the club trial marathon exactly one month before, moved into third. Soon they hit another series of hills, and now Lermusiaux suddenly tired and veered off the side of the road, where his handler lowered him gently to the ground and began giving him an alcohol rubdown in hopes of reviving him.

This scene may be visualized as a painting by Goya. The exhausted Lermusiaux, no doubt suffering from cramps and dehydration, lies prostrate on the side of the road, his handler working on him as though ministering to the wounded, while Flack moves on past, intent on his own discomforts and troubles. Eventually the game Lermusiaux would regain his feet. He seems actually to have revived, because he ran well for another eight kilometers.

Meanwhile, Spiridon had passed Vasilakos. Not much later, he caught the seemingly revived Lermusiaux, at thirty-two kilometers (32-K), and passed him. The move may have been the last straw, for now Lermusiaux collapsed and allowed himself to be transported to the stadium by cart. A mere kilometer later, Loues moved around the faltering Flack. The two raced each other for some four kilometers, with Flack sticking to within twenty meters of Loues before the shepherd picked up the pace outside

Ambelokipi. Finally the pace and straining to stay with Loues did Flack in, and he too collapsed. That put Kellner into second place and Vasilakos into third, with Belokas, a teenager, in fourth.

Papadiamantopolous, who had been forcing his horse to stay ahead of the field (for horses, having much more sense than human beings, do not take easily or well to running forty kilometers), waited at the Rizarios School outside of Athens. As Spiridon Loues ran past him, moving inexorably toward the stadium and glory, the colonel fired his pistol in excitement.

Covered with dust, Papadiamantopolous spurred his horse ahead and they raced into the stadium, where the last track-and-field events had concluded well before the scheduled finish of the marathon. The crowd had been getting periodic reports, but the last one they'd received had Lermusiaux still enjoying a commanding lead.

Papadiamantopolous blurted out his news to the king, and the word spread, causing vast excitement. As the tough little shepherd from Maroussi trotted into the stadium covered with dust and sweat, weaving slightly, the murmurs turned to roars.

On receiving the news of Loues's lead, Prince George (all six feet, five inches of him) and Crown Prince Constantine had rushed to the entrance to the stadium. Now they ran beside Loues to the finish line as the partisan crowd went mad, thousands of hats filling the air. Loues crossed the finish line, then turned to his king and bowed. The king waved his naval cap at Loues in salute.

Vasilakos entered the stadium more than seven minutes later, to be followed by Belokas within thirty seconds. Kellner, who finished fourth, stopped at the finish line to protest that Belokas had passed him by taking advantage of a carriage ride. Crown Prince Nicholas, hearing this, took it upon himself to investigate the matter, and found that Belokas had indeed cheated. Third place was duly awarded to the Hungarian, while Belokas was stripped of his medal.

Loues, who had finished the course in 2:58:50—the first sub-3:00 (under three hours) marathon—was called before his king while the rest of the runners were finishing, with the crowd continuing to go wild. There, following his formal congratulations from the king, the new Greek hero was embraced by several members of the Greek Olympic Committee, and then humbly accepted the gifts offered to him.

Although the marathon was the last of the track-and-field events (it is, of course, technically not a track event), there were still several events in other sports to be contested. After the excitement of the marathon, these were, however, almost anticlimactic. Captain Sumner Paine of the United States won the revolver match at 30 meters, and his brother took second place. To point out the wide-open aspect of entry into the first Olympic Games, Dick Schaap reports that an English tourist entered the tennis tournament on a whim and won.

On the seventh day of the games, King George threw a breakfast for all the competitors. Midway through he asked that the Americans repeat their Boston A.A. cheer, which they did, to the amusement and enjoyment of all. Later, out on the lawn, the king and crown prince played leapfrog with some of the athletes, and the Americans attempted to teach the royal family how to play baseball by using a stick and an orange. When struck by Thomas Curtis, the orange showered the crown prince, who thought it all quite a riot.

On the tenth day, the games were officially ended. The king presented each of the winners with a gold medal and an olive branch. Spiridon Loues also carried off with him the silver cup Michel Breal had offered as a special prize for the marathon, plus another prize of an ancient Greek vase.

Following the games, King George asked Loues what he would like as a gift. Thinking but a moment, Loues asked for a horse and cart so that he could carry fresh water more conveniently from his village to Athens, a distance of some seven kilometers. It seems that his village had excellent, cool, clear water, which Athens was badly in need of. Every day, Loues was in the habit of making trips to Athens with his mule carrying barrels of fresh water. He would run the seven kilometers to Athens and ride the mule back to his village, once in the morning and once in the afternoon. The horse and cart would make the trip easier for him, for then he could ride both ways.

By running from his village to Athens twice a day, Loues had stumbled upon the twice-a-day training method now used almost universally by world-class marathoners.

No fool in the way he trained, and no fool in his career moves, Loues retired from running following his Olympic victory and settled back into a quiet life in his village.

In 1936, Loues visited the Olympic Games in Berlin as a guest of Adolf Hitler. For all his wisdom in matters close to him, Loues was an innocent in world affairs. Until his death, he held the German fuehrer in awe and respect.

Clarence DeMar wins his seventh and last Boston Marathon on April 19, 1930.

3.

CLARENCE DeMAR:
Against the Odds

The Greeks were not the only people impressed by Loues's feat.

The American Olympic team had come primarily from Boston and New York, and, although a hastily-put-together and very much jerry-built group from the start, their successes were overwhelming. The creation of the marathon specifically for the games seems to have had the most profound impact on the American spectators, though.

The Boston contingent was so fired by the marathon race that, on their return to America, they straightaway set about putting together a marathon for the Boston area. And, of course, it is well known, even in non-sporting circles, what became of that particular endeavor.

What is not so well known is that the Boston Marathon was *not* the first marathon in America, even though its inaugural running came the year after the Athens Olympic Games.

In 1896, the first marathon held in America was run from Stamford, Connecticut, to the Knickerbocker Athletic Club at Columbus Circle in New York City. The course was about twenty-five miles long; among the thirty entrants there were ten finishers, a dismal completion rate, but not downright embarrassing considering that the race was run in mud and slush under some of the worst possible conditions. The winning time was 3:25:55 by John J. McDermott.

McDermott would travel to Boston the next spring to win the first Boston Marathon. There a measly fifteen starters would take the signal to have at it, instituting the most famous annual marathon in the world. The Boston course would run from Ashland to downtown Boston and would measure almost 25 miles; McDermott's time would be a respectable 2:55:10. It would be another eleven years until the now-standard length of 26 miles, 385 yards was arrived at—in the 1908 Olympic Games in London, and then by royal decree. In the meantime, Boston was run annually as a sort of blue-collar macho-fest.

The marathon was not an event ardently embraced by track specialists. Fortunately for its future, Boston and New York sported a very ardent—if very small—cadre of road racers, and their fascination with the marathon assured its persistence. The road racers in the Boston area were frequently members of local athletic and social clubs, often ethnic in nature. The members were fervently physical. Between its inception and 1911, the Boston Marathon was variously won by a student, a blacksmith, a carpenter, a clerk, a plumber, a farmer, a mill hand. All the winners were in their late teens (Boston has a minimum-age limit of eighteen) or early twenties.

In 1911, the race was won by a printer from Melrose, Massachusetts, by the name of Clarence H. DeMar. He was five feet, eight inches tall, weighed one hundred twenty-seven pounds, and was twenty-one years old. It was not the young man's first Boston Marathon. The previous year, he had placed second to Freddy Cameron, who had led from the start. Cameron had won in 2:28:52 with DeMar less than a minute behind, closing on Cameron at the time. In 1911, DeMar won in a time of 2:21:39.

Clarence was born near Cincinnati and, despite legends that grew up about his boyhood after he had made a name for himself in marathoning, he was not a speedster as a child. In fact, in his autobiography, entitled simply *Marathon,* he states that, despite entering quite a few races as a youngster, he never made much of a showing.

Not unlike Spiridon Loues, however, he was laying the groundwork for his later distance-running prowess in his daily life. The school he attended at age seven was a mile away, and he found it more pleasant to dogtrot there than to walk. He quickly developed a reputation as the kid who never walked anywhere.

Later, however, he took to walking in a big way. His father died, and in order to help his mother meet expenses for themselves and his five younger brothers and sisters, he sold pins, needles, thread, and soap around his hometown. Such a sales trip would involve ten to twenty miles of walking.

When he was ten, his mother moved the family to Warwick, Mass., and young Clarence roamed the new neighborhood selling little things to help make ends meet. He also did quite a bit of hiking on and around Mount Grace. During his first winter there, he injured his ankle skating over the crusted snow. The ankle subsequently became infected and he nearly lost his foot.

Even though they had free use of the house in Warwick (it belonged to relatives), the DeMars still could not make ends meet. The family was forced to break up. Clarence was placed in a home called the Farm School, on Thompson's Island in Boston harbor. The only "running" he managed to do on the small island was when he and a few friends attempted to run away by swimming a mile to shore while holding onto a rowboat; the gang of escapees was ultimately recaptured by the personnel of a life-saving station. "The failure of the effort to escape caused me to crawl into my shell tighter than ever and take to story books and study," DeMar wrote in his autobiography.

When he graduated at sixteen, DeMar was allowed to leave the island. He secured a job working for a fruit farmer in South Hero, Vermont, putting in long and hard hours for less than twenty dollars a month. Meanwhile he continued his education at Maple Lawn Academy. He also managed to send some money home. During that period, Clarence dreamed of becoming a great athlete like those in the storybooks. He tried all sorts of sports, but in each one he failed.

Clarence ultimately entered the University of Vermont, an environment where athletes were the heroes-about-campus. But he had no illusions of becoming one of them. He studied and worked: on the experimental farm, in print shops, beating rugs—anything he could get—and he continued his dogtrotting between jobs and classes. In fact, he used his constant dogtrotting to get out of gym classes by convincing the instructor that he was getting enough exercises. Using this logic, Clarence managed to pass his physical education courses without ever attending a class.

DeMar almost never attended a sporting event because, as he put it, he was never "bitten by the bug of 'spectatoritis.' " What Clarence wanted was to take part in a sport; everything else was merely waiting around.

He finally stumbled into running while delivering milk. On Thompson Island there had been no way of keeping up with world events because no newspapers were allowed there except the one the boys themselves printed, *The Transcript*. But in his sophomore year in college, Clarence developed a hazy idea from casually reading newspapers that there were races of great distances run in foreign countries where he might make a name and reputation for himself. To a young man passionately starved for a sport in which he could participate, dreams came easily— especially dreams of a hazy, half-formed sort. "One morning the thought came to me," he wrote years later, "that I could run a marathon, and perhaps go abroad to represent my country." Of such vague dreams are destinies formed. The dream grew as he dogtrotted between the experimental station and the State Hygiene Laboratory, delivering small samples of milk for testing (one of several jobs he held simultaneously). He ran the mile in each direction to save time and to keep warm.

In his junior year, a Professor Stetson, speaking before a group of young men at a college smoker, put into words what DeMar had assumed: that there was some sport somewhere suited to everyone and that, when one found that sport, if one dedicated oneself to it, one could become a champion.

The next day Clarence was out, trying to make the cross-country team. His running was finally taking on a sharper focus. DeMar's ground-eating, efficient, low-slung running style didn't sit well with the team captain. "Run on your toes, on your toes!" he admonished Clarence. Clarence tried to comply but eventually came to a simple and profound conclusion that is generally subscribed to today: the most important ingredients of good distance-running are endurance and the ability to get done with it as soon as possible, in whatever way is most efficient for you.

In his first inter-class meet (of 4 miles) he placed fourth. The next week, at a meet at Union College, he came in fourth, beating out the team captain who had admonished him to run on his toes.

DeMar's college career was interrupted halfway through his junior year, however. Upon turning twenty-one he was legally able to help support his mother, so he went to live with her in Melrose. There he remained for twenty years, working as a printer in the Boston area.

Although college was behind him, Clarence did not allow his dream of becoming a marathon runner to fade. He adopted the practice of running to and from work, carrying a dry shirt to change into so he would not offend his colleagues. He also purchased a book on running for ten cents. During this time DeMar formulated the idea that he did not need a coach, because a coach would only upset his concentration. Clarence felt he could better work out his problems himself without someone forcing outside prejudices upon him.

The would-be marathoner had never run more than ten miles in his life. During the Christmas vacation of 1909 he decided to try the marathon distance. He ran through Reading to a section of Andover where a road sign indicated that Boston was twenty miles away. He started his run into Boston and then came back out to Melrose, which was seven miles from downtown. He covered approximately twenty-six miles in about three hours and, as he recalls, "without much exertion and so [I] felt very confident." His ground-eating shuffling style seemed ideally suited to the distance.

Clarence ran his first open race on February 22, 1910. It was a 10-mile handicap race from Boston to Chestnut Hill and back, held in rain and sleet. He won, posting the second-best time of the day, and was thrilled to see his name and picture in the Boston papers. His attitude toward publicity would soon change, though. His usually taciturn nature was to rebel against the attention (and the subsequent intrusion of strangers into his life) which surrounded him.

There was at that time a general misunderstanding of long-distance running. For example, when DeMar came home from that first open race, his prize of a silver tea set in hand, his sister expected to see him covered with blood. This dread of the dire consequences of running such long distances was a recurring theme during DeMar's career, with most of the warnings coming from people supposedly better educated in such matters than his sister.

DeMar's sights were now set on April 19. His first 10-miler and subsequent races had been mere warm-ups for his first marathon—the fabled B.A.A. (Boston Athletic Association) Marathon.

The starting field that year was inordinately large—over two hundred. (In subsequent years, due partially to the coming of World War I, the field would shrink to about seventy-five; it would experience its next growth spurt around 1928.) The day was fairly hot, and DeMar's neophyte strategy was to pace himself carefully in hopes that the rest of the field would fall by the wayside. He related in later years that his secret was concentrating on the distance yet to go and metering out his energy accordingly. He claimed that this method always worked, "barring accidents like the loss of confidence, a gambling spirit, or mild sunstroke."

The course during that period was twenty-four miles long (it underwent many changes over the years, eventually being set at the standard Olympic Marathon distance of 26 miles, 385 yards), starting at Ashland instead of its current starting point in Hopkinton.

As the runners entered Wellesley, about ten miles into the race, DeMar was some seven minutes back of the leaders. But, as he had anticipated, some of the runners ahead of him had misjudged their pace, and he found them strewn along the side of the road, burned out. Clarence continued to run steadily, precisely, almost mechanically, his concentration intense, his head held straight. A newspaper reporter said that he ran as if his head were held by a check. His relentless and studious racing put him into second place, and as he came down Commonwealth Avenue, just before the turn into Exeter Street, he finally caught sight of the winner, Freddy Cameron. Cameron, from Nova Scotia, finished the course in 2:28:52. DeMar finished less than a minute behind him and was closing the gap at the finish.

It was a common practice in those days to have handlers on bicycles accompanying each runner. Each handler could give his charge a sponge soaked in water, or exhort him on to greater efforts. This was before the days of stationary aid stations for the runners. Open cars for the press usually drove in front of the leaders, spewing lung-numbing exhaust clouds and generally getting in the way of the runners. After the race, one of DeMar's co-workers at the printer's commented that Clarence had run right past the handlers and sponges without ceremony. DeMar stated that he thought such distractions to be a handicap to a serious runner. In later years at Boston, he would make his distaste for people forcing him to share the road quite clear.

He ran a slew of 10-milers during the rest of the season; his first one was in May at Lynn, where he finished tenth. The theory was put forth at that time that no one was ever the same after he had run a marathon, so Clarence should expect to finish back in the pack from now on. On July 4, however, he placed second in a 10-miler held at Haverhill.

At about this time, against his better judgment, DeMar allowed two men, Colclough and Jordan, to talk him into letting them coach him for a trip to Nova Scotia to run against Freddy Cameron, behind whom he had finished at Boston. As DeMar put it, "They talked about eating plenty of meat, getting a long stride, taking breathing exercises, and having the guts to fight to the finish." As an experiment, DeMar let them direct his career. They took him to an antiquated doctor in Roxbury who, upon listening to Clarence's heart, declared that he had a heart murmur and should not continue to run for more than a year or two. To continue running would endanger his life, the doctor told them. (Two years later the doctor died of a heart attack, while Clarence lived forty-eight years more.)

Despite pep talks and all the rigorous training, Clarence finished well back in both the 10- and 15-mile races. He used the dismal placings to once and for all banish coaching from his career.

That fall he ran his second marathon at the Brockton Fair and placed third. During the race he let some speed he'd developed over the summer overcome his self-reserve and, as a result, burned himself out for the final ten miles.

During the winter, DeMar worked to get himself in peak condition for his second Boston Marathon. He ran about one hundred miles a week and threw in some twenty-mile workouts. As a tune-up he entered the 10-mile Armory A.A. race held on Washington's birthday. And as the BAA Marathon approached, he developed a knee problem. He administered everything he could think of, hoping that one or two of the ointments and greases would help.

A few nights prior to the marathon, Clarence dreamed that he won the race. Not being superstitious, he took it as a good omen but a coincidence all the same.

At the pre-race medical examination, the doctors listened intently to his heart and confirmed the old Roxbury doctor's suspicion that he had a heart murmur. They advised him that this should be his last race, and they further advised him to drop out of the race should he become tired. He shrugged his shoulders, not sure how to run a marathon *without* getting tired, and lined up at the start.

Clarence's dreaming—on top of his training—paid off. He ran a textbook-perfect race, completely under control. He took the lead at nineteen miles and won by a half-mile with a time of 2:21:39, knocking about three minutes off Tom Longboat's course record. The soreness that had plagued his knee stayed with him during the race but did not become any worse, so he ignored it. The next day he was back at his job as usual, putting in more than a full day by modern standards. DeMar's philosophy was that running should not interfere with one's work.

Clarence continued to race throughout the summer, winning regularly. The fact that he had run three marathons did not lead him to ruination, as many had warned him it would. In fact, by the middle of August, when he won a race at Manchester, New Hampshire (that had been advertised as a 10-miler but that was, in fact, 7 miles), he had won all eight distance races he had entered since the Boston Marathon.

It was during this summer that Clarence heard from a Dr. Kellogg of Battle Creek, Michigan (not the cornflake king), who wanted him to experiment with training on a special diet. Kellogg wanted Clarence to spend several weeks at his sanitarium, but because Clarence couldn't afford to miss the time from work, he offered to have Kellogg direct his diet by mail. As he had been willing to experiment with the two coaches at one point, so now he was willing to try a carefully controlled diet that required him to abstain from all meats—except at Thanksgiving.

An examination of the diet makes for interesting reading, and shows the progress of science over the years. For the morning of the 1911 Brockton Fair Marathon, Kellogg advised Clarence to eat the following: one dozen oranges, one-quarter pound of pine nuts, and one pound of high-grade caramels. Clarence reported that it took just about the entire morning to eat all of the stuff. After his eating marathon, he ran the marathon itself and, although he didn't feel full of pep (it is remarkable he had any strength at all, with most of his blood being diverted to his stomach to process all that food!), he did feel full of endurance and won the race. Dr. Kellogg wrote a paper on the success of the experience, but Clarence felt he had won *despite* the force-feeding.

Clarence's record at the end of 1911 was ten for ten, including the Boston and Brockton marathons. In conference with A.A.U. officials, he decided to back off racing for what little remained of the year; the officials felt sure that he was a shoo-in for the 1912 Olympic Marathon team. A man whose life revolved around establishing goals and working to achieve them, Clarence H. DeMar had set out to win the Boston Marathon and had done so. In the world of running, there was only one goal higher—the Olympic gold medal for the marathon.

Although his intuition told him that the theory of "the more marathons you run, the less chance there is of winning them" was inaccurate, Clarence wanted to cover all bases, so he continued to cut back on his racing in the spring of 1912. So strictly did Clarence adhere to the theory, he watched the Boston Marathon from a press car instead of running it, lest he run himself out before the Olympics. It was won by Mike Ryan, a big, strong runner who broke Clarence's record by twenty-one seconds.

The Olympic team selection process involved a 10-mile exhibition race for Clarence, and on the strength of his 1911 performances and the 10-miler, he was selected. There were less strict and selective rules for picking the U.S. marathon team in those days. Today, an actual marathon is run, and the top three make the team. In 1912, the United States took a team of twelve marathoners. And from the beginning there were problems.

It would not be an exaggeration to say that, of the athletes on an Olympic team, the marathoners have always been the least understood. They are profound individualists. Although it is possible to train 100-meter sprinters as a group because the requirements to get individual runners through the 100 meters do not vary much, the same is not true of the marathon. Over such an extreme distance, one man's talents for getting through in the fastest possible time may be completely different from those of the man who lines up next to him. Over many thousands of training miles and many hundreds of racing miles, a marathoner learns about himself and adjusts his own training and racing to stress his strengths and overcome his weaknesses. Preparing for an important marathon, one runner may feel the need for one long run a week before the race and two track workouts in order to put an edge on his speed, while another may find it best to engage in a gradual backing off of running entirely so that he will be properly rested for the big race. Marathoners, in other words, would not make good soldiers, because each marches to his own drummer.

Unfortunately, the coaches selected for the U.S. Olympic teams have seldom, if ever, appreciated or understood the needs of their marathoners. So it was in 1912. As the entire Olympic team gathered in New York prior to boarding the *Finland,* which had been chartered for the trip to Stockholm, an official of the Olympic Committee addressed the team as though they were school children going on a day outing. He emphasized that the team members had better do as they were told, as no one was indispensable, and that it would be easy to send any disobedient athlete home. Understandably, a man like DeMar—who worked a full-time job, supported his mother at home, and trained like a demon on his own time—was insulted by the speech.

The insult went even deeper as, on the boat, schedules were set giving times during which each group of competitors was to train. There would be no team prior to 1936 with more potential, but the coaching and organization promised to undermine that talent.

Because he had set the American marathon record that April at Boston, Mike Ryan assumed a position as leader of the marathoners and led them in their training. Although, as DeMar stated, everyone tried to respect him for his feat, they all also found him quite domineering and overbearing. "For instnce," says DeMar, "he would try to trip me up if I talked and he would bawl me out if I kept quiet for not saying anything."

DeMar was continuing on Dr. Kellogg's no-meat experiment. There was no friction on that count, but there was a growing concern on DeMar's part that this running with the group was undermining his competitive edge, which he gained by training at his own pace, working to stay relaxed. The boat stopped at Antwerp and the marathoners trained about twenty miles a day in a hay field, under the eyes of head coach Mike Murphy and marathon coach Johnny Hayes. This training under the supervision of coaches was also contrary to DeMar's regular patterns. By the time they piled back on the boat and were back underway, DeMar was feeling rather tired.

When the boat docked in Stockholm, DeMar headed for the gangplank, hoping to stretch his legs. Mat Halpin, the team manager, turned him back, which further upset DeMar. He was becoming very disenchanted with the treatment he was receiving.

The pressure was intensified when an official declared that either Ryan, DeMar, or Sockalexis (who had taken second at Boston) *must win* the gold medal in the marathon! The situation was further strained when Hayes made disparaging remarks about how DeMar ran and tried to cause him to change his style. DeMar vowed that when he got through with amateur running, at least he'd get out of the way and stay there and not hamper the future champions by trying to tell them something which they didn't want him to.

A week before the race, with all the pressure and with training at a pace that was not wise for him, DeMar began to go stale. The staleness took the form of chronic tiredness. In addition, he ruptured a blood vessel and began to go lame from too much practice.

The marathoners on the team, along with Jim Thorpe, were housed several miles outside town. While the marathoners were constantly run ragged, Thorpe refused to be pushed and spent most of his time resting.

The day of the marathon came. There was a drawing for positions. The course was an out-and-back, and the day was hot.

Soon after the turnaround point, Mike Ryan dropped out. A Portuguese runner suffered sunstroke and died the next day. The American team had a rather dismal showing. DeMar was so lame and exhausted that for one of only two times in his career of some sixty-five marathons, he broke his running stride and walked for nearly a mile.

South Africans, used to running in extreme heat, took first and second. Gaston Strobino, the last member of the U.S. team— who had only made the squad when Sidney Hatch had decided not to come, and who had therefore been ignored by the coaches—took third place. The Americans placed seven men in the top dozen finishers (DeMar was twelfth), but most had become too tired to be near the top of those dozen. DeMar claimed that he had never before or since been so lame following a race, and he and several other members of the team had to walk with the aid of canes for a week afterwards.

The team training paid off in the shorter events, where such methods are appropriate; the Americans swept the 100 meters.

Camped out with the marathoners, Jim Thorpe took the entire event as rather a lark. According to DeMar, King Gustaf's fabled remark to Thorpe, "Sir, you are the greatest athlete in the world!" was never uttered, for although King Gustaf sent word following the games that he'd like to meet the great Indian athlete, Thorpe "meditated a moment, yawned, stretched, and said, 'I guess I won't go!' and so the king has not yet met Thorpe!"

Clarence's dismal showing in the Stockholm Olympic Marathon—a race much more important to him than the Boston Marathon—had profound and far-reaching effects.

Immediately following his return from Stockholm, Clarence wrote to Kellogg that he was discontinuing the experimental vegetarian diet. "I could not see that the self-denial did one iota of good and it was a tremendous bother," DeMar told Kellogg. His return to a regular American diet did not have adverse effects on his racing. He ate his meals with printer's ink on his fingers and went out on several occasions to beat everyone that a race promoter could throw against him, including Sockalexis (who had placed fourth at Stockholm), whom he ran against in a 20-miler from Old Town to Bangor.

The fall came, and with it, the Brockton Fair Marathon, which

Clarence had handily won the previous year. In 1912, however, he did not take the day off from work to run the race.

Clarence H. DeMar had entered a period that frustrates statisticians of the running game and that completely throws off one's evaluation or judgment in answering the question: "Who was the greatest marathoner of all time?"

The commonly quoted fable is that Clarence took an extended break from racing marathons under the mistaken impression that he was saving himself from a heart attack. That is one-third of the reason why, during the next five years (some of the prime years for a long-distance runner like DeMar), he did not run another marathon.

The three reasons DeMar admitted to are as follows:

1. The repeated warnings of doctors and fans that running marathons with any regularity was hard on the heart and could cause irreparable damage or death.

2. Clarence had begun formulating an idea that, for a member of the Baptist church, running was a vainglorious affair. It came home to him profoundly when, before or after church services, men in the parish would come up to greet him and, instead of asking him about the condition of his immortal soul, would ask him about the condition of his legs for the next race. Clarence reflected that perhaps his fame in running was selfish.

3. The third factor was simply one of time. As well as working full time as a typographer, DeMar was taking extension courses at Harvard and Boston Universities, and the studies cut into his training time. Knowing the rigors of training for a competitive marathon, he decided he didn't have time during that period to train properly, for Clarence DeMar hated to do anything halfway.

It should not be assumed that Clarence stopped running entirely. He did not. He still ran from North Station in Boston to work at 117 Franklin Street and back, nearly a mile each way, in under six minutes, through traffic, wearing his street clothes and shoes.

He even ran some races, but they were not at the same level as the races he had run in 1912. Everyone pronounced him through with running. During this period he received his A.A. from Harvard and became superactive as scoutmaster of troop 5, Melrose.

After five years, Clarence resumed serious running with his entry in the Boston Marathon of 1917. Clarence prepared for the 1917 marathon by running only three times a week, half his training level of five years before. The day of the race was hot, and the course had been lengthened by two miles since his last competition there. Despite the factors working against him, Clarence finished third, one place in front of Hannes Kohlemainen, who would win the gold medal in the marathon at the 1920 Olympic Games in Antwerp.

In the fall, Clarence took off a day from work to run the Brockton Fair Marathon. He won, breaking the previous record. But he was making a comeback just in time to get caught up in the war. The navy rejected him because he was near-sighted, a common occupational hazard for printers, but the army came along and swept him up in their draft not much later, despite their findings that he had a "runner's heart." DeMar was sent to England and then to France and had little time left for running.

Eventually, Clarence managed to do some running while in the army and even ran some races outside the military during the occupation of France. Most of his time, however, was just spent being restless to go home.

Having returned stateside, Clarence spent April 19, 1920, the day of the Boston Marathon, canoeing on the Shawsheen with his scouts. He did not train for or make the U.S. marathon team going to the Olympic Games, which was probably just as well because Mike Ryan was marathon coach, and Ryan was up to his old tricks. Clarence's friend Frank Zuna, who had won the Brockton Marathon in 1915, reported the same kind of bad experiences with Ryan in 1920 as had occurred in 1912. Zuna had not been able to prove his fitness to Ryan's satisfaction, and so was not allowed to start the event.

As though to put Ryan in his place, Zuna ran the 1921 Boston Marathon and broke Ryan's record by nearly three minutes. And on the day Zuna was doing damage to Ryan's precious record, where was DeMar? Up making repairs at the Boy Scout cottage in North Reading so it would be ready for the next set of boys.

On July 4 of that year, DeMar trained for and won a mile race at Melrose in 4:47:6, one of a handful of times he'd ever run a mile in less than five minutes.

For the upcoming year, however, he planned to dedicate himself to his Scouts. His only run of note came in November when it sleeted so badly he could not ride his bicycle for four-and-a-half miles to work in Medford and so jogged instead. There was a fly in the ointment, though. At Millers, the print shop where he was then working, there was a foreman named Bob Campbell, who was enthusiastic about all sports. Campbell was about to be instrumental in ending DeMar's respite from running—and winning—marathons, especially *the* marathon, Boston.

With the encouragement of Bob Campbell and Campbell's promise to ride a bicycle and accompany DeMar as his handler, Clarence decided in late 1921 to once again run the Boston Marathon come April. He began a very gentle training season, running the four-and-a-half miles to and from work each day, usually at about an eight-minute-per-mile pace. Several weeks before the marathon he did a long, fast run from Wellesley Square to the finish of the marathon course and then jogged back home to Melrose. It had been five years since he had competed at Boston, and six years before that since he had won. But, as in 1911, he went into the race having just had a dream that he would be the winner. The press, which did not share his dream, pretty much dismissed his chances.

The only people with faith in DeMar's chances were Campbell and DeMar's Boy Scouts, who took it for granted that their leader would win whatever he wished to win—including a marathon he hadn't won in eleven years.

Campbell rode rough-shod on traffic and fans along the course, using a brand of military language to harangue any would-be intruders (the course was not yet closed to traffic as it would eventually be). In Wellesley, an open car made a turn and grazed DeMar, who reacted by throwing a punch at the occupants of the car. The punch caught a passenger in the rear seat in the ribs—causing DeMar to hasten his pace over the next few miles for fear of retaliation.

On the Newton Hills (later to have its last pinnacle dubbed Heartbreak Hill), DeMar finished off his rivals, and headed home alone, except for the press and officials in their cars, who, having monitored his time, found him within easy reach of a new course record. Ignoring the urgings of the officials, he sailed in smoothly and confidently, clipping forty-seven seconds off Zuna's record from the previous year, to complete the Boston in 2:18:10.

Subsequent invitations to make speeches at receptions cut into Clarence's time for training and for the Scouts, but eventually he got back onto the right track.

DeMar decided to train again the following year for Boston. His training for 1923 began in the middle of February. The rather late start was due to ten days spent in bed suffering from erysipelas caused by a gash on the upper lip; the gash had been administered by an irate man whose dog Clarence kicked when it lunged at him on a training run.

With his brand of training, however, DeMar was in shape by April 19. His own drawback was a slight cold . . . and the absence of a dream telling him he'd win. However, the night before the race he received a special delivery letter from a man in Green-field, Massachusetts, who said he'd had a dream that DeMar would win, but that he'd be challenged by Zuna near the end.

The day of the marathon was hot, and DeMar began feeling tired at Framingham; his recent sickness was catching up with him. He was never a quitter, however, so he continued to run. With dogged determination, Clarence passed his last opponent on Chestnut Hill and moved into the lead, only to be the victim of a bizarre accident which could have cost him the race.

Coming into Cleveland Circle an automobile hit a cyclist, throwing him into Clarence. The impact pulled his shoe loose from the heel. Pheidippides, patron saint of marathoners, was on Clarence's side, however. Before the race he had safety-pinned his socks to his shoes to keep them from sliding down and caus-ing blisters. The pin now kept the shoe attached to his foot, but his heel was on top of the shoe instead of inside it. The fans tried to give Clarence advice on how to solve his problem, but with typical self-reliance he ignored them and continued to shuffle along, his concentration allowing him to eat up the remaining miles.

True to the special delivery dream, Zuna finished in second place behind DeMar. Considering his shoe problem and the heat, Clarence ran a very good race—only five minutes slower than the year before. And an added bonus was that he managed to sweat out his cold in the process!

In 1923 DeMar raced more frequently than he had the previous year, but always somewhat nonchalantly. At that point he wished to concentrate his training only on Boston. During the winter he accepted an invitation to run the Baltimore Marathon, but, training for it, he vaulted a snowbank and went lame in his back and hip. He managed to struggle into third place, while Zuna won. After two treatments from an osteopath he was much improved and resumed training for Boston 1924, continuing the formula that had worked for him the past two years: running a great deal, but cautiously, so as not to exhaust himself.

Again, he had a dream that he would win and in fact confided this to a group of young people in Wilmington, Massachusetts, before whom he spoke the day before the 1924 race.

The 1924 Boston Marathon was the first one that conformed to the now-standard 26-mile, 385-yard distance set for the Olympic Games. Running with supreme confidence, assured by yet another dream of victory, DeMar completed the course in under 2:30, winning by several minutes. The victory gave him an unheard-of three Bostons in a row, with his 1911 victory bolstering his total wins to four. He had, in effect, become a legend. Before his feat, it was commonly felt (how common such "commonly felt" limits are!) that no one would ever win twice. The unprecedented victory automatically put Clarence DeMar on the Olympic team, a position he had not held for a dozen years.

Instead of an army of contenders to represent the United States, the marathon team in 1924 consisted of six runners and one alternate. Remembering his own bad experiences in 1912 and recalling Zuna's complaints about the 1920 race, DeMar set out to guarantee himself a situation in which he could run and train the way he knew to be right for him. He made his demands known to Lawson Robertson, the head coach. Robertson said he couldn't agree more and cited his own experiences with Pennsylvania cross-country team members. Mike Ryan was again marathon coach. DeMar wrote him a letter warning that he would not abide interference from coaches on this trip. Eventually, Ryan wrote back agreeing to his ground rules.

The marathoners were to leave early. The officials came to see them off and, in an officious way, told them that they would at all times have to abide by the rules laid down by the coaches and train like one big, happy family. DeMar stormed up to Robertson, demanding his rights. Robertson shushed him and told him that the officials weren't talking about him. Feeling that if the others couldn't speak up for themselves, he wasn't going to champion their cause, Clarence trained by himself. The other six fell under Ryan's heavy hand.

In a last-minute decision, the officials of the U.S. team entered Ralph Williams, the alternate, and held back Carl Linder, a more experienced runner. This move undermined any morale the marathoners had had up to that point.

It was July, and it was hot. The conditions of most Olympic marathons are bizarre enough to make winning the contest almost a hollow victory. Under conditions more appropriate, the results would often be much different from those which appear in the record books. This time was no exception. DeMar's strategy was to hold on, to control his pace, in order to survive the incredible heat. Stenroos of Finland won in 2:42, an Italian took second place, and DeMar was right behind him for third. The next American was sixteenth, another indication that Ryan's training methods were absurd.

Before the race, the runners had agreed that whichever of them finished highest would draft a paper to the U.S. Olympic officials. The runners strongly urged the officials to drop the job of marathon coach and threatened not to participate in any future Olympic Games if their conditions went unmet. All but Frank Wendling of Buffalo signed it. Before he turned it in to the officials, DeMar read it to Mike Ryan, who had nothing to say. Although the officials never directly responded to the paper, the job of U.S. Olympic Marathon coach was missing from the 1928 roster, when DeMar was back again on the team.

Meanwhile, Ryan turned in *his* report, blaming the heat for the failure of the team. He also claimed that DeMar had been yellow and didn't have the guts to run harder in an attempt to win.

In the 1925 Boston, DeMar was second to Chuck Mellor by a

mere thirty-seven seconds. The next year Clarence was third as Johnny Miles won the race in a world-record time of 2:25:40. Stenroos, Olympic champion in 1924, took second. As though to prove that placing third to the likes of Miles and Stenroos was almost as good as a win, DeMar used it as a jumping-off point in winning his next five marathons: Baltimore in May 1926, the Sesqui-Centennial at Philadelphia in June, Port Chester in October, Baltimore again in March, 1927, and the Boston Marathon again in April of 1927—a phenomenal feat!

For the first time in three years, DeMar had dreamed of victory prior to the 1927 Boston Marathon. He repeatedly stated that he was not superstitious, and that the dreams merely gave him a little added confidence going into the race—something a good marathoner never has too much of.

The 1927 race was a classic because Miles was back to defend his title, and he was expected to repeat. Who wouldn't pick the holder of the world record to repeat? As though from a deep well of pride, DeMar, for the first time in his career, raced against another runner instead of against the course and the weather and the time.

The day was hot. DeMar describes it colorfully for a man of such restraint: "It was hot, so hot that the tar was like flypaper. . . ." He took the lead immediately. Each time Miles challenged him and took the lead away, DeMar would sprint ahead again; the tactic, combined with the heat, was Miles's undoing. At about six miles, he dropped out.

The tactic had not been without its effect upon DeMar, however. He had tired himself considerably and still faced twenty miles of torturous road. He continued to lead but developed the paranoia that all marathoners experience when they are depleting themselves. Every time he heard a motorcycle cop approaching from the back, he would turn that way to make sure he was not run into. That merely added to his exhaustion.

Fortunately, Clarence came across one of the cars accompanying the lead runners; there was a bucket of ice water sitting on its runningboard. He took a few swallows. This helped him so much, he started to plot his course through the traffic so he could repeatedly find the car and continue to take ice water as the sun drained him. At Kenmore, about a mile from the end, he felt a bit dizzy and faint but overcame this by slowing the pace for the final few hundred yards.

It was DeMar's first Boston win in three years. He'd again proved that he was not a man to count out of the competition until the bell. The win generated a lot more publicity, which Clarence was not fond of but tolerated as part of the price to be paid for winning.

Through the end of the 1920s, Clarence spent more and more time with the Scouts and with Sunday classes, and he cleaned out his trophy cases several times over by giving his racing prizes to Scouts and students who performed well.

Jock Semple, a man who competed against him often, puts Clarence's unique qualities in perspective: "At one time he ran for the Melrose Post American Legion, and, although he had all the patience in the world with kids who wanted autographs, he had no time for those sycophants and drunken Legionnaires who used to bother him with inane questions and handshakes."

Although DeMar spent more time with the Scouts and Sunday-school classes and worked his printing job full time, still he had fair success in his running. In the spring of 1928 he won both a 44-mile race from Providence to Boston and—again—the Boston Marathon! In both instances, he had favorable dreams about the event.

But this was the last time that dreams of victory coincided with victory itself. Having heard of his luck with dreams, people began telling him they'd dreamed of his victory in 1929 at Boston, but he already knew differently before he started the race. He did come back the next year, however, to score his final victory at Boston. For that one, there was no dream predicting his performance.

His first six Boston victories, up to and including the 1928 win, had been previewed by dreams of victory. That span covered the ten Boston Marathons in which he participated between 1910 and 1928. The four Bostons he did not win had been preceded by absolutely no dream activity. DeMar wrote it off to coincidence and never really held much stock in the predictions. Such superstitions were too far outside the realm of his strictly regimented life.

The disappearance of those dreams after 1928, however, may have had some effect upon his mental outlook. More and more, quite realistically, he began to feel there was no way he could continue his level of performance. Age was encroaching, and, although he had managed to hold it off well, in the final analysis, no one beats age.

In his autobiography, DeMar attempted to pinpoint where he began slipping as a competitor. He felt it may have been in 1927, when, for the first time in his running career, he ran a marathon and did not place in the top three (Olympic Marathons excepted), despite being able to train as he felt necessary. Just about the only bright spot in his slipping career was a third-place finish at the New England Championship Marathon from Boscawen to Manchester, New Hampshire, on October 12, 1932, when he finished behind Johnny "Jock" Semple. Semple would emerge in the marathoning world as one of the trustees of the famed Boston Marathon.

At Boston in 1933, Clarence placed eighth; in 1934 he placed sixteenth, and he was eighteenth in 1935. The next year he ran the race eleven minutes faster than in 1935 and placed sixteenth, but from that point on he began to run mainly for the fun of participation. That year the Boston race was won by John A. Kelley, a tough little Irishman who would become as well known for his tenacity in running Boston Marathons as DeMar had been in winning them.

"He was," Kelley would say of DeMar, "a very determined person. Brought up on hardships, a man of high moral standards."

Although his racing career declined, DeMar continued to enjoy running. His printing career took some nice upturns. He married in late 1929, and at about that time also changed jobs, becoming the printing teacher and the school's printer at the Keene Normal School, a position he enjoyed thoroughly.

He also continued his own education. In 1934, after taking courses on weekends and at nights, he received his master's degree from Boston University.

Clarence H. DeMar died on July 10, 1958, four days after his seventieth birthday. He did not die from a heart attack as a result of damage caused by running, as doctors had warned him; in fact, pathologists who examined DeMar after he died found his heart to be larger than normal and incredibly healthy. Instead he died from simple old age, leaving forever unanswered the question of how many Bostons he'd have won if he hadn't taken such extended vacations from running.

Jock Semple puts his assessment of it simply: "I feel he would have dominated the Boston Marathon for those many years he laid off." Semple goes a bit farther in according DeMar his place in history: "He was a great athlete and, although his seven wins were not as fast as today, with the conditions in those days [one had to overcome], only runners like myself and Old John [Kelley] can appreciate that, after all, he beat the best in the world during his era."

Johnny Kelley (the elder) completes his forty-eighth Boston
Marathon in 1979 at age seventy-one.
(COURTESY MATTHEW M. DELANEY III)

4.

JOHNNY KELLEY (the Elder): The Mayor of Boston

April 20, 1981. Patriot's Day in Boston. It was one of those days Bostonians point to with perverted pride as they comment for the millionth time: "Don't like the weatha'? Wait a few minutes 'en it'll change."

The eighty-fifth running of the Boston Athletic Association Marathon had begun nearly four hours ago in the quaint, pleasant village of Hopkinton, precisely 26 miles, 385 yards from the middle of Ring Road in front of the Prudential Center. It had been nearly two hours since Toshihiko Seko of Japan had broken the blue finishing tape, setting a new course record. Seko had battled Craig Virgin and Bill Rodgers and then had broken loose. He was no longer at the press conference or the awards ceremony or even at the site of the race. All that was far behind him.

The day had started in Hopkinton with a temperature in the forties and a light drizzle, but as the flotsam of runners struggled toward the finish line, the weather seemed to have a demonic intent. On one block along Commonwealth Avenue, a runner would pass through a downpour of chill rain, while in the next block he would be subjected to bright sunshine, and then in the next, pelted with sleet. The bodies of those runners still on the course seemed always one block behind the weather, their internal thermostats going crazy trying to adjust.

Along the course, nearly a million people had watched the race. Although the fastest runners were long gone, the crowds were still there, expectant, almost as though anticipating an instant replay.

The crowds were waiting, as they did every year, for one man. A man more important to them than the winners. A man who would take nearly twice as long as Seko to cover the course. A man the size of Seko, but, to residents of Boston, a man of much greater stature. Their patience this year was especially poignant.

It was the fiftieth Boston Marathon start for Johnny Kelley, who literally owns Boston every Patriot's Day. Kelley had won Boston in 1935 and 1945, had placed in the top ten nineteen times, and had placed second an incredible seven times! A bandylegged, high-spirited man who doesn't fight his way through life but rather runs in concert with it, he is someone whom life has kissed and bestowed with a degree of invincibility. Kelley the runner, Kelley the indomitable, Kelley the artist, Kelley the philosopher. Seventy-three years old, going on a thousand, running in his fiftieth Boston Marathon. The crowd loved him and waited in the foul weather to see him, to applaud him as he worked his way on down the road, a symbol to them of what man can do when he puts his mind—and body—to it. Only then would they go home. Only then would the current edition of the Boston Marathon be officially concluded.

Kelley was born on September 6, 1907, in West Medford, Massachusetts, the eldest child in a family of five boys and five girls. His father was a mailman. Kelley recalls that the family was neither destitute nor wealthy, just sort of getting along OK. As a youngster, he used to accompany his father on the mail route. "We used to walk, walk, walk," Kelley says. His first knowledge of the Boston Marathon came in 1919 when he came across a faded copy of the *Boston Globe* that proclaimed in bold headlines: CARL LINDER WINS BOSTON.

During his twelfth through sixteenth summers, Kelley and his brother Jim went to Maplewood and Bethlehem in the White Mountains of New Hampshire, where they served as caddies. "We used to earn seventy-five cents for a round of eighteen holes, so sometimes we carried two sets of clubs each around the course. The bags were bigger than me. They were great, terrific summers," he remembers, "and all we did was walk, walk, walk, getting stronger and stronger. Kids today don't get to do that.

Kids today don't walk much. Cars, cars. I never had a car until I was thirty-two."

At school, he tried playing football but found it wasn't for him. He loved sports, so he persisted, next trying baseball. One day he was standing at home plate trying to outguess the pitcher. "He threw the ball and it began coming at me. 'It's gonna break. It's gonna break,' I kept saying to myself," Kelley recalls. He smiles. "It didn't. It broke my head. So that was the end of my baseball career. Oh, I still played, but it was in the sandlots. A little later, someone put on a footrace for the kids and some of my friends talked me into trying it. I took second place and I won a baseball bat, so I said to myself, 'Hey, maybe this is what I ought to be doing.' "

His interest in running—especially in the Boston Marathon—increased in 1921, when his father took him to the fabled race. "My father says to me, 'If you behave, I'll take you to the marathon.' I didn't even really know what a marathon was, except what I'd read in that copy of the *Globe* that day. But we went," he says.

"We got in with the crowd near the finish line, and this big cop held up the rope and said to me, 'Here kid, come under here so you can see better.' So I went up, and pretty soon Frank Zuna comes through in record time. 'Look at him,' my father said to me, 'he doesn't even look tired.' I can still remember Zuna today, sixty years later, the look on his face, as he won."

Kelley started high school in Medford, where he ran track; then the family moved to Arlington and he ran track and cross-country there. When he graduated, he tried to find work. But work was hard to find in the middle of the Depression, so Kelley spent his free time training and running in local 5- and 10-mile road races.

He tried his first marathon at age twenty-one—on St. Patrick's Day, 1928—on an out-and-back course in Rhode Island between Pawtucket and Woonsocket. He went out too fast and, although during the second half he could see the town of Pawtucket up ahead, it never seemed to get any closer, no matter how hard he ran. He finished in 3:17.

The following month Kelley ran his first Boston Marathon. He dropped out at Cleveland Circle. It was 1932 before he tried again. Again, he dropped out, this time while with the leaders at about the halfway point in Wellesley. The next year he ran the Boston even though he was still recovering from the flu and finished thirty-seventh. In 1934 he placed second. Kelley attributes his finish in part to a custom pair of shoes made by a seventy-year-old shoemaker who had begun making the shoes for several of the marathoners, including DeMar and Semple. In 1935 he won his first Boston in 2:32:07.4.

The following year, Tarzan Brown won Boston and, as a result, made the 1936 Olympic Marathon team. To round out the team, a marathon was held in Washington, D.C. The first two finishers were to be assured a place on the team. The race was won by "Biddie" McMahon, a runner who'd been competing for only two years, while Johnny Kelley took second place.

The trip over on the *Manhattan* was especially memorable for Kelley. "Today," he says, "the team gets into jet planes all over the country and *whoosh*"—he shoots his arm toward the ceiling—"and they're already there. We went on the slow boat and we became one big, happy family. We put on shows for the whole boat. I sang some songs, and this shotputter, he did magic tricks. It was really something. When you'd walk into the dining hall, you'd be walking into a hall filled with champions."

Johnny took three pairs of the custom-made shoes along with him. Jesse Owens wanted to try out a pair, even though his feet were larger than Kelley's. Johnny tried to talk him out of it, but Jesse insisted. He put them on, ran in them, and split them down the back. Johnny hunted up a crew member who, for fifty cents, repaired them somewhere down deep in the bowels of the ship. Owens, Johnny still contends, was the greatest track athlete he'd ever seen, and a good friend.

"I didn't do anything in Germany," Johnny says. "I was the only one from our marathon team to finish—Brown and McMahon dropped out—but like I told my father and brother, who were there to see me, I'd have finished if I had to walk. As I finished, Hitler waved to me, but I refused to acknowledge his presence." He pauses a moment and again becomes animated. "Oh yeah. You wouldn't believe the jerseys they made us wear. They were like sandpaper. Tarzan didn't want to wear his, but I was patriotic and I wanted to. Boy, they were terrible. They rubbed my whole chest raw and my nipples were bleeding at the end. I sat down on the grass when I finished. I was beat. And suddenly, my two arms went up in the air. These two German soldiers grabbed me and hauled me off the field. The rule was you had to leave the field as soon as the event was over. But those shirts, even the 5000- and 10,000-meter men didn't like them. They were terrible."

Kelley admits to never doing well in international competition. "I've been in love with the Boston Marathon all my life," he admits. "Boston is my race." He becomes wistful for a moment. "Jerry Nason [the dean of Boston Marathon journalists]—he's my agent but he isn't feeling too well lately—he feels, and I agree, that mistakes I made—mainly impatience and being hasty—cost me three wins. I should have won three more Bostons, turned three of those seconds into firsts. I believe this and so do others.

"Here's an example. In 1937 they had a 20-mile race in Medford. It was in mid-March, and it was the best race of my life or career. I never felt better. I had all my guns going. I ran 1:52:59, three minutes ahead of the second-place finisher, Walter Young of Canada. Everyone said, 'Hey, you're in geat shape, cut back.' I did and I finished second that year in Boston—to Walter Young of Canada."

In that Boston Marathon Kelley and Young, an amateur boxer from Quebec, dueled for twenty-three miles, the lead changing sixteen times. Eventually Young used his strength and pulled away, leaving Kelley nearly six minutes behind at the end.

His second and last victory at Boston came in 1945. Kelley was one of the few to win in the 1940s, an era Quebec's Gerard Cote dominated with four wins. Kelley's wins, coming a decade apart (he was thirty-seven years old for his 1945 win), reflect his persistence. He won the Yonkers Marathon fifteen years apart, first in 1935 and again in 1950. He rememers Yonkers, which he ran twenty-nine times, for its start and finish on the Empire City Race Track. "We started by running one lap around the track, which was a mile. The track was like sand, it was like running through sand. And at the end of it, they had us come back onto the track and run the *last* four miles through this sand stuff. That was some marathon!"

Kelley made the U.S. Olympic Marathon team in 1940, but the games were cancelled because of the war.

Although Kelley believes that a marathoner peaks at thirty and can hold his peak until age thirty-five, he goes against his own theories. He made the U.S. Olympic Marathon team for the third time in 1948 at the age of forty-two and finished twenty-first in the London Olympic Games.

"The Olympic Games, they were really something," he says. "I felt really bad that we didn't go to Moscow, that Carter boycotted the Moscow games. We didn't boycott our own winter games. We should have boycotted Russia in other ways. We deprived five hundred boys and girls of taking part. Carter made a terrible mistake."

Johnny and his wife, Laura, now live on Cape Cod, in East Dennis. They've been there ten years. Two days after the 1982 Boston Marathon (which had been run in seventy-degree heat), Kelley offered some reflection on his life and his running career. It was raining hard on Cape Cod as he spoke about his current running.

"Year after year, I manage to get a little slower. I go along for the ride—I'm part of the furniture at Boston. But I love it. The girls are terrific. When I'm running along, they'll come up to me and they'll say, 'Mr. Kelley, is it all right if I run along with you? I've heard so much about you and I want to be like you when I'm your age.' I love them. They never touch me, they just run along with me. It's great. Some of the men, though, they're different. They'll come up behind me and they'll slap me on the back, not meaning any harm, you understand. I'm going to be seventy-five in September, you know. I don't know why they do that. Then they want to talk and talk. When I'm running I want to concentrate on my run. I don't want to talk. It's always been difficult for me to do both."

Kelley talks about the Ohme race in Japan, which he attended in 1982. The Japanese invite the top two American finishers at Boston to come to the race, and they also pay for a manager to come with them. Bill Rodgers and Craig Virgin, the top two Americans at Boston in 1981, turned down the trip, so it reverted to Malcolm East and Kyle Heffner. Will Cloney, the businessman behind the Boston Marathon for more years than he'd care to remember, traditionally goes as the manager, but in honor of Johnny's fiftieth Boston, Cloney had Johnny go in his place. "It was the best trip of my life," Johnny says. "It was wonderful. I ran in the 30-kilometer race [Ohme also features a 10-kilometer race], and I did 2:35. That's comparable to a 3:30 marathon. The Japanese were wonderful to us. Laura and I almost cried when we had to leave. I'm always being asked to come to races to talk at clinics and to run. They want me to come and Kelleyize them. But I only go to twelve to fifteen races a year now. But I'll go back to Japan any time they ask! That was the most wonderful trip of our lives."

As of the 1982 Boston, Johnny Kelley had run 1,401 races. The 1982 Boston Marathon was his 100th marathon. He has dropped out of only 3 marathons in his life, all of them at Boston. He has a saying that the newspapers like to quote: "My painting [which he took up late in life, at which he is quite successful] and my running shoes are the children I never had."

Kelley has a stock answer to people who ask him why he keeps running: "Because I love it. Some people like to go bowling, or horseback riding. I run because I like it, and I like it more now than I ever have. I run to please myself."

He claims that the things which keep him going these days are: the serenity of his life and the terrific places to run on Cape Code, the fact that he covers his legs with Vicks Vapo-Rub before a marathon and takes a hot bath afterwards, and the fact that Laura takes care of him by feeding him properly and seeing that his life remains relatively uncluttered. Johnny doesn't like to talk to reporters the day before the Boston Marathon, because it interferes with his training. After the marathon, he's more than happy to talk with people.

He feels that all the publicity surrounding his fiftieth Boston in 1981 robbed him of the chance to do a good time. He ran 4:01:25.

On that day, people a half-mile away could tell where Johnny was on the course because they could hear the crowds cheering for him. The crowds at Boston have their traditions, and one is that they don't leave until Johnny Kelley crosses the finish line. And on that cold, windy, miserable April day in 1981, they stood eight and nine deep at the Prudential Center as Johnny Kelley, the mayor of Boston on every Patriot's Day, ran down Ring

Road. The officials had a special finishing tape stretched out that was identical to the one Seko had broken, but Johnny's had the historic occasion printed on it.

"I could have done a much better time, you know, on my fiftieth, if I hadn't given in to all the people who wanted some of my time before the race. I'm still learning lessons about my running," he says. "This year it got hot and I was overdressed, and I lost a lot of time taking off my racing singlet and then my shirt and then getting rid of the shirt and fighting to put my racing singlet back on. The number [he wore number 51 for 1982 to commemorate his fifty-first Boston] got tangled, and I stood there fighting with the singlet to get it back over my head. I lost time at other spots, too. I could have done a better time this year, because I trained for it and I was ready. But the heat, and losing time here and there—that's what did it." He finished in 4:01:18.

Kelley pauses a moment, glances out the window at the pouring rain and at the birds coming by the feeders outside. "To commemorate my fiftieth Boston last year, my club, the Cape Cod Athletic Club, got permission down in Nickerson State Park in Brewster, about five miles from here, to get a big boulder placed and they put a plaque on top of it to commemorate number 50. I guess maybe it's like my tombstone," he says, winking. "But I'll tell ya, they're going to have to wait to put it to use."

Jim Peters at the famed "Race of Champions" at Boston, with winner Karvonen (number 2).

5.

JIM PETERS:
Time Tripper

Jim Peters was born on October 24, 1918, in Homerton, a poor section in the East End of London. His father was a railroad worker who earned just enough to keep his family barely alive. Young Jim took solace in sports and was almost hyperactive in soccer and cricket. "I was all energy when I played," he said recently. "I never used to stop."

His talent as a runner emerged as an offshoot of his training for soccer, and he embarked on a career as a middle-distance runner. In 1946, under coach Johnny Johnston, he won the Amateur Athletic Association (English national title) 6-mile crown, and the following year took the 10-mile title. His goal at that time was to become a good enough runner to represent his country in international competition, but although his times were fast enough to gain him notice on his home turf, they were not really at the world-class level. That was still down the road.

Peters found this out when he competed against the rest of the world at the 1948 Olympic Games, held at Wembley Stadium in his hometown of London. His event was the 10,000 meters, in which he lined up against the Czech track whiz, Emil Zatopek. Zatopek blasted through the 6.2 miles in 29:59.6. Peters finished in 32 minutes, in ninth place, and was lapped by the Czech in the process. Embarrassed and deeply depressed by his loss, Peters retired from running at the ripe old age of twenty-nine.

Through the insistence of his coach, however, Peters allowed himself to be talked into training for the marathon. For the next two years he raced little but began a training regimen that would, when unleashed on the road-racing world, forever change the amount of discipline necessary to run and win the marathon.

Until then, the marathon runner for the most part was a man trained for extreme endurance. He did lengthy workouts to constantly build upon that endurance, allowing his natural abilities to provide what speed they could. That type of training could not be sustained day in and day out, so most marathon runners ran a long distance on alternate days, running perhaps three or four times a week. (Clarence DeMar was certainly an exception, running every day that he could, and this may have contributed greatly to his success at the distance.)

Peters trained very intensely, and he trained every day. Of course, he did not train intensely at great distances, because his regimen of training every day (usually in two segments) and practice running just slightly slower than race pace combined to give him mileage equal in quantity to his competition, while his quality was light-years beyond them.

"I rarely ran more than sixteen miles a day in training," he explains. "But I did good, fast quality miles. You see, speed and stamina are yoked together. And if you do a lot of speed work, the more you do, you build up the stamina to do a marathon.

"At lunch time, I would go to a track and run six miles, working against the clock until I could run five-minute miles. It took me several years before I could do it. But, once I could, if I was off the pace by thirty seconds for six miles, I was fit to be tied. Then at night, I would run ten miles at a five-fifteen pace.

"In later years, I never trained on the track. I was running eighty to one hundred twenty miles a week broken down into eleven to thirteen timed sessions. There was no mucking around. I was running at a five or five-fifteen pace. And I always ran shorter distance club-level races. You see, jogging will never make a champion.

"I had a terrible rolling-gait style—they used to say 'If he's rolling, he's all right.' My head went back and forth. But I'll tell you what, Johnston took a film of my leg action and he said: 'Don't be fooled by anything above the legs.' Apparently, my power was in my legs and I never used to raise them much off the ground.

"The other secret I had was deep breathing. Once I got into an even pattern of running, I'd take a deep breath and hold it as long as I could. I'd do this over and over for five minutes or so, and that increased the size of my lungs."

Peters was aiming for a goal comparable to Roger Bannister, who, in the same era, was training to break the four-minute mile. He felt it was possible to break the 2:30 barrier in marathon racing at the Olympic distance of 26 miles, 385 yards. No one had ever accomplished that feat. Hannes Kolehmainen of Finland had approached it back in 1920, but there it had stayed, an invincible barrier.

But Johnston and Peters were too ambitious to spend several years training merely to slip under 2:30. The British record had been set in 1929 by Harry Payne at 2:30:57.6. Johnston and Peters were training to break 2:20.

Peters entered the year 1951 with a terrific training behind him. But Johnston decided to enter him in some shorter road races as sharpening drills before unleashing him at the marathon distance.

In the spring, Peters won the Wigmore 15 in 1:26:55, and in April, he finished second to Britain's reigning marathon great, Jack Holden, in the Finchley 20-miler. The next month he entered his final tune-up race, the Essex 20-miler. In this race he revealed a strategy that would characterize his marathon career: go out fast, beat the competition down early, and then race to the end. He led the Essex 20 from start to finish, winning in a spectacular time of 1:47:08. The time—and consequently the course distance—was questioned, and upon careful remeasurement, it was found to be six hundred yards short. Adjusting for the discrepancy, his time would have still been an unprecedented 1:49!

It was the kind of emergence race-watchers hope for. As word came out that the sensation Jim Peters had entered the Polytechnic Marathon (from Windsor Castle to Chiswick), speculation was rife. It was especially fueled by the fact that Jack Holden was also entered in the June competition.

Peters, true to his off-at-the-gun strategy, went through five miles in twenty-eight minutes flat, but Holden was there stride for stride, sticking with him through thirteen miles. At that point, the aging Holden threw in a surge and by eighteen miles had opened a two-hundred-yard lead on Peters. However, Peters made his move and closed the gap, passing Holden, who shortly afterwards dropped out. Later Holden cited a bad side stitch as the reason. He retired shortly afterwards.

His opposition vanquished, Peters kept pushing himself, coming through the tape of the Polytechnic Marathon in 2:29:28 for a new British record. Ironically, Harry Payne, whose 1929 record has just been broken, was one of the finish-line referees and was among the first to congratulate Peters. Stan Cox took second place with a fine first marathon of 2:34:34.

Five weeks later, Peters was back at the starting line, this time at Perry Barr in Birmingham, at the hilly and tough British A.A.A. championship course. Cox was injured, so Peters was virtually alone. He went through ten miles in fifty-nine minutes, winning the race in 2:31:42, five minutes in front of the second-place finisher. The two victories in his first two marathons announced to the road-racing world that Peters's retirement was definitely over.

Meanwhile, that same year, in Korea, a runner by the name of Choi Yoon Chil set a new world record in the standard-distance marathon, turning in a 2:26:07. In order to be the best in 1952, Peters was going to have to prove his theory that it was possible to push the record down to the 2:20 range.

The methods Peters had been using to train not only affected his performance in longer road races. As 1952 opened, he took fourth place in the national cross-country championships; in his first running career, his best finish had been forty-sixth. On the roads in early 1952, Peters was beyond reach—and beyond belief. He did the Finchley 20-miler in 1:49:39 and the Essex 20 (now accurately measured) in 1:48:33. With those kinds of tune-ups, it was expected that he'd excel at the Polytechnic Marathon on June 11. (For 1952, the race was also the A.A.A. championship and served as the trials for the British Olympic Marathon team.)

Peters took the lead immediately, going through ten miles in 51:35 despite the fact he'd had a slight altercation with a car at eight miles. At ten miles, Stan Cox was forty-nine seconds back. At fifteen miles, Peters's lead was 1:49, and he went through the marker in 1:17:23, moving with relaxed confidence. By the time he crossed the finish line in Chiswick, Peters had a stranglehold on the world's best time. He'd run it in an astonishing 2:20:42.2; Stan Cox was second in 2:21:42, and Geoff Iden was third in 2:26:53.8.

Naturally, the cry of "short course!" went up immediately. The course was remeasured and found to be two hundred sixty yards too long!

It was understandable, then, that the next month Peters and Cox left for the Olympic Games at Helsinki as favorites to sweep the gold and silver medals.

The biggest fear Peters had at Helsinki was that, because of his reputation, the other marathon runners would attempt to "nobble" him—box him in and slow him down—in the early stages of the race. It would have been understandable for other marathoners to use that tactic in self-defense. Chris Brasher, British Olympic gold medalist in the steeplechase, puts Peters's position into clear perspective: "[He] was the absolute clear favorite for the marathon. He was way ahead of everybody else in the world."

There were two things working against Peters, however. Peters and Cox were transported from Britain to Helsinki in an antiquated York transport plane left over from World War II. The plane had only temporary seating arrangements, and bad weather dragged the trip into a nine-hour ordeal that included no hot food, nothing to drink, and a pronounced draft coming in through the old fuselage. The other factor was Emil Zatopek.

Zatopek of Czechoslovakia had caused Peters seriously to contemplate premature retirement in 1948. Now, like a ghost rising from Peters's past, Zatopek won both the 10,000-meter and the 5000-meter gold medals and then announced he would also run the marathon. Although Zatopek had never in his life run a marathon, Peters had enough respect for the Czech as a competitor to know that any race he entered would be a serious event indeed.

It was little wonder, then, that Peters elected as his strategy the one that had become characteristic: he took the lead immediately and set a blistering pace. The sixty-six marathoners did three-and-a-half laps of the cinder track at the stadium, as spectators sat under a warm July sun. Peters went through five kilometers in 15:43, already asserting a nineteen-second lead over teammate Cox, Swedish marathon titleholder Gustaf Jansson, and the unbelievable Zatopek. The spectators along the route shook their heads in wonder, figuring that Peters had taken leave of his senses. Slightly behind the trio of pursuers came Soviet champion Yakov Moskachenkov, world record holder at 30 kilometers; eighteen seconds behind him were the South Americans Flores and Gorno.

At ten kilometers (10-K), Peters was still in the lead, but the incredible pace had not shaken his pursuers. In fact, although he went through the 10-K mark in 31:55, Jansson was only sixteen seconds back, and Zatopek was sticking with Jansson, while Cox was only eight seconds back of them; Gorno had moved up to fifth. At 15-K, Jansson was behind Peters, while Zatopek clomped along with him. The trio had opened a sixty-four-second lead over Gorno and Cox.

Just before the turnaround point at 20-K, Jansson moved along with Zatopek as the Czech began to move away from Peters. Peters fell ten seconds behind. A few minutes later, as Cox came to the turnaround mark, he collapsed and was taken away in an ambulance.

By the 25-K mark, Zatopek began to make his move, opening a five-second lead on Jansson, while Peters hung in twenty-eight seconds behind the Swede.

At 30-K, the handwriting was on the wall. Zatopek was invincible that day. He had gone through the checkpoint in 1:38:42, Jansson in 1:39:08, and Peters in 1:39:53. Peters was struggling to dredge up some reserves of strength to overcome the feeling of deadness that had developed from his fast early pace, but in the marathon, what is used up early is never found again. The pace and the drafty plane trip had caught up with him. Before he reached the twenty-mile point, his left leg cramped up, and he was forced to hobble along the side of the road. Sam Ferris, a former running luminary, was standing at almost the exact spot where Peters peeled off the road. Ferris shouted encouragement, and Peters reposed by hobbling another two hundred meters, but it was too much. He retired from the race.

Peters's departure moved Gorno into third. The race that was unfolding behind the beast-like Zatopek—who was running along, his head cocked characteristically to the side, his face contorted in apparent pain—was a dramatic one. Zatopek went through 35-K in 1:56:50, sixty-five seconds in front of the still-game Jansson. Gorno was less than a minute back of him, and Gorno's teammate, Cabrera, was thirty-one seconds behind him. Choi Yoon Chil had moved into fifth, and went through 35-K in 2:00:57.

Zatopek went through 40-K in 2:15:10, continuing his relent-less assault. In trying to keep up, Jansson became fatigued; Gorno passed him, but he was still 2:15 behind the Czech. Choi was challenging Cabrera for fourth, and in the closing two kilo-meters, the Korean almost did catch Gorno as they closed to within thirty seconds of Jansson.

The twenty-nine-year-old Zatopek crossed the tape in 2:23:03—a new Olympic record—and smiled for the crowd. He had his track suit on and was chomping on an apple by the time Argentinian Reinaldo Gorno crossed the line. Zatopek had done the unbelievable by winning the Olympic long-distance triple, while Peters had once again failed in his bid to shine at an Olympic Games.

As though to erase the 1952 defeat from his mind, Peters re-trenched and came out fighting in 1953 with a season that shines as one of the most incredible ever in marathon history.

He captained the English cross-country team that entered the world cross-country championships, and placed a creditable eleventh. He followed that up with a personal record of 29:01.8 for six miles, set a record of 1:45:23 for twenty miles at the Southern Counties 20, and broke the British one-hour track record on a day with temperatures in the eighties and high hu-midity, breaking Walter George's sixty-nine-year-old record. His feet blistered badly, and the effort exhausted him. But nothing would deter his training for the marathon season.

His 1953 marathon rampage is exquisite.

On June 13, he again entered the Windsor-to-Chiswick mara-thon. The day was clear and cool. For once Peters started at a relaxed, conservative pace. His high-intensity training made the pace too tame, however. Just after five miles, he began to move away from the field, opening a two-minute lead over Cox by the ten-mile mark. He went through twenty miles in 1:45:07, still running smoothly and strongly. He was five minutes in the lead. When he breasted the tape at Chiswick stadium, marathon history had been rewritten. Looking fresh and chipper, he heard the news that the elusive 2:20 barrier had been broken on a certified course. He had run a 2:18:40.4. In an effort to reverify the distance, the course was remeasured. It was found to be one hundred fifty-six yards longer than the required 26 miles, 385 yards. Cox took second place in 2:26:39.

Peters spent the summer further sharpening himself by running track races to maintain or better his speed. On July 25 he was again lining up at the starting line of a marathon, this time at Cardiff. It was the British Championship race, and the day, with a downpour at the start, was a miserable one for spectators. Peters again went out fast. Bob McMinnis was the only man able to stay with him, and then only for the first five miles. From there on, Peters had the out-and-back course to himself. When the rain slowed at about ten miles, a headwind began to build. On the return trip, Peters battled the weather and the headwind, and also had to pick his way through two herds of cows that had wandered onto the course! Despite it all, when he entered Maindy Stadium, he had run 2:22:29, a new world record for an out-and-back course, bettering Zatopek's Olympic time from Helsinki. The second-place finisher was more than seven minutes back.

The method seemed to be working. Peters continued to enter track races and shorter road races over the summer to keep up his leg speed, so that when he and Cox traveled to the Netherlands for the fourth annual Enschede Marathon on September 12, he would still be primed. Peters had hoped to meet some of the Olympic marathoners on the course, among them Karvonen and Gorno, but they had withdrawn. So he and Cox went out confidently, and at ten miles, quicked the pace to toss off the rest of the field. The move left Cox behind, too. On the return trip the course became reminiscent of Cardiff. The rains came and Peters worked his way into a headwind. But he was on record pace and wasn't slacking off for anything. The wind and rain slowed him somewhat, but he did manage a 2:19:22, a new course record and a new world record for an out-and-back course. Cox finished in 2:24:38, with the third-place finisher ten minutes behind him. The British were obviously in the driver's seat.

Three weeks later Peters traveled to Finland to race in the Turku Marathon. He went to Finland with a hostile atmosphere prevailing. Other marathoners were claiming that he had been competing on only favorable courses, and that some of those courses must have been short. In short, plenty of top-level marathoners were riding into Turku gunning for Peters.

The course was unique. It started in the stadium at Turku and then went out into the country for a large loop, returning to the stadium at the midway point for a lap of the track. It then headed out once again into the loop and finally returned to the stadium, where twelve laps of the track were needed to complete the required distance.

The field was not lacking in quality. It appears that the other runners were so anxious to "get" Peters that they ended up falling all over one another. Peters handled the entire field with incredible ease. He went through 10-K in 32:02, through 20-K in 1:03:16. By the midpoint (13.1 miles), he was two hundred meters in front of Karvonen, one of the local gunslingers. In a commanding lead, he slowed a bit on the second loop through the country.

He came back into the stadium running confidently and strongly, did his dozen laps, and left the spectators sitting slackjawed. He had beaten his own world's best by five seconds, turning in a terrific 2:18:34.8.

The crowd was almost embarrassed as they waited some seven minutes for the second-place finisher, Veikko Karvonen, their hero and one of the marathoners who had been vocal about the shallowness of Peters's accomplishments. Karvonen did a very respectable 2:25:47, but he had been so humbled on home ground that he swore revenge on Peters.

Looking back at the race, Peters puts it simply: "I beat the nearest runner by one-and-a-half miles . . . but it was no consolation. It was a year too late. You see, it isn't always the best that get it. It's the best man on that day. My biggest problem always in the marathon was to run the first six miles slowly. You see, I was in an absolute class by myself in the years '52, '53 and '54. In fact, Zatopek said I was the fellow to beat. But I just chucked it away."

Peters's reputation spread to the United States, and he was invited to come to Boston for Patriot's Day to race in the famed marathon. It was shaping up to be a formidable race, with Karvonen coming, hoping for revenge, a large contingent of Japanese marathoners planning to attend, and the 1948 Olympic Marathon gold-medalist Delfo Cabrera making plans to come too. Nineteen fifty-four was shaping up to be a very, very competitive year at Boston.

Peters arrived the day before the race and was taken in tow by the fabled Jock Semple, who drove him over the course. Peters remembers Semple as the personification of kindness and consideration. During the trip in Semple's car over the course, Peters learned that the Finns and the Japanese had been there for eight weeks training for the big race.

It was not a good year for Peters to try Boston. The winds, if there are any, usually come at your back at Boston as you make your way eastward from Hopkinton. On this day, the winds were coming from the ocean. And then there was the heat. Although Boston can be counted on to be hot one out of three years, the heat became especially trying when coupled with the headwinds.

In the race, Cabrera took the early lead, but the pace began to wear down the forty-seven-year-old Olympian, and Peters soon asserted himself, assuming his typical front-of-the-pack position. Karvonen had run Boston before, and knew the struggle that lay in the hills between sixteen and twenty-one miles at Newton Falls. He stayed with Peters, but let Jim do the pacing, occasionally harassing him by moving into the lead. "I never found Finns very talkative," Peters would say in an interview in 1978 with Mike Spear, a reporter for *Stars & Stripes.* The two raced on in profound silence, the half-million people along the course being treated to a classic duel which met all the expectations of the Boston race directors.

At about twenty miles, deep into the hills, Karvonen made his move, opening a five-yard lead. At about the same time, a small dog dashed out of the crowd and got tangled in Jim's feet. "It didn't bite me but it stopped me running and I couldn't get going again," he said in talking with Spear.

By the time Karvonen topped the last of the Newton Hills, known less than affectionately as "Heartbreak," Peters was one hundred yards behind. Karvonen was clearly acclimated to the temperature and, fueled by his passion for revenge, overwhelmingly peaked for the race. He turned in a sterling 2:20:39 and seemed to feel very good, reveling in the cheers and congratulations of the crowd. Peters crossed the line in second place in 2:22:40 and collapsed. Karvonen's teammate, Erkki Puolakka, finished third, in 2:24:25, in as wretched shape as Peters.

The question now arose as to Peters's ability to come back after giving himself such a beating. On the horizon was what had clearly become one of his favorite races, the "Poly." It was scheduled for June 26, and for 1954 it was combined with the British title race. There were 181 starters, and the field was a good one. Peters soon put to rest any doubts about his ability to bounce back. He and Cox went through ten miles in an astounding 52:53. Cox backed off soon after, hoping to conserve his strength, perhaps sensing in Peters a fierce desire to erase the Boston experience.

Cox ran the best race of his career, a 2:23:08, but his accomplishment was far overshadowed by Peters's new world record of 2:17:39.

As in the previous years, Peters began to mix in some track races to keep up his speed and in fact ran his best-ever six-miler (28:57.8) at White Stadium soon after the "Poly."

He was a man with astounding records under his belt. He had repeatedly lowered the world's best time for the marathon between 1952 and 1954, lowering it by eight minutes after it had remained unchanged for years. Yet, the major international glories eluded him. He had done badly in the 1948 Olympics at 10,000 meters, and, the favorite for the marathon at the 1952 Olympic Games, had dropped out, letting a marathon novice beat him. He felt desperate to prove himself on the international level.

It was with a great deal of determination, then, that he traveled to Vancouver, British Columbia, to compete in the British Empire and Commonwealth Games.

Early in the competition, he had distinguished himself with a third place in the six-mile race. He had been in marvelous condition, but had run conservatively, saving his strength for the marathon, where he hoped to take first place and set a new world record in the process.

Peters wanted everything to be just right, so he and Cox took a car to measure the course. They measured it at twenty-seven miles, much too long for an attempt at the world record. They complained to the Canadians, who checked it themselves and determined it to be only two hundred fifty feet too long; they consequently moved the finish line inside the stadium up two hundred fifty feet. Cox and Peters agreed that it was not going to be a record-setting marathon.

As though a long course weren't enough, the day of the race dawned hot and humid—and the starting time was noon.

Peters went out like a man obsessed. Although he fully appreciated what damage a bare sun and high humidity can do to a marathoner, he refused to compromise his race and set out for his usual position—well into the lead and going away.

"I planned to come into the stadium in two hours, twenty, and I did," says Peters, looking back on that day. "I was capable of 2:15, but not in that heat. All told, there were about eighteen runners and Stan [Cox] was especially out to beat me, because he never had.

"It was sort of fun, really. Stan and I trotted along and got rid of everybody. I looked around and I could see him about three hundred yards behind and I didn't like that. My philosophy was always: kill or be killed.

"So I put it on a little but I didn't want to do too much because I knew I had this race coming up in Bern (scheduled for eighteen days later). Well, I thought around the twenty-three mile mark I heard someone say Stan Cox had collapsed. So I said to myself: 'Don't be bloody ridiculous!'

"Because all the time you are fighting a losing battle with fatigue and your mind goes. It was absolutely boiling hot. It was a very hilly course and it was in the nineties. So I said to myself: 'You know you're being a coward. You're just imagining he's out.' "

In actuality, Stan Cox had been profoundly affected by the heat. He had become groggy and disoriented and had run into a steel telephone pole.

The stadium crowd was in a pandemonium. They had just witnessed one of the greatest mile duels ever between Roger Bannister and John Landy. Both had just recently astonished the

entire world by running sub-4:00 miles. Now they had met in
battle and had both broken four minutes, Bannister taking the
win when Landy performed a tactical mistake in the final lap by
looking behind him for Bannister, while the young physician
ducked past him on the inside.

Peters was approaching the stadium well within his plan of
getting there in 2:20. He was rapidly developing near-fatal heat-
stroke, however, and his perception of things was rapidly becoming distorted.

"Then, when I got just outside the stadium," he says, picking
up the story, "a young Canadian couple looked at me in amaze-
ment. If my coach had been there he'd have said: 'You've got
time to take a shower.' "

Indeed, Peters was seventeen minutes ahead of his closest
competitor, but in his confusion, he was still expecting Cox to
come running into view to rob him of his day.

"I came to the stadium ramp and it seemed a very big incline.
Then, when I came into the stadium, I thought: 'What are you
working so hard for? Get on with it. Get around, you've got to do
that lap.' And as I ran onto the cinders, they seemed like quick-
sand. It was only my legs getting rubbery, you see. I thought:
'Get on with it you coward. Finish it!'

"I moved from the left side of the track to the right toward the
shade. That was where the Duke of Edinburgh was watching.
And I remember falling."

Assuming the course was really as long as he suspected, Peters
had, ironically enough, already finished the marathon distance
before he entered the stadium.

He was less than three hundred eighty yards from the finish
line. The scene was nearly a carbon copy of the 1908 Olympic
Marathon, when little Dorando Pietri came into the stadium well
in the lead and fell repeatedly before being carried over the finish line by sympathetic officials.

Not wanting to repeat that incident, officials stood by help-
lessly as Peters fell, crawled forward, clawed his way back to his
feet, collapsed again. If they touched him, he would be disqualified. The spectators watched in horror for eleven minutes as
Peters covered a mere one hundred eighty yards, repeatedly falling, lying there twitching, then crawling forward.

"Apparently, there are various stories that I fell down twelve times," Jim Peters remembers. "I don't remember going down more than three times. What I did remember, though, was that I had to finish. I knew I hadn't felt the sensation of the tape breaking so I got up."

When he was still two hundred yards away from a finish line he couldn't even see, officials could stand his horrible efforts no longer and voted to end it. John Savidge, a former shotputter who was the English team's masseur, walked onto the track and carried Peters off. Chris Brasher, who was standing there that day, describes it in graphic terms: "He collapsed, got up, and collapsed all again. It was a hell of a scene, one of the most horrific in athletic history. I was on the side of the track and saw it all. They took his temperature right there and his brain temperature was about 107 or 108 degrees. It is something that is still absolutely unbelievable in medical circles. He was on the verge of cooking his brain."

Savidge carried Peters to the dressing room and from there to a waiting ambulance. Peters was already gone from the track by the time Joe McGhee, who'd stopped along the road to take a rest, came into the stadium. He won the race in 2:39:36.2, followed by two South Africans who, mindful of the hot sun, had run the course very conservatively.

Jim Peters woke in a recovery ward in a Vancouver hospital.

"The first bloody bloke I see is Stan Cox laying in bed. So I look at him and say: 'What the bloody hell are you doing here?' And when he said he'd collapsed, I realized that I hadn't imagined it, that I hadn't been a coward.

"I said, 'You didn't win the race, then?' And he said, 'No.'

"So I said, 'Who the hell did then?' And he didn't know."

Ironically, Jim was one of the first patients of Roger Bannister, for after his sub-4:00 mile race against John Landy, Bannister had come to the hospital to see Peters. The specialist on the case likened Peters's condition to that of a man in an open boat for two weeks in the sun, and claimed it was only his tremendous physical condition that saved him.

When he recovered, despite being afflicted by headaches and giddiness from his trial in the sun, he had every intention of going into training for the 1956 Olympic Games in Melbourne.

His coach, in fact, encouraged him, claiming that he'd run forever. Intellectually, however, Peters felt he'd have to train three times a day to accomplish that, because by 1956 he'd be thirty-eight years old. Moreover, his doctor attempted to discourage him from trying, even though he admitted that he'd recovered beautifully.

What finally swayed Peters from making the attempt was a conversation with John Landy, Australia's premier miler. He told Jim how hot it was likely to be in Melbourne. Jim knew that if he went to Melbourne, he wouldn't be able to hold himself back. "I was a different man on the track," he admits. "I liked to run them into the ground. I ran for my wife, my club, and my country, and I was absolutely dedicated. I told Landy, 'If it's a hot day in Melbourne, you know what I'm going to do. I'm going to tear the floor down like I did before.' "

He wound down his career gradually, easing off over a six-month period, and spent his time studying to be an optician. He opened his own shop and today works there with his son, Robin.

At the end of Mike Spear's 1978 interview with Jim, Mike asked him if he'd change it if he had it to do over.

"If I had me life to live over," he said, "I'd have another go, I suppose. I remember meeting the [light heavyweight] boxing champion Freddie Mills, who later was supposed to have committed suicide. I was introduced to him at an East End London boys club and he said: 'What a wonderful chap you are, Jim. I don't mind taking a punch on the jaw for a grand, but I'll be damned if I'd run a marathon for a medal. I don't know how you do it.'

"I'd be a hypocrite if I didn't say it. But I wish there'd been some money in it."

Emil Zatopek (left) leads Chris Chataway and Herb Schade in
the 1952 Olympic 5-K.

6.

EMIL ZATOPEK:
Triple Play

It seems preposterous to number among the best marathoners in history a man who competed at the marathon distance only twice, and who placed sixth in one of those two races. Yet it is that seeming contradiction which exemplifies the entire career—and legend—of Emil Zatopek.

Zatopek was born in Koprinivince, Czechoslovakia, the son of a poor carpenter, and moved to Zlin at the age of sixteen. Short and wiry, with straight, straw-like hair, he was a young man filled with ambition and good humor, and a tireless worker. At Zlin he worked in a shoe factory and went to school in the evenings.

The diverse strands of fate that would allow him to fulfill his ambitions were coming together. In 1941 the shoe company for whom he worked sponsored a race through the streets of Zlin. Emil had run a few races for fun against his fellow workers but had never competed formally. He actually tried to get out of the race, but as an employee of the company, he had no choice but to run along with about one hundred other young men. He finished second, probably motivated more by the desire to get it over with than the wish to shine in the event.

In the year that followed, Zatopek ran a few more races but did not develop any burning interest in the sport. By the end of the year, however, trainers and coaches had singled him out as a young man with a future, despite his rather awkward running style. Although outwardly nonplussed by the selection, inwardly,

Emil was happy. Running provided a road upon which his ambitions could travel.

His first official race was a 3,000-meter contest in which he finished only three seconds behind his trainer, recording a 9:12. The local newspaper carried these words: "A good performance by Zatopek." It was the spark that would account for Emil Zatopek's burning down the track world. His poor beginnings had primed him to take advantage of the first opportunities that came along to become someone. He read that single sentence in the newspaper over and over again.

Training became the mainstay of his life. His interpretation of what it took to excel at running quickly took on its own unique flavor. Instead of looking for races with inferior competition which he could win, he sought out the toughest competition available, and, through doing so, his times improved dramatically.

Zatopek also began studying other runners and their methods, dismissing what he found unworkable, modifying and customizing what seemed to make sense to him.

From this studious approach to running came what is today referred to as "interval training."

"When I was young, I was too slow," Zatopek said in a 1979 interview. "I thought, 'I must learn to run fast by practicing to run fast.' So I ran one hundred meters very fast. Then I came back, slow, slow, slow. People said, 'Emil, you are crazy. You are practicing to be a sprinter. You have no chance.' I said, 'Yes, but if I run one hundred meters twenty times, that is two kilometers and that is no longer a sprint.' "

Other distance runners at that time were training strictly for endurance and stamina. Emil's reaction? "Why should I practice running slow? I already know how to run slow. I want to learn how to run fast."

Although he is credited with developing the interval training method, he claims that he merely modified methods being used by the Flying Finn, Paavo Nurmi, his inspiration and hero.

Coaches, trainers, and track enthusiasts watching him train all contended that he was a fool.

His training was interrupted somewhat by his joining the army after the Russians drove the Germans out of Zlin. He continued to train, however, running in place in his military boots while on guard duty.

After the war, Zatopek signed up for officers' training. His first race outside his native country came in the 1946 European Championships at Oslo. He ran the 5,000 meters, and, although he did not win against the stiff international competition, he did run 14:25.8, setting a Czech national record. Encouraged by this achievement, he found a spot in the woods near the military base where he measured off a course a quarter-mile long. It was not the traditional oval, however; he used a straight line. Zatopek ran his course daily, through wind and rain and mud and snow, all the time wearing his heavy military boots, and, when it became too dark to see, carrying a flashlight.

In 1947, in his first 5,000-meter race, he lowered the national record to 14:08.2. Almost immediately he went into international competition again, where he turned in a brilliant 14:15.2 to beat Finland's Heino by one yard, a terrific accomplishment against one of the world's greatest runners.

By now he was swamped with invitations to race. He graduated from officers' training school and spent his month's leave taking on every race he could fit into his schedule. Zatopek finished 1947 undefeated in 5,000 meters and ranked number one in the world.

Zatopek went into the 1948 Olympic year in sterling condition. No one worked harder or against such odds. His style has been described as similar to a man just stabbed in the heart. When he ran, his head would roll back as though his eyes were attempting to see over the top of his head, his tongue would loll out of his mouth, and an expression of pain would cross his face as though he were about to drop to the ground from a mortal wound. His arm movements were usually spastic; often, one would drop so low that it looked as though he were trying to scratch his knee. Each step appeared to be torture, and the next step after it seemed impossible for the wiry little man. Yet, through it all, Zatopek was covering a tremendous amount of ground. Further, he did not consider it important to have a classic, beautiful style in the upper body—what was ultimately important was happening with the legs.

Journalists loved to write about him and to create colorful

nicknames for him. His animal-like pain and desire inspired the appellation Beast of Prague, while the force of his late-race charge through the finish, his legs driving like pistons, earned him the title of Human Locomotive.

Zatopek's most endearing qualities were his love of running, his good humor, and his almost naive enthusiasm at winning or at participating in a good race. It was this feeling of animal joy at the competition that helped drive him on to superhuman efforts in training and racing.

The level of fitness he exhibited going into the 1948 season was reputedly the result of as many as sixty repetitions of four hundred meters in one day with a mere two-hundred-meter jog between.

The Olympic Games were coming up at Wembley Stadium in England. Zatopek was favored to win the 5,000 meters, but was considered a dark horse for the 10,000. He had only run his first 10,000 in Budapest in May, his time of 30:28.4 setting a national record by two minutes. He followed that with a terrific 3,000 meters and then ran 29:27 for 10,000 meters at Prague on June 17. Five days later he ran a 5,000 meters in 14:10.

Zatopek went to London as something of an unknown, certainly an unknown in the 10,000 meters. The English had never seen him run before. When they saw him start in the 10,000, they agreed that he was probably the worst runner they'd ever had the misfortune to watch. He was wearing a faded Czechoslovakia shirt; although young, his corn-colored hair was already thinning, his tongue hung limply out of his mouth, he made noises that sounded like tortured huffs and wheezes, and his face contorted into such a pained grimace that people in the stands winced to see him.

He was almost a sideshow for the crowd. His tremendous accomplishments had not been reported outside the Iron Curtain, and his obvious near-exhaustion did nothing to give the spectators a hint of the performance they were about to see. He was running back in the pack, obviously there only to fill out the field and to appease the Iron Curtain bloc.

At each lap, he would look into the crowded stands at a certain spot, and for seven laps a Czech supporter stood up and held a white sock in the air. After the eighth lap, however, the Czech fan stood up and displayed a red vest, the signal to Zatopek that the pace had slowed to below seventy-one seconds per lap. Zatopek responded immediately, seeming to limp up into fifth place. Like a battered dog, the crowd took him to their hearts as a sentimental favorite, although they all knew that against the great Heino his chances were nil. Viljo Heino held the world record at 10,000. The crowd was generally unaware that the previous month Zatopek had come to within 1.6 seconds of that record in only his second 10,000.

Czech fans in the stands who knew his prowess began chanting, "Za-to-pek, Za-to-pek, Za-to-pek!" The chant was soon taken up by non-Czechs. He closed on Heino at four thousand meters and moved past him. The crowd responded. Heino fought back and retook the lead and again the crowd went wild. The Czech fan with the red vest displayed it again, and again Zatopek took off with a sprint that was truly uncommon in a distance event. He opened a thirty-meter lead on Heino, and now much of the crowd was chanting, "Za-to-pek, Za-to-pek, Za-to-pek!"

The heat of the day was becoming oppressive, adding an element of confusion to the affair. Zatopek was secretly shooting for a 29:35. The Czech fan kept waving the red vest, indicating that the pace was too slow. Zatopek became more confused. "Where is Heino?" he asked an official.

"Heino is out," came the answer.

Zatopek moved on through the heat. He crossed the finish line, and as he did, it was discovered the lap counter had counted one lap too short. Zatopek rolled into his awkward gait and continued on, finishing with an awesome sprint. He was ecstatic, and his fans mirrored that genuine excitement—they were singing the Czech national anthem as Alain Mimoun of Algeria, representing France, took second place, forty-seven seconds behind Emil's new Olympic record of 29:59.6.

The following day, the crowd was again with him as he ran his qualifying race for the 5,000 meters in a competitive style, winning by thirty seconds, a show of excess that would ultimately catch up with him.

Two days later came the 5,000-meter final. The race was run in a downpour. For the first eight laps, Zatopek led with almost machine-like laps of sixty-eight or sixty-nine seconds. The rest of the field was content to follow. At 3,500 meters, Gaston Reiff of Belgium made his move.

Zatopek seemed too tired to respond. Seeing his sluggishness, Willi Slykhuis of Holland also took advantage of it. Emil was soon sixty-five yards behind Reiff, with Slykhuis securely in second place. Zatopek fought back bravely, but his legs were tired and he kept slipping on the slick track. As he went down the backstretch of the last lap, he was still thirty yards behind Reiff. But his courage had risen, and he began an awkward sprint that soon turned into what would stir the press to refer to him as a runaway locomotive. He rushed past Slykhuis, seemingly heedless of the man's very existence. He ran ahead madly. The crowd was on its feet, going crazy.

As Reiff turned onto the homestretch, Zatopek was twenty yards behind, building momentum. Reiff was completely zoned out, wearied to his bone. But as soon as the crowd again began chanting "Za-to-pek, Za-to-pek, Za-to-pek!" Reiff was roused from his weariness enough to turn his head. What he saw was enough to frighten him to a final surge, enough to hold the charging Czech off by a mere two yards. The stands went wild, and never again would anyone in the track world ask, "Who's this Zatopek?"

"Witnesses who have long since forgotten the other events," wrote American sports columnist Red Smith, "still wake up screaming in the dark when Emil the Terrible goes writhing through their dreams, gasping, groaning, clawing at his abdomen in horrible extremities of pain."

In October of the same year, Emil married a young Czech girl who had placed seventh in the women's javelin at the Olympic games. Dana Ingrova was a fit companion for Emil; she shared his enthusiasm, high spirits, and love of life and athletics. Ironically, they were both born on the same day, September 19, 1922, with Emil the elder by six hours. Legend has it that on the morning of their wedding day, Dana's parents forbade her to participate in a handball championship, so she went cycling with Emil and they crashed while kissing. They arrived late for their wedding, but once they had arrived, they danced until dawn, hours after the last of the guests enjoyed the peace of exhaustion.

Zatopek took to his married life well, and began working even harder at his running. Over the next four years, he began breaking world records, racing frequently—sometimes too frequently. He set one 10,000-meter world record after another. Following one of his world records, Dana described his state of mind: "He glowed like a meteor and couldn't fall alseep all night for excitement."

During 1949, except for one loss at 1,500 meters, he went undefeated.

On August 2, 1950, he set a personal record of 14:06.2 for 5,000 meters, and two days later, this time at Turku with Heino a spectator in the crowd cheering him on, he ran an incredible race: finishing with a wild sprint, he broke the world record in 10,000 meters by eighteen seconds, running an astonishing 29:02.6.

Some time later, he developed food poisoning from eating a tainted goose. He was admitted to the hospital, had his stomach pumped, and was told by his doctor to pull out of the upcoming European Championships. Emil ignored the doctor. During the month that followed, he ran two of the best 10,000-meter races in history, and the second, third, and fourth fastest 5,000s recorded to that time. He finished 1950 unbeaten.

Relatively speaking, 1951 was somewhat disappointing. He decided on a rather radical departure from past winters, in that he set out to train indoors. He concentrated on building strength through weight training and building cardiovascular endurance by riding a stationary bicycle with four-and-a-half-pound weights on each foot. The ever-enthusiastic Emil got a little bit over his head skiing that winter, however, and suffered an accident that put one of his legs in a cast for a month. With the indoor training and the accident, he didn't have an opportunity to run until April.

Once he got rolling, Zatopek promptly lost a 3,000-meter race. Although he did win all of his 5,000-meter races, they were done in—for him—mediocre times. He remained unbeaten at 10,000 meters. In the fall he decided to try the longer distances, and set out after Heino's world records in the one-hour track run. He went through the 10-K in 31:06, and, feeling good, picked up the pace a bit, going through the second 10-K in 30:10. His distance for one hour was 19,558 meters (twelve miles, two hundred sixty-eight yards). His 20-K time of 1:01:16 destroyed Heino's record. When he heard of the performance, Heino's reaction reflected his respect for Zatopek: "Believe me, Zatopek could run twenty kilometers in one hour."

That comment got the track world talking. Only six men in the world had run under thirty minutes for 10-K, Heino and Zatopek among them. To break the 20-K record to the extent of bringing it below sixty minutes would mean two sub-thirty-minute 10-K performances back-to-back.

Zatopek did not share Heino's faith, but two weeks after setting the one-hour record, he was back on the track going after the incredible 20 kilometers in one hour. Seventeen runners participated. From the start Emil led, as he knew he had to in order to break the mark. The day was warm and windless; the track was cooperative. He went through 5,000 in 14:56, 10,000 in 29:53.4, and 15,000 in (a world record) 44:54.6. Suddenly, he felt a stitch in his side. For once the pain apparent in his face was real, but he fought it with characteristic courage, passing ten miles in 48:12, another world record.

The pain left in a few minutes but it was replaced by a bone-deep tiredness. He knew that there would be a gunshot at 59:00. Zatopek felt it was going to be very close as he approached the marker indicating four hundred meters remaining. If he could reach the post, he was certain he could reach down within himself to sprint the final four hundred meters in one minute. He passed the pole and there was no shot. He kept going, pushing into the curve, hoping that the man with the gun was not asleep at the trigger. Finally, the shot! He went around past the finish line, passing the 20-K mark in 59:51.8. He kept going, getting in fifty-two additional meters before the gun fired to signal one hour. He had broken the 20-K record and had also set a new record in the one-hour run.

Zatopek finished the year by running three 5,000s; he also got some rest, ice-skated with Dana, and took runs in knee-deep snow.

By that point in his career, he had racked up four of the five fastest 5,000s in history, and six of the seven fastest 10,000s. It was time to think about 1952 and the Helsinki Olympics, the

Olympic Games that would be the closest in spirit to those held in Athens in 1896.

Things did not look promising for Zatopek at the games after he suffered a bout of flu that put him in bed. And as he made a comeback, he found his performances somewhat lackluster. Zatopek was not overly confident of his chances. He felt fairly sure he would win the 10,000 meters but did not allow himself to hope for more.

Zatopek started the race tucked in among thirty-two runners, maintaining a conservative pace. After six laps he made his move, methodically picking up the pace and keeping his lap times between sixty-eight and seventy-two seconds. The Czech had shaken all but two courageous runners by the 5,000-meter mark. Then Gordon Pirie of Britain dropped off the pace, and the one man left was the Algerian, Mimoun, who had been second to him in the 10-K at the 1948 Olympic Games. Mimoun, who had not lost a race at the distance except to Zatopek, trained by using Zatopek's methods.

The crowd cheered Zatopek and they cheered Mimoun, but Zatopek felt it necessary to put down all competition. For six laps he worked Mimoun over until the little runner dropped back. Emil kept the pace in the range of seventy-one seconds per lap and then, for the last lap, increased his speed to sixty-four seconds. His time was an Olympic record and his third best time at 10-K, a 29:17.0. He won by ninety yards.

Two days later he was in good spirits as he ran in the third heat of the 5,000 meters. He very much wanted the pole in the race. To take it, he would have to place fifth. He also wanted his friend, the Russian Aleksandr Anufriev, to make the final. During the race, he accelerated and decelerated, hanging in with different runners, admonishing them to run faster. He pulled up next to Curt Stone of the United States and spoke to him in English: "Hurry up, Stone, or you'll miss the bus." He moved to the side of Anufriev and spoke to him in Russian: "Sasha, come on, we must get a move on." As the race became a contest between Zatopek and four other runners, he continued his playfulness. On the final lap, with only the five men in contention, Zatopek ran from one to the other, holding up five fingers, dropping the field into an easy pace, finally grabbing Anufriev by the back of his shorts and pushing him across the finish line.

Speaking in English, French, German, and Russian to his fellow competitors, Zatopek was still in excellent spirits for the final two days later. But for all the warmth and light spirits he showed, he was very serious inside, as well he might have been, for the race turned out to be one of the greatest track battles in history. Journalists of the period referred to it as the race of the century.

The line-up was virtually a who's who of world-class track stars: Chris Chataway of Great Britain, who later that year would help to pace Roger Bannister to the first four-minute mile; Zatopek's archenemy, Reiff, who was Olympic defending champion at 5,000; Herbert Schade of West Germany, the fastest qualifier, who had won his berth in the final in Olympic record time; Anufriev of the USSR; the indomitable Gordon Pirie of Britain; and Mimoun, second to Zatopek in two Olympic 10-Ks.

It was Schade who took the group out—fast! He hoped to use the intimidation of his Olympic-record qualifying time to scare the rest of the field into staying with him. Mimoun, Reiff, and Chataway went after him, while Zatopek lay back in sixth place. Reiff, a tough and confident veteran of the 5,000, was still the favorite; his classic stride and his tremendous speed seemed the necessary ingredients for victory, and they were augmented by his experience. Schade, everyone agreed, would have his work cut out for him to hold off the hungry pack.

At the midway mark, Zatopek moved up and made his push for the lead, but Schade saw him coming and was still strong enough to fight him off. Zatopek tried again—and again—but failed to get past the German. On the next try, he barely edged past Schade, took a deep gasp, and tried to assess the field. In that moment the race blew apart. As though they were turning his reputation on him and imitating his tactics, Chataway, Reiff, and Mimoun went past Zatopek, and past Schade, like a runaway freight train. Zatopek tucked in behind them in self-defense; Schade stuck with Zatopek because of a survival instinct. For the next several laps the five of them exchanged the lead innumerable times. The crowd was going crazy. Anyone was capable of taking it at that point. With five hundred meters to go,

Reiff—inexplicably—stepped off the track; he had quit. Now there were four left and four hundred meters to go.

Zatopek squirted out of the tight group and took the lead, but on the backstraight the red-headed Chataway moved past him, followed by Schade and Mimoun. Zatopek was, within a matter of seconds, six yards behind the trio and looking very tired and lost.

But it was in such situations that Zatopek—the real Zatopek, the Zatopek of courage unbounded, strength incarnate—came to the fore. With two hundred meters to go, he became a running beast, his head back, his shoulders hunched, a look of near-terror on his face, his stride awkward and seemingly painful—but enormously effective. The crowd turned hysterical.

Zatopek moved out to the third lane, the longer way through the turn but an effective position for coming into the straight. He went past Schade and moved up on Chataway and Mimoun. Mimoun moved out to go around the ailing Chataway, bumping into Zatopek, but Emil was running wild and didn't notice. The interchange between Mimoun and Zatopek had somehow an effect upon Chataway—whether physically or psychologically, it is difficult to say—for he fell into the inside of the track. Mimoun put on a tremendous effort to catch Zatopek, but the Czech was moving too fast. Mimoun finished second to Zatopek for the third time in Olympic competition.

At the bold move, the hysterical crowd had fallen silent. Even after Zatopek crossed the line, they were still too awed by his performance to speak. Emil, exhausted, made his way toward the Olympic Village amidst a strange quiet. Because of his exhaustion he failed to see the finals of the women's javelin, in which Dana won the gold medal. When he heard of her accomplishment later, he was excited. "This gold one pleases me more than all the other ones so far," he said. "But," he added later, "at present, the score of the contest in the Zatopek family is two to one. This result is too close! To restore some prestige I will try to improve on it—in the marathon race." Actually, he had decided prior to Dana's gold that he would attempt the marathon, for the first time in his life.

The marathon was scheduled for three days after the 5,000,

and track fans were mystified by his desire to try the distance, a distance at which he had never competed and one that had been, for two years, the province of England's Jim Peters.

Zatopek was no fool, however. He had two precepts of strategy: first, since Jim Peters was the best in the world, he had best follow Jim Peters; second, since the marathon was run at a slower pace than he was used to, he must practice patience (something he was not noted for in competition).

He had never met Peters, although he had humbled the man four years before by lapping him in the 10,000 meters at the London Olympic Games. Zatopek read the newspapers and learned that Peters would be wearing number 187. He wanted to be very certain this information was correct, though, so, before the race, as the sixty-eight starters milled about, he walked up to number 187, extended his hand, and said, "Hello, I am Zatopek." Number 187 in turn extended his hand and said simply, "I'm Jim Peters." Peters had endured a drafty, difficult, cramped ride to Helsinki in a surplus World War II plane that had worked its way slowly through bad weather. He was feeling somewhat under the weather.

When the gun sounded, Peters, like the competitor he was, took off for his usual position—out front, the vantage point from which he could destroy the competition and, once rid of them, see if he could perhaps destroy himself. When Peters took off, Zatopek was caught by surprise. He was shocked by the fast pace at which marathons were actually run. It was almost ten miles before he finally caught up to Peters. It must have been quite a sight, for neither of them had a classic running style: Zatopek looked pained and Peters flopped from side to side in a rolling gait.

He moved up beside the Englishman and said, "Jim, the pace—it is too fast?" Peters, already suffering terribly, hoped to discourage the seemingly naive Zatopek and with him, Gustaf Jansson of Sweden, who had challenged Zatopek to move up with Peters and who now ran between but slightly behind the two.

"Emil, the pace—it is too slow," Peters said, hoping Zatopek would pick it up and burn himself out.

Although he and Jansson were running relatively comfortably, it came as a shock to Zatopek to hear Peters say such a thing. He was sure he had heard wrong. "You say 'too slow'?" Zatopek said. "Are you sure the pace is too slow?"

"Yes," Peters answered.

Emil shook his head in disbelief and picked up the pace. "Come with us," he said to Peters, "it's much easier when there are three together." Peters did not reply.

Zatopek and Jansson reached the tunaround point running side by side, with Peters already falling behind. When they turned, it was into a headwind. The second half of the race became a competitive ordeal, something Zatopek was used to.

By 25-K of the 42-kilometer race, Jansson, tiring, had fallen five seconds behind the Czech after stopping to take some fruit juice at an aid station. Zatopek had ignored the chance to drink. The Czech approached the hills in the course, took them at speed, looked back at the top, and saw that he had broken Jansson's tenacious attachment to him.

As he ran, he chatted with cyclists and spectators, whether or not they understood him.

Now came the hard part: fighting against his own weariness and the remaining distance. Such fights were an everyday occurrence in Zatopek's training, however, and he held gamely to his pace. He went through 30-K in 1:38:42, some twelve seconds in front of the world record for that checkpoint.

Zatopek now began to feel the pain and exhaustion encroaching on his remaining competitiveness. He began to develop blisters, he was gasping for air, and he was getting a headache from the crowd noise. Ten minutes from the end, he had a two-and-a-quarter-minute lead. His confidence built with each step that took him closer to the stadium.

His exhaustion was written plainly on his face and he was too tired to employ his characteristic grimaces of pain. His scarlet Czech racing singlet was hanging out of his shorts and he moved with an old man's shuffle. The distance and the challenge of the marathon had almost done him in, something the world's best distance racers had not been able to do for years.

The crowd had been appraised of the marathon's progress, and they were prepared to witness one of the greatest feats in athletic history: a clean sweep of the Olympic long-distance events.

As he came through the marathon tunnel and burst onto the track, the crowd began chanting as one: "Za-to-pek! Za-to-pek! Za-to-pek!" Instead of his usual outrageous grimace of pain, he smiled. He loved the crowds to love him, and they loved him with a vengeance perhaps never equaled in track history.

As he reached the tape, he raised his arms in victory. He limped to the side of the track, sat down, removed his shoes, checked his bloodied feet, and breathed a sigh of relief that the ordeal was over. The announcement of his time came: 2:23:03.2. It was a new Olympic record and a world record for an out-and-back course.

He rose, put on his sweats, and walked to the finish line, where he ate an apple and handed orange slices to the other finishers. Reinaldo Gorno of Argentina, who had passed Jansson, took second place, two-and-a-half minutes behind Zatopek; Jansson took third. After the official ceremonies for the victors in the marathon, Zatopek jogged a victory lap to an ovation that set its own world record.

He left Helsinki to go on a rampage of breaking world records.

Amidst less-than-ideal conditions (a hard rain was persistent), he set out, on October 26 at Houstka, Czechoslovakia, to take the 30-kilometer world record. He covered 18,970 meters in one hour, and then went through fifteen miles in 1:16:26.4, a record by more than a minute. At 25-K he hit 1:19:11.8, a minute under the record previously held by Mikko Hietanen. He hit the 30-K mark in 1:35:23.8 looking fresh and chipper, having taken one-and-a-half minutes off the record. He now held every distance record of consequence from 10 kilometers up to the marathon.

The next year Emil's performances were not up to par, due in part to a tonsillectomy. He ran some good races in the late summer, but again became ill—this time for six weeks. He made a comeback on October 17 in Prague, where he won a 5-kilometer race in 14:09. He ran the final lap in 57.8 to come from thirty meters behind going into that lap. On November 11 he looked like the old Zatopek, racing a 10-kilometer in which he set a world record for six miles and in which he pushed during the last lap, breaking his own world record by one second. On New Year's Eve he traveled to Sao Silvestre in Brazil, where he won handily in their tradition-laden road race before nearly a million spectators.

While he was being Zatopek the Terrible, smashing records wherever he went, the rest of the world was taking note of the success his training methods had produced. The young lions were suddenly taking up his techniques and turning them on him as they snapped at his heels on those occasions when his age began showing.

As though to prove to them that he was still a man to be feared, Zatopek ran a 5-kilometer race on May 30 at Colombes Stadium in France before a meager crowd of 6,000. With his characteristic blast in the latter stages of the race, he went one second under the twelve-year-old record of Gunter Hagg. That race secured for him every world record above three miles.

After resting a day from his labors, he was on the track in Brussels, powering under his own 6-mile and 10-kilometer records, setting new standards of 27:59.2 and 28:54.2, respectively.

On July 3, in highly partisan Budapest, Kovacs beat Zatopek at the 10-kilometer distance by six meters, Zatopek's first loss at a distance over 5,000 meters in many years. He had been slightly ill and feverish, but he saw it as the first true signs of age, something he dreaded. His indomitable spirit would not admit defeat, however, and at the European Championships, he threw away his usual race tactics and ran hard from start to finish, beating Kovacs and the rest of the field by more than half a lap. The effort weakened him for the 5-kilometer race, and he placed a disappointing third, while Vladimar Kuts of the USSR set a new world record of 13:56.6. Emil tried to gain it back in early September but could come only within sneezing distance with a 13:57.

Seven weeks later, Kuts set another 5-kilometer record of 13:51.2 while Zatopek finished a half-lap behind.

He felt that by increasing his training he could—at least for a time—counter the age that was robbing him of victory. In 1955 his 10-kilometer performances earned him only a fourth-place ranking in the world standings, a terrific blow for the man who had ranked first for seven years in a row, six of them undefeated.

The year did have a bright spot, however. On October 29, after Albert Ivanov had broken his 25-kilometer record, Zatopek went out to regain it and lowered the mark by nearly half a minute.

The Olympic year of 1956 was a semi-disaster for Zatopek. Plagued by the urge to keep winning against the odds of age, he determined to pursue the philosophy that more work would overcome the otherwise inevitable. He began training for the Melbourne Olympics by running with Dana on his shoulders, hoping that by doing so he would get the old strength back into his legs. Instead, he gave himself a hernia that literally destroyed his summer of training. He had it surgically repaired later in the year, and, still recuperating from the operation—and against his doctors' advice—he entered the marathon and placed sixth. Ironically, the race was won by the Algerian, Mimoun, now thirty-six years old and one of the earliest disciples of Zatopek's methods—the same Mimoun who had placed second to Zatopek three times in Olympic competition. Mimoun crossed the finish line, turned around, waved away the press and photographers, and, out of respect, waited for Zatopek. As Emil crossed the line, the two embraced warmly.

Emil entered some races in the next few years. In fact, he won half of the 10-kilometer races he entered in 1957—at the age of thirty-five. He accepted an invitation to San Sebastian, Spain, to run a cross-country race of 12.5 kilometers in January, 1958, and won by thirty seconds. "I was surprised," he recalls, "but it was useless to stay active and try for a new world record. That was my last race." In a typical Zatopek gesture, he relinquished his position in the army sport club Dukla Prague to make room in the limited-membership club for the upcoming young lions who were making his life as a runner miserable.

He stepped back into the daily life of Czechoslovakia. Zatopek embodied a sort of paradox. His country hailed and revered him as its hero, yet he personally stood for individuality. "I am not Czechoslovakia. I am me," he said in a 1979 interview. "I always liked the American athletes because they owed nothing to the state. In Russia, athletes have everything handed to them, much more so than here [in America], but they are expected to win. In my country, the same. Before Helsinki, I said, 'I think I can win the 10,000 again.' They said, 'Only one gold medal?' It is not good that way. Better to be given nothing by the state and owe nothing in return. Sports should be a free activity."

His penchant for speaking his mind on individuality placed him in a unique position. During his years of competition, he was followed by agents everywhere he went and, due to such restrictions, never competed in the United States. He once commented to a Western competitor that he had to get permission to go to the toilet.

It is little wonder then, that when Alexander Dubcek rose among the Czechs, preaching personal rights and freedoms for his people, Emil was right beside him. When the Russian tanks rolled into Prague in the summer of 1968, Zatopek donned his colonel's uniform, walked into Wenceslas Square, and faced the oncoming Russians. "Why are you invading our country?" he demanded.

Manfred Steffney, a former Olympic marathoner and publisher of the West German running magazine *Spiridon,* believes that if it had been anyone but Zatopek they would have shot him down on the spot.

Instead, in an attempt to belittle him, they shipped him and Dana to a trailer deep in the woods where he was required to dig wells and mine for uranium. But rather than being belittled in the eyes of his countrymen, Zatopek, by his devotion to his new job, rose even higher in their esteem. Unable to break him, the Russian and Czech officials eventually designated him as rehabilitated and brought him back into society, giving him a low-level clerical job dealing with sports information.

Things have loosened up somewhat in Czechoslovakia, however, and, as if to prove it, the regime allows Zatopek to travel frequently to help promote sports. Those who meet him today find him charming, warm, intelligent, filled with humor, guileless, and totally unaffected by his fame as well as undaunted by his frequent turns of fortune. To those who have become champions in the sport of running, Zatopek is their champion.

Johnny Kelley (the younger) at the midway point of the 1961 Boston Marathon.

7.

JOHNNY KELLEY (the Younger):
Constant Companion

It is impossible to tell the story of the younger John Kelley (who is no relation to the other John Kelley) without telling the story of Johnny "Jock" Semple.

John Semple was born in Glasgow, Scotland, on October 26, 1903, in a second-floor apartment not far from the steel mill called Dixon's Blazes because of the hellish light its furnaces cast through the closely built, nondescript apartment buildings both day and night. John was one of three sons born to Frank and Mary Semple. At age four, John and his family packed up and moved to Clydebank, a shipbuilding city on the River Clyde.

With more than a little encouragement from his father, Johnny worked part time for a local butcher. He'd get up at 6:00 A.M., walk from house to house, taking orders from the butcher's customers, and deliver the goods on his way home from school in the evening. He earned fifty cents a week for his work.

His father was a strong believer in the benefits of going to school, but Johnny was of the belief that it was better to have a nickel in your pocket now than to have the promise of a quarter after you got out of school. Quitting school at fourteen, he went to work at the Singer Sewing Machine plant, where his father also worked. The war was on and there was plenty of work available.

Singer sponsored an annual sports day, and, with the help of a soccer trainer who lived in the apartment below his, Johnny got some valuable training tips. He won the 100-yard dash, and it was not long before he was recruited by the Clydesdale Harriers, a local running club that stressed the social rather than the competitive end of running. The Clydesdales liked to win, but they felt that the fun was in the running and the physical exercise.

As Semple recalls, "I improved rapidly as a runner until the day before my sixteenth birthday, when I broke my arm in a qualifying race for the Scottish National Championships. Though my arm was placed in a cast, I did not want to reduce my training. So I invented a workout at my job. I had many spectators each day as I slipped down to the main gate at the Singer plant to wait for the noon bell. Each day I tried to get a little extra running in by timing my exit more closely with the bell, but one day I missed, and my foot touched the ground outside the gate one second before the bell. That afternoon I got a call up to the boss's office. He was an old fuddy-duddy with a personality like a fish, and he fired me. He also had seen me running my weekly soccer-score pool."

Johnny decided to try going back to school to learn a trade. He chose the profession of a joiner (a carpenter who uses a fine-grain wood). His apprenticeship paid only three dollars a week, however, and with this he had to buy his own tools. He left that job and took one at a shipyard while he continued to train as a joiner. He worked at the shipyard for two years, but then a strike was called, and he was again out of a job.

Times were tough, and Johnny couldn't see that things were improving greatly. One evening, over supper, his father gave him quite a shock. He asked Johnny if he would like to go to America to try his luck there. Johnny jumped at the chance.

Johnny landed in Philadelphia full of enthusiasm—due partially to being on dry land again—and, after looking for work for a few months while living with relatives, he secured a job as a carpenter at a shipyard. Although he loved the job, he eventually lost it and had to go knocking about looking for other work. However, he was soon able, by landing odd jobs, to get a place of his own. He also once again became involved in athletics by joining the Kensington Athletic Club.

Philadelphia was working on putting together a major exhibition to celebrate its sesquicentennial. Semple worked laying floors for the Japanese exhibition.

One of the events the exhibition planners had scheduled was a marathon run. Johnny decided to train for it and began immediately by running ten miles through the streets of Philadelphia that night after work (as "Rocky" Balboa would do at dawn fifty years later). He upped his training to ninety miles a week, and even a dislocated shoulder suffered at work did not stop his training—he ran with his shoulder in a sling.

The day of the race, Johnny hitchhiked out to Valley Forge for the start. The marathons in the United States at that time could be counted on the fingers of two hands, with some fingers left over. The marathoners all knew one another and they ran in most of the country's marathons.

Johnny started off the race enthusiastically. At one point, a spectator yelled out to him that he was in tenth place. That egged Johnny on because there were trophies waiting at the finish for the first ten finishers. At twenty-two miles, however, he got a cramp in the leg. He worked in vain to recapture tenth place, finishing eleventh, one place out of the trophies.

After crossing the finish line, he wobbled to the grass, dropped onto it, and lay there for a half-hour recovering. "You did well," one of the competitors said to him, coming by to see if the young newcomer was still alive. "Stay with it. But don't be surprised if it takes you at least three years to run a decent marathon." For Johnny Semple, Bill "the Bricklayer" Kennedy's prediction was highly accurate.

"We were considered oddballs, yet we put up with it," Semple recalls. "We put up with it for the camaraderie. I would try to do everything I could to beat the man next to me in a race, summon every competitive juice, but the minute it was over we shook hands and we were friends. But not on the roads. On the roads we gave each other no quarter. That's how life was in the Depression, anyway. Most of us found ourselves in and out of jobs, and our running served as ventilation for that frustration. We carried the lesson of the road over into our lives: if a man could be tough out there, he wouldn't succumb under normal circumstances. Most of us were laborers. Once in a while a college man

tried the marathon, invariably without success. We were praised
for our sportsmanship and camaraderie, but we weren't considered serious athletes. Except in Boston, but then only for one day
a year."

When he was twenty-seven, Jock decided to give the Boston
Marathon a try. It was the start of the Depression and work was
spotty at best. He left Philly at 7:00 A.M., hitchhiking, and made
it to Cambridge by 9:00 A.M. the next day. It was 1930, the year
Clarence DeMar won Boston for the seventh time. That day
Johnny was in fifteenth at ten miles and began moving up; he
very badly wanted one of the prizes, which were being given to
the first eight finishers. Ultimately, he finished seventh. For
Johnny, it was the greatest day of his life. His mother had come
to visit his brother in Lynn, and both of them were standing at
the finish line. The Philadelphia newspapers put his accomplishment under the headline WEST PHILADELPHIA IRISHMAN HITCH-
HIKES TO BOSTON AND FINISHES SEVENTH. Johnny was furious.
To be a Scotsman and be called an Irishman!

He hitchhiked back to Philly and two days later was fired from
his job. It was one of those times in life when you feel things
happen for a purpose. Nothing held Johnny in Philadelphia, and
Boston was the mecca for running: he packed his kit and moved.

Semple obtained a job as a locker-room attendant at the Lynn
YMCA which paid eleven dollars a week. Someone suggested to
Johnny that he start a running team, which he did. The team
began to perform well, winning championships up and down the
eastern seaboard. To get money for gas for the team's trips,
Johnny (or "Jock" as he was now usually known) would speak to
local service clubs; the twenty or twenty-five dollars he got for an
appearance would pay for gas for the team car.

He didn't run Boston in 1931, but in 1932, he placed tenth; the
next month he won the Pawtucket Marathon for the second year,
breaking DeMar's record for the course. He wanted to try out for
the Olympic team but was not allowed to because he was still a
citizen of Scotland. In 1932 he defended his New England Marathon title.

The Depression was deepening, however, and it was not long
before the "Y" felt that even at eleven dollars a week, Johnny
"Jock" Semple was a luxury it could not afford. He was let go.

Having nothing to do, Jock decided to hitchhike out to join C.C. Pyle's transcontinental run, but he was talked out of giving up his amateur status by "Monty" Monteverdi, when he met him during a stop over on his way to the West Coast. "Don't throw your amateur status away on a crook," Monty advised him.

Jock turned around and headed back to Boston, where he applied for work at the United States Shoe Machinery Company. While he was waiting in line, one of the company's officers recognized him. The shoe company wanted to put together a road race in conjunction with their annual carnival. Ultimately, the young officer and Jock came to an agreement: a job for his services and for offering his expertise on behalf of the company's running efforts. Jock began his association by sharpening dies and sweeping floors; he earned sixteen dollars a week.

Semple had received his job partially on the strength of his promise to put together a running team, and so he began recruiting members of the Lynn YMCA team. Pretty soon, United Shoe was making itself felt on the road-racing scene.

Then Jock got himself married to a very lovely Scottish girl, on New Year's Eve 1938.

The year 1939, although a good one for him and Betty personally, began going downhill work-wise. The United Shoe team took second in the Nationals, and the bosses felt that wasn't good enough. Jock revealed the state of affairs at United Shoe to Walter Brown of the Boston Athletic Association, who urged him to come on over to the B.A.A. Jock did just that, bringing along most of his runners from United Shoe. The team did very well, but then the war came. Jock enlisted in the Navy.

After he got out in 1945, Jock wanted to continue in sports in some capacity, so he set his sights on being a physical therapist. He talked to Win Green, the Boston Bruins' trainer, about a job, but Win told him to go back to school. Win sent him over to see Walter Brown, the man who'd formed the Boston Celtics basketball team. Walter used his influence to get Jock into Boston University and further arranged a carpentry job for him at B.U. to help supplement his income. Walter also hired him part-time to guard doors at the Boston Garden, always making sure he got doors high up in the building so he could study during his working hours.

Jock's life gradually became meshed with Walter Brown's. He began doing everything from taking the Celtics out on early morning runs to officiating over his own rubdown room. He became also the main man of the B.A.A. When it started, the B.A.A. had been a wealthy club, with its own building; now, its fortunes diminished, the B.A.A. was down to one telephone—in Jock's rubdown room. Affectionately dubbed Salon de Rubdown, this room was hidden away in the bowels of the Boston Arena. After that burned down, it was relocated to the Boston Garden.

Jock had been set up in his work by Walter Brown. Brown had purchased the equipment he needed to get started and had given him the room to use. Therefore, Jock never forgot when, during one rubdown under Jock's practiced fingers, Walter mentioned that he hoped a B.A.A. boy would someday win the Boston Marathon. As he attempted to revive the club, Jock kept searching for the one stand-out runner who might become the club's star and bring Walter's dream to reality.

It was at this point that the stories of Jock Semple and the younger John Kelley came together dramatically.

The B.A.A. road-racing team continued to improve under Jock's direction. Jock acted as a talent scout when he went to races. Although his principal job was to get his team there and to see that they had what they needed to make their best competitive effort, Semple was always on the lookout for new talent to lure under the B.A.A. umbrella.

Jock's approach to prospective talent was interesting. "I employed a standard approach in my recruitment efforts in the 1950s," he says. "I sought out a man's wife or girl friend first. While the men were out on the course during a race, I'd take the lady aside. 'The great advantage to having a man run for the B.A.A. is that my B.A.A. boys come home tired after I'm finished with them,' I said. Usually this elicited a polite nod, but little interest. 'After men get out of work . . . you know the diversions that exist for a man,' I repeated each weekend [at races] in towns such as Haverhill, Belmont, and Somerville. 'Some men don't come home at all. Soon after they get married they discover the gin mills, and the elbow-bending, and soon their wives have to trek down to some dark men's bar in their housecoats. Never my B.A.A. boys. They come home every night, very tired.'

"If I got the ladies hooked on the elbow-bending, I didn't have to say anything more. I gave them an application, which they asked for, and by the next race a dozen women would run up to me with completed forms for their husbands or fiancés."

It was at one of these races that Jock first saw Johnny Kelley. The year was 1948, an Olympic year. The 15-K race, at Fall River, Massachusetts, on July 4, would be the last major road race before the American team left for the Olympics in London. Vic Dyrgall was brought in for the race. He was then the best 10,000-meter man in the United States. It was assumed he'd be a shoo-in, that no one would be foolish enough to challenge him.

Dyrgall went out at the gun on a pace that was supposed to shake anyone foolish enough to give him a go. It didn't work. Two high school kids pasted themselves to him, one on either side. The smaller of the two wore track shoes from which he'd removed the spikes, and, in order to accommodate the road, he'd wrapped them all around with adhesive tape. The temperature was about one hundred degrees. The heat and the abrasive road, combined with the kid's pounding, began to loosen the tape; pretty soon it was coming apart in strands, and as it came off, so did the thin spikes, which began to disintegrate under the pounding. By two miles there was nothing left of the shoes; they'd fallen away, and the kid was keeping up with Dyrgall in his bare feet! The heat and the rough road became too much, however, and at four miles the kid dropped out to nurse his bloodied feet. He sat down on the side of the road, picking pieces of asphalt and grit out of them. Jock, who had been driving behind the leaders, had watched the entire drama unfold. He stopped to ask the kid if he wanted a ride. "Yes, sir, thank you, sir," the kid said. Jock asked him what his name was. "Johnny Kelley, sir," he said. The almost-too-polite high school kid bore the name of one of the Boston Marathon legends, one of the three men who would soon represent the United States in the Olympic Marathon at London. Jock muttered to himself: "Say hello to the new generation."

Johnny Kelley didn't know who Jock was, and, in his fairly

discombobulated state, didn't much care. The race he'd just dropped out of was only his second race on the roads; his first had come the previous year at Littleton, Massachusetts. Here he'd met his namesake the elder Johnny Kelley, who'd turned to him before the start of the race and had made his day by saying, "You've got runner's legs, kids." The young Johnny Kelley did not finish that race.

His friend George Terry, by the way, had gone along with him on that one, and it was friend George Terry who'd been running on Vic Dyrgall's other shoulder at Fall River.

Here are Johnny's recollections of the race: "I had sent away for legitimate shoes from a mail-order house, but they had not arrived. So I had taken a pair of my track flats, removed the spikes, and wrapped them around and around the toes with adhesive tape. First came the blisters, then came the unraveling tape, and finally the shoes burst. Soon I was relegated to a ditch before a kindly official picked me up in his car."

That was probably the only time in his life Jock Semple had been referred to as a kindly official. Jock's reputation was based chiefly on his scathing tongue and his quick—often unrehearsed—comebacks.

It would be a mere ten days until the paths of John Semple and Johnny Kelley would cross again at the Sons of Italy Ten-Mile Handicap Road Race in Haverhill.

Handicap races were very popular during the period. Faster runners were given handicaps based on their previous performances. They were required to stand at the starting line for the number of minutes of their handicap while other, slower runners were given the gun and a headstart. There was one prize at the end for whoever took first place and another prize for the best time.

Johnny Kelley took a train to Haverhill. It was a Tuesday evening and the streets of Haverhill were fairly deserted, but soon Johnny saw two other fellows carrying gym bags. Johnny asked them if they were runners, and, as they made their way to the race, the three struck up a wise-guy banter, most of it centering on the impossibility of this kid's name being the same as that of the great John Kelley.

The two runners were George Waterhouse and George Pike;

the former ran for the North Medford Club while the latter ran
for what he called "Semple's outfit."

The three of them assembled with the mass of other runners in
the second-floor hall. A television set in the corner was bringing
a Red Sox-Senators game to the Sons of Italy hall. Johnny was
fascinated by seeing something that was going on forty miles
away.

"You won't run far watchin' that thing all night," someone
behind him said.

Turning around, he encountered, but did not recognize, the
man who'd helped him out of the ditch in Fall River.

"Where's your sidekick?" the man asked. "The other fella that
put the scare into Dyrgall?"

Johnny made the connection and explained that Terry had
had to work. Jock went into an harangue about how he didn't
know runners worked, and this led to an interchange with Fred
Brown of the North Medford Club. Pretty soon they were both
getting the business from the rest of the runners, who were used
to the two of them going at each other.

Semple offered to go out and see the race director on Johnny's
behalf. He told the race director it was Kelley's first race and got
him a five-minute handicap. He brought the kid's number back
and reported that Waterhouse and Pike would be on scratch—
the last to start. Jock spent a few more minutes with the kid,
pumping him up, telling him that the two races he'd dropped out
of were only dress rehearsals. "Tonight's your big performance,"
Jock told him.

By the time he crossed the finish line, Kelley knew he'd taken
both the time and place prizes.

Because of the somewhat complicated mathematics involved
in handicap racing, there is a lot of standing around after the
race, waiting for the official results. In this instance, there was
quite a bit of additional dickering going on, because the Haverhill Sons of Italy were not anxious to give prizes to a new, unknown squirt.

One official wanted to give the Hamilton watch for best time to
a veteran racer from Somerville; another felt George Pike should
get it. Meanwhile a third official was trying to change the results
around in order to drop this John Kelley fellow down a few

notches. Jock watched the maneuvering while maintaining an uncharacteristic calm.

After twenty minutes Jock had had enough. His voice boomed above the confusion, and his voice carried the sound of the Lord with it.

"For cripes sake!" he roared. "This man is unquestionably your time-prize winner."

"What? The boy?"

"Use your noggin, man. Your head isn't just a hat rack. If he didn't win the time prize, how in the hell did he start five minutes ahead of your scratch man and finish seven minutes ahead of him? Answer me that."

No one could answer that one. And there had been absolutely no way for them to deny the place win—he'd obviously finished first.

So at 10:09 that night, Johnny Kelley stood on the train platform wearing a bright new watch and lugging a trophy. He'd been thrust across the threshold into another world. Into a world inhabited by "kindly officials" like Jock Semple.

A unique relationship developed between Jock Semple and Johnny Kelley. Kelley had lost his father early in his running career, and Jock contends even today that he was more a father figure for Johnny than a coach. During Johnny's college career, certainly, Jock wasn't just his coach.

Johnny went to Boston University on a running scholarship. He entered college in 1950 and was housed at Myles Standish Dormitory. Although he was still going with a girl back in Groton, he dated at school too, his interest centering on a music major by the name of Jacintha Braga. His scholarship was not a full scholarship—running scholarships seldom are—so Johnny made ends meet by working fifteen hours a week in the dorm cafeteria. His coach at B.U. was Doug Raymond. Raymond had some things in common with Jock Semple: he was a Scotsman and an ex-navyman. But their methods of coaching, and their interests in running, were poles apart.

Johnny became adept at playing both sides of the fence. Raymond wanted him to become a miler; Semple wanted him to be a marathoner. During the week Johnny trained at the track with Raymond, doing gut-wrenching workouts day after day with no let-up; on Saturdays he'd head down to the Boston Arena and let Jock throw him on one of the massage tables so Jock could work the sore spots out of his legs. Then Jock would send him out on a twenty-mile run with the B.A.A. regulars down to Jamaica Pond and back.

A constant battle, then, raged around Johnny's head over his potential talent. He needed the scholarship to continue his studies in English, so he was required to submit to Raymond's training techniques; yet his heart was with the pavement pounders and Jock. He ran with a B.U. jersey, but he and his heart belonged to the B.A.A.

Johnny conducted a constant campaign to get Doug Raymond to introduce other methods into his training regimen, which consisted only of repeating laps. It didn't work.

Fred Wilt, an F.B.I. agent who also happened to run—very well, as a matter of fact—went to Europe to compete and came back touting *fartlek* training (i.e., "speed play"). When Johnny broached the possibilities of the B.U. team trying *fartlek*, Coach Raymond replied, "If it weren't for those years of quarter-mile repeats, he wouldn't know *fartlek* from my grandmother's pickle jar." Johnny broached the subject to Jock, who replied, "Oh, he's onto somethin', all right, Johnny. It's a far more natural way to train than all that in-and out quarter stuff. But we knew it, the idea of it, in the Old Country when I was your age."

The battle continued apace.

While his battles with his courses raged in college, and the battle between Jock and Doug Raymond raged, and the battle between Joanie in Groton, Connecticut, and Jacintha in Boston raged, the Korean War was also moving along rather briskly.

Johnny's college career was coming to an end. There had been some track victories and some defeats. The Korean War and army drab were staring him in the face. And then, to complicate matters, Emil Zatopek exploded onto the scene.

"I run until I can't run anymore. And then I run some more," Zatopek said as he set the running world on its rear with his triple victory in the 1952 Olympic Games.

To Doug Raymond it justified massive repeat quarters; to Jock, it was Zatopek's far-ranging runs through the countryside that were important.

Johnny modified Zatopek's training principles somewhat and began working harder at his running, but he never grew to enjoy the track. One of the reasons may have been that B.U.'s track, indoors and made of boards, was less than inviting.

Zatopek's success changed theories about training in most of the world. Unfortunately, as far as road racing went, the United States had a lot of catching up to do—even in its own premier race, the Boston Marathon. The last time an American had won was in 1945, when the other John Kelley had won his second Boston.

Young Kelley decided in 1953 that he'd begin training for that year's Boston. Obviously, Jock was ecstatic. Johnny knew that Doug Raymond would not be so favorably disposed. Jock decided to keep a low profile, because he wanted any decisions on Johnny's future to come from Johnny himself. He didn't want to jeopardize the kid's scholarship—yet he did want to see Johnny take his cracks at Boston. And he still had the dream in the back of his head that he would see Johnny winning Boston. That would fulfill Walter Brown's dream, also.

Jock spent his time hammering Fred Brown and his North Medford Club, while Doug Raymond spent his time hammering Jock. Just as mention of Fred Brown would set Jock off into a harangue, so the mention of Jock Semple in Doug Raymond's locker room would send the B.U. coach off on an harangue against what he called "those ham-and-eggers." Nowhere was the distinction between the college boys—the track man, the pure athlete—and the laborer—the road racer, the plodder, the pavement-pounder—drawn more succinctly than in Doug Raymond's ranting and raving, which invariably ended with: "Don't bother me with this nonsense; I don't want to hear the word 'road' again!"

Johnny continued to engage in a very precarious balancing act that was further complicated by his studies and his part-time jobs. He worked as a short-order cook in the evenings and in the basement of a jewelry store on Saturdays.

His tenacity about Zatopek's methods eventually broke Raymond down, and the coach allowed Johnny to work some of Zatopek's continuous running with speedwork thrown in; while the rest of the team ran the board track, Johnny ran around Braves Stadium—at a fast pace. On Saturdays and Sundays he'd take long, easy runs for endurance unless there was a college meet on Saturday. He worked in a little extra mileage by running from the college to his short-order cook job at nights.

Poor Doug Raymond. You have to sympathize with him. Johnny didn't break the news to him that he was going to run the 1953 Boston Marathon until two weeks before the event. And to add to that, he'd made other decisions in his life, too; in January he announced to his track coach that he planned to get married to Jacintha Braga.

He didn't make his announcements himself, however. Instead, like the Myles Standish his dorm had been named after, he sent his old high school buddy, George Terry, to break the news. Johnny pumped George for Doug's response. It had been fairly simple and direct: "Jeepers Crow, I can't believe it!"

Johnny and Jessie got married on the evening of January 17; that same night Johnny also ran anchor on a two-mile relay team at the Knights of Columbus track meet at the Boston Gardens. They moved to a third-floor room on the Back Bay; it featured a hot plate for a stove, and, not having an ice box, they put perishables on the windowsill and hoped the winter cold would preserve them. The rent was sixty-four dollars a month.

As spring came along, Johnny's enthusiasm grew, and even Doug Raymond, seeing that he was fighting a losing battle, came around.

The Boston Marathon was going to be no parade in the park. The Japanese were sending a team, and the Finnish team had been in the United States for weeks getting ready for the race.

The United States was—rightfully—given little hope of winning or even of making a dent in the foreign running machines.

The press began billing Johnny as America's only hope and even got poor, beleaguered Doug Raymond into the pre-race publicity. One shot showed Raymond and Kelley together at Braves Field; instead of going berserk, Doug came out in support of the whole affair.

Jock took stock of things, looked over the entry lists, and told Johnny that he was picking him to finish fifth. "No offense," he said. "You're goin' to do OK; but Johnny, I watched those Japanese practicin' out on the course today, an' jeez, nobody's goin' to beat them."

When the race started, Johnny kept up with the leaders, hanging with a little Japanese runner through the halfway point in Wellesley, where the Japanese runner relentlessly moved away from him. Johnny had run faster than he'd anticipated, and he had to play the rest of the race as a hang-on affair, while he watched Veikko Karvonen of Finland move past him, then another Japanese runner, and then Karl Leandersson of Sweden. Jock's prediction had come true: Johnny finished fifth. Top American, but to the rest of the marathoning world, it was still just fifth place. Jock and Johnny were both quite thrilled by the performance—especially since the little Japanese runner, Keizo Yamada, ran a course record of 2:18:51.

As Jock helped Johnny away, wrapped inside a warm army-surplus blanket, the two glowed in their accomplishment. Jock found a place for Johnny to sit down in the Soden Building, and Johnny felt a hand clap him on the shoulder. It was Doug Raymond ready with congratulations. "For gosh sakes, you really were America's only hope," his track coach said.

Jock, down at Johnny's feet unlacing his shoes, did a slow burn, grumbling enough so that Raymond noticed him. "What d'ya think of him, Jock?" Raymond said. "Wasn't he great? Wouldn't you say his performance is worth my talking to the athletic director at B.U. about our getting him a special jersey for the race next year?"

"Yeh," Jock spat out, "one wi' a unicorn on it!" (The unicorn was the B.A.A.'s symbol.) The battle between B.U. and the B.A.A. had taken another significant step toward open warfare.

Johnny was back the next year, all right. A month before the 1954 race, he ran the course as a practice workout and did it in about 2:28—complete with commuter traffic. He felt ready. His performance, which was again best American, and which was close to the previous year's time, placed him seventh. From the start, the race was between England's Jim Peters, the best marathoner in the world, and Finland's Karvonen. There was a lot of excitement about the entry of 1948 Olympic Marathon champion Dolfo Cabrera of Argentina, but he was now thirty-seven. Cabrera lost the lead early to the duelists, Karvonen and Peters. Karvonen won in what was a grudge match to get back at Peters for an earlier humiliation in his homeland. Johnny was pretty much overlooked. Even by Jock, who had paid money out of his own pocket to bring Peters over. Jock wrapped Peters in the army-surplus blanket meant for Johnny as Peters staggered across the finish line, completely exhausted.

Jock's role at the Boston Marathon had escalated from being merely one of the officials to being the majordomo. He hustled, cajoled, brow-beat, and bullied runners onto the busses; he scanned entries, was empowered to accept or reject them.

Jock, with his Scottish brogue and brusque manner, had become as much a story as the marathon itself. Reporters loved him because he was never stingy with a quote—quotes usually directed at their heads as he told them what he thought of people who interrupted the training of his runners, or who got in the way of the machinery of the Boston Marathon.

To someone unfamiliar with the Jock Semple legend, he could be incredibly intimidating. He dispatched cheaters, fakes, and phonies who tried to sully the Boston Marathon. His verbal invective was similar to a bolt from the blue or the bite of an enraged shark.

On the other hand, his treatment of authentic, serious runners was like that of a mother taking her child to her breast.

Toward Johnny Kelley, whom he referred to as his star, he was downright fatherly. Johnny's continued success at road racing was an unspoken affirmation that he and Doug Raymond were going to split, and that Johnny was going to be all Jock's.

But first, a word from Uncle Sam. Uncle grabbed Johnny up when his four years of college were over, even though Johnny was still two courses and eight weeks of student teaching short of graduating. He stayed in the army a year and a half and then returned to Boston with $120 a month from the G.I. Bill, a job as a twenty-five-year-old stock boy at Thomas Long's jewelry store, and membership on Jock's B.A.A. team.

Even though he had not been gone long from the marathoning scene, things had changed radically. In the 1955 Boston, Nick Costes had placed fifth and had been first American, while Japan's Hideo Hamamura lowered Yamada's record to 2:18:22.

During that furious race, Costes had run some nine minutes faster than Johnny's best.

Jock was supremely confident on behalf of Johnny, and he set out a formula for success: "Get yer mileage up, inject the right amount of interval work, race every so often, an' come in fer regular massages an' diathermy treatments, an' you'll run wi' the best of 'em, mark my word."

Among his training improvements, Johnny was running a sixteen-mile workout along the Charles River five mornings a week. To Johnny and the rest of the United States runners, the 1956 Boston Marathon was going to be very imporant: it was going to be one of two marathons used to pick the U.S. Olympic Marathon team. At the same time, the Boston Marathon was becoming increasingly important to foreign runners as a meeting place where the world's best could sock it out early in the season. Johnny Kelley's work was obviously cut out for him, but Jock was all confidence.

The 1956 race was a barn-burner. Antti Viskari, a military man from Finland, ran 2:14:14, a new world record. Johnny Kelley was again first American. But this time he was in second place overall, a mere twenty seconds over Viskari's incredible time. He'd stayed with the Finn through twenty-five miles and was still running exceptionally well at the finish line, but Viskari had pulled a kick out of somewhere, and Johnny couldn't match it. Johnny was assured a berth on the U.S. Olympic team, as were Nick Costes (fourth place, 2:18:01) and Dean Thackwray (fifth place, 2:20:40).

There was understandable merriment in the B.A.A. for two full weeks—until the course was remeasured and found to be 1,-100 yards short. The times were disallowed for world's best performances, but it did not in any way negate the Olympic team selection.

Unfortunately, when the team traveled to Melbourne in December for the Olympic Games, their results were dismal. England's Jim Peters had given up his running career after learning that Melbourne was going to be extremely hot. Hot it was. Johnny finished twenty-first, one place behind Nick Costes; Dean Thackwray did not finish. The indomitable Zatopek had finished sixth, despite just having recovered from a hernia operation.

Johnny returned to his home in Mystic, Connecticut, seriously considering giving up running. He'd taken second place with a sterling performance at Boston; he'd won the A.A.U. marathon championship the following month on the tough Yonkers course; but the Olympic Marathon had devastated him. He had two weeks left of teaching reading at the junior high school in Groton before Christmas vacation. Johnny stopped training and looked forward to a much-needed holiday season—during which time he hoped to make up his mind about what role, if any, running would play in the rest of his life.

His disenchantment with running was only temporary, however. If it hadn't been, it is likely that Jock Semple would have made it temporary, whether Johnny wanted it to be or not. Besides, once the weather begins breaking in the Northeast, it breaks the hold of gloom on people as well; then spring brings to mind thoughts of Boston. And Jock hadn't yet kept his promise to Walter Brown to have a B.A.A. runner win the Big One.

Because Patriot's Day fell on Good Friday, the race was moved to Saturday, April 20. There were one hundred forty entrants for the 1957 race. Among them was an impressive foreign field: Veikko Karvonen (winner in 1954) of Finland, his teammate Olavi Manninen, Koreans Soong Chil Han and Ching Woo Lim (the Koreans didn't bother coming if they didn't think they could win), Keizo Yamada (winner in 1953) and Nobuyoshi of Japan, Canadian Gordon Dickson, and Pedro Peralta of Mexico.

The day before the marathon, the young Johnny Kelley and his wife Jessie spent the night with the elder Johnny Kelley and his steady date, Laura Harlow. (Jock thought it was a terrific idea, because Johnny the Elder was in the habit of going to bed at nine o'clock, which would assure Johnny the Younger he'd get a good night's sleep.)

Young Kelley awoke at 4:45 in the morning, stared at the ceiling, and soon heard the other Johnny tapping at his door to see if he wanted to go out for a little workout to vent some of the nervous energy that builds up before a race. They went to the Belmont Golf Course and ran the slopes easy. Johnny the Elder was

Mr. Boston Marathon, and the early-morning golfers greeted him warmly, urging him to a good race. "Thanks, pal," he would answer. "Don't forget my son here."

The unrelated father and son got back, had a hearty breakfast, and went to Hopkinton for the checking in. The runners were herded inside a snow-fence and their names checked off as they were shouted off. As the names rolled out, the quality of the field became apparent. It had been a dozen years since an American had won Boston, and the elder Johnny Kelley held that honor.

Young Kelley's life-long friend George Terry, who was also running along with their friend Rudolpho Mendez, told Johnny that he felt one of them would win it.

When Walter Brown aimed his sawed-off shotgun into the air at noon and fired, he didn't realize that he was putting the finishing touch to his most cherished dream: a B.A.A. runner in the winner's circle.

The temperature was in the high sixties, just the way Johnny Kelley liked it. The race was truly a nationalistic affair. There were segments of Japanese fans cheering their contenders on, and the van attending the Finnish team leapfrogged from one checkpoint to the next, urging on their runners. In the lead pack, the three Americans ran coolly and under control, rattling the Finns; it was a matter of turning the tactics on the Finns and Japanese, who usually ran as a team instead of as individuals so as to be able to set a favorable pace and set up strategy moves and blocking techniques.

George Terry began developing blisters and dropped off the pace just beyond Natick. Before the fourteen-mile point, Rudy Mendez dropped off the pace, and Johnny was the lone American left in the lead pack. But the Japanese had also dropped back. The only runners left were the Finns, the Koreans, and Johnny Kelley.

Jock had been on the press bus, but the pace had been too fast to allow the bus to stop at checkpoints so that members of the press could get out and watch the race up close. The oranges and sponges Jock had stuffed into his pockets for Johnny's use were merely ruining the inside of Jock's pockets. Finally, at sixteen miles, Jock leaped from the moving bus, passed a sponge to

Johnny, and asked him how he felt. "Terrific, Jock! I can't believe it!" Johnny yelled.

The leaders went into the Newton Hills and Karvonen put on a desperate surge, hoping to break the pack and gain some control of the pace so he could ultimately slow it down; he wasn't looking all that good. Johnny responded to the surge, going with him; Manninen, Lim, and Han did not respond, and dropped behind.

Kelley and Karvonen ran along Commonwealth Avenue in Newton together, with nine miles to go. Johnny decided to gamble. On the second of the Newton Hills, Johnny threw in a surge and the Finn fell behind. Johnny continued to blast the hills, topping Heartbreak and feeling fine. He was all alone.

In the press bus, Jock was going wild, pounding the side of the bus, shouting, "There's nobody in sight!"

At the twenty-one mile point, the press bus had sped up to get the reporters to the finish area at the Lenox Hotel. Jock bounded off the bus, clenching his woolen army-surplus blanket. Walter Brown was with him. They were trying to see over the heads of the crowd. "Think he can hold it?" Walter asked.

"Sure," Jock said.

"You know that's all I ever wanted," Walter said.

"I know," Jock answered.

"It's all I want, to see a B.A.A. boy win the Boston Marathon."

"I know," Jock repeated. Walter regarded Jock strangely.

"You told me," Jock said. "Years ago."

Walter smiled upon realizing that Jock had remembered so well.

The crowd began to get restless, and then there was shouting, and then there was specific shouting—the leader was coming and he was an American.

From Johnny's perspective, it was like this: "I remember also catching a glimpse of Jock as I pummeled down Exeter Street over those last delicious yards. He opened and closed his arms with the blanket, and behind him I saw Walter Brown, beaming. As I crossed the line, I saw them both, and we were all smiling. Years later—so many Bostons between then and now—I realize we made a triangle."

Johnny went on to retain the A.A.U. Marathon Championship the next month, when it was again held at Yonkers. Incredibly, Kelley would win this race eight years straight!

But he would never again win Boston. In fact, no American would win Boston again until 1968—and then it would be one of young Johnny Kelley's proteges, Amby Burfoot of New London, a student at Wesleyan College and a roommate to Bill Rodgers, who would himself win it four times. And so the line from Jock Semple to his racing companion Johnny Kelley the Elder passed to the next generation, Johnny Kelley the Younger, and from there would extend to Amby Burfoot, and on to Bill Rodgers—to men with road racing in their blood, men who keep running long after track runners' competitive days are over.

Jock Semple continues to preside over the Salon de Rubdown, having less and less to do with the Boston Marathon as it goes through radical changes that are breaking his heart.

And Johnny Kelley the Younger? He has quit teaching school and is a free-lance writer with a big and happy family. He still runs Boston, consistently under three hours, and he continues to love running.

Abebe Bikila, one of the most natural runners ever to grace the marathon distance.

(COURTESY ALLSPORT PHOTOGRAPHIC, SURREY)

8.

ABEBE BIKILA:
The Tragedy of Excellence

There is an image that sticks in the mind of every marathoner who has ever seen it. And at certain times, especially at times when a training run is going sour, the image has a way of returning like a balm, as though dredged out of a common subconscious of all the marathoners who had ever lived.

The image is stark, and it is gently-edged at the same time. There are no fancy colors, there is no sound when the image ricochets up out of the well of souls, in slow motion. And there is that fascinating, incredible, tenacious sweat dropping ripe as an autumn pear.

The scene is from Kon Ichigawa's marvelous documentary film, *Tokyo Olympiad,* and the image on the screen is a head-and-shoulders shot of Abebe Bikila. The shot is taken from the side by one of Ichigawa's cameramen who was traveling at precisely the same speed as Bikila—about thirteen miles per hour.

Bikila is wearing a dark racing singlet. His concentration is intense, equaled only by his supreme, almost animal-like relaxation. He stares ahead, looking toward an as yet invisible finish line. He is either unaware of the camera or he studiously ignores it.

It is well into the race and Bikila is perspiring freely. He has broken away into a staggering lead. He is on his way to making history: the first man to win the Olympic marathon twice. In the process he is setting a new world record.

As he sweats—nearly half the heat loss in a marathoner is dispersed through the head—perspiration runs down his Roman nose and hangs persistently on the edge of that nose, the motion of his running just above five-minute miles too precise and smooth to dislodge it. Occasionally Bikila's hand comes up to grasp his nose in a smooth wiping motion that, for a short space of time, sweeps free the perspiration.

The film runs and Bikila runs, the embodiment of an animal that runs free, relaxed, and naturally. Bikila is the running animal everyone who takes a step wishes to be.

His running is seemingly effortless; he is frail but incredibly strong. He is like a personification of everything the marathon runner should be. He is the most natural world-class runner anyone has ever seen.

It is a tribute to the producers of the film *Marathon Man* that it opens with this image of the marathoner incarnate.

Bikila broke into the limelight at the Rome Olympics in 1960 as he and a Moroccan, Rhadi ben Abdesselem, put the world on notice that Africa would bring forth the new generation's distance stars.

Although Bikila and Rhadi were new faces to the regular followers of distance running in Rome, Bikila was far from a marathon novice. The machinery that would put Bikila at the forefront of the world's distance runners began turning in the years following World War II, when Onni Niskanen of Sweden accepted an appointment with the government of Ethiopia. In that remote country, Niskanen set up a training camp for the Ethiopian armed forces and for Haile Selassie's Imperial Body Guards. The camp was at six thousand feet, an ideal altitude for training athletes.

One of the privates sent to the camp to train was Abebe Bikila. Incredibly, he did not begin running until he was twenty-four years of age. Niskanen's idea of training included rugged cross-country runs, sometimes as much as twenty miles at a time, with interval workouts of fifteen-hundred-meter repeats. The rugged schedule was perfectly suited to the rugged soldiers with whom he worked. Sometimes the soldiers would wear shoes when they trained, and sometimes they would train barefooted.

Ethiopia, then as now, was somewhat closed off from the rest of the world. It is understandable, then, that the spectators gathered in Rome in 1960 for the marathon did not realize that the shoeless Bikila toeing the line had come off two marathon trials in July and August, held within his country at the capital, Addis Ababa. In the first he had recorded a 2:39:50, while in the second he had turned in a 2:21:23, putting him nine minutes ahead of his countryman, Abebe Wakgira. Addis Ababa is, of course, at a high altitude, so the latter performance was rather significant.

The Rome Olympic marathon was interesting in several ways. It was the first time in the Olympic Games that the race neither started nor finished at the stadium where the other running events were being held. Also, in consideration of the September heat, the race was to begin at 5:30 P.M. and continue into the darkness. To enable a celebration of the fabled city, the course was laid out to run by and through various Roman landmarks.

The race started near Capitoline Hill. Within a few miles, spectators saw that they were in for a unique event. A group of four runners had moved to the front, taking control of the pace. One of the men was Arthur Keily of Britain who had been the first Englishman since Jim Peters to break the 2:20 barrier, a feat he'd managed in April. Another of the leaders was Aurele Vandendriessche of Belgium, who'd been that country's marathon champion for five consecutive years. The third and fourth members of the front-running group were Africans, neither of whom was well known outside his native continent. One of them was Rhadi ben Abdesselem of Morocco, who'd placed fourteenth in the 10,000 meters two days earlier; he was a 31-year-old military man. The final member of the quartet was a nut-brown, bare-footed runner who had tried shoes but found that they gave him blisters and pinched his feet: Abebe Bikila, twenty-eight years old, running relaxed and with confidence.

The group went through 10-K in 31:07. At that point Brian Kilby of Britain caught up with them, as did Allal Saoudi, another Moroccan. Keily and Vandendriessche dominated the pace, while the rest seemed content to sit back and wait. Also in the field, but back by more than thirty seconds, was the current world record holder, Sergey Popov of the Soviet Union, running in a group of five.

Between 15-K and 20-K, a dramatic change took place. The Europeans began wilting while the Africans began putting on a surge. Bikila and Rhadi went through 20-K in 1:02:39; Vanden-driessche was nearly thirty seconds back, while Keily was fifteen seconds back of him.

While the Africans kept up their relentless pace, there were changes taking place behind them. New Zealander Barry Magee and Popov had moved out of their pack-of-five and worked their way together into third place, running step for step, but they were more than three minutes behind the Africans.

At the 30-K point, the course turned onto the Appian Way. Magee and Popov were closing the gap, working their way to within two-and-a-half minutes of the leaders (1:34:29 to 1:36:52). Magee began breaking away from Popov, and in fact had closed to within two minutes by 35-K, while Popov was more than a minute behind him. Magee continued valiantly to push his pace, closing to within less than ninety seconds by the 40-K mark. It was at that point that the Africans consummated their duel. Running up a tunnel of light engendered by the thousands of torches and lights, Rhadi moved from Bikila's shoulder and made his move, but Bikila fought back and threw in his own surge, pulling away by twenty-five seconds in the final two kilometers and winning in 2:15:16.2. Bikila had broken Popov's world's best mark by less than a second. Magee finished third, and Konstantin Vorobiev of the Soviet Union took fourth, having passed countryman Popov in the final kilometers.

Following his incredible victory, Bikila embarked on a marathoning spree around the world, but only after a quiet recovery back in Ethiopia.

On May 7, 1961, Bikila traveled to Greece to run the tough original marathon course in the fourth annual International Classical Marathon. He won in 2:23:44.6 on a very warm day, on a very hilly course. Aurele Vandendriessche finished a minute behind.

On July 25 Bikila traveled to Osaka in Japan for the Mainichi Marathon. The day was extremely hot, and the forty-six runners performed before a crowd of seven hundred thousand. Bikila won in 2:29:27, certainly not an astounding time, but very good considering the heat and humidity; second place was taken by another Ethiopian, Wami Biratu, some ten minutes behind Bikila. Only fifteen runners finished the race.

On October 12, Bikila showed up in Czechoslovakia at the famed Kosice Marathon, where he dominated the race, winning in 2:20:22, having broken Vaclav Chudomel of Czechoslovakia at 20-K and never being challenged after that.

He returned to Ethiopia and news of him faded.

On February 17, 1963, at Beppu in Japan, one of the most impressive marathon races in history took place, with Toru Terasawa running 2:15:15.8, breaking Bikila's world record by less than a half-second. The top ten runners in the race were all under the 2:20 barrier!

This beginning of the 1963 season threw an extraordinary amount of attention on the Boston Marathon, where the undefeated Bikila, and also his rapidly emerging countryman Mamo Wolde, joined one of that race's most talented fields on Patriot's Day, April 19. Adding to the interest was the fact that no Olympic Marathon champion had ever won the Boston race. Eino Oksanen of Finland was back to defend his title. Brian Kilby and Aurele Vandendriessche were there. So was America's amazingly consistent performer, John J. Kelley of Connecticut. It was shaping up to be a classic confrontation between many of the world's best.

The temperature was perfect—in the fifties—although there was a crosswind. The Ethiopians took the field out at a formidable pace, soon breaking away. They were running at a record pace, but they were not used to the cold, and it began cramping them. The Newton Hills couldn't have come at a worst time. The rest of the top runners were catching them as Bikila began to put his moves on Mamo Wolde, who was cramping badly.

Vandendriessche had caught up with them, and at Coolidge Corner, he caught and passed Bikila. To add to Bikila's defeat, John Kelley, Brian Kilby, and Eino Oksanen also passed him. Vandendriessche's 2:18:58.2 was a new course record. Mamo Wolde finished twelfth.

Bikila was obviously vulnerable, and some observers saw it as the end of a glorious—but brief—time in the marathon limelight.

He returned to Ethiopia and again vanished as he had between October, 1961, and the Boston race. It was reported that he was taking part in races within Ethiopia, which was likely quite true, although much of his time may have been taken up by his military duties, which caused him to spend a great deal of time on his country's eastern frontier (where there were continual alerts due to uneasy relations with Somalia).

Reports finally filtered out about a warm-up marathon run on May 31, 1964, at Addis Ababa in which Bikila ran 2:23:14.8. The Ethiopian Olympic Trials Marathon was held on August 3, and the race, held again at six thousand feet, featured performances unmatched in the world of running. Bikila ran in 2:16:18.8, beating his friend Mamo Wolde by four-tenths of a second, one of the closest marathon finishes in history. Taking third place was Demissie Wolde (no relation to Mamo), with a 2:19:30. Obviously, the little country of Ethiopia had an awesome team ready to go to Tokyo.

Six weeks before they were to depart, however, Abebe was forced to undergo an appendectomy. Although he would travel to Tokyo with the team, it seemed certain he would not race—and certain that he would not win. The pressure was on Mamo and Demissie Wolde.

Abebe came back into training soon after the operation, however, and when the field of sixty-four marathoners toed the starting line on October 21, on a day well-clouded to screen the sun, with temperatures in the high sixties, Abebe was among the group. The phenomenal Australian, Ron Clarke, already the veteran of three Olympic races that week, decided to run the marathon also. A multiple world record holder at distances below the marathon, Clarke took the field out at an ambitious pace, covering the first 10-K in 30:14. At that point, Clarke was paced by Jim Hogan of Ireland, while Bikila, wearing shoes this time, was close behind them. The trio went through 15-K in 45:35, with the pursuit group a minute behind. Mamo and Demissie Wolde were not faring so well, and as Demissie fell farther off the pace, Mamo dropped out.

Bikila, feeling relaxed and in control, began moving away from Clarke and Hogan within a few miles, going through 20-K in 1:00:58. Hogan was five seconds back, while Clarke was tiring and was forty-one seconds behind the Ethiopian.

At the halfway point in Chofu City, where the runners turned to come back toward National Stadium, Bikila was at 1:04:28, smooth as fog moving over the ground, with Hogan trying desperately to keep him in sight. The pursuit pack was closing on Clarke, who had grown increasingly weary. At 25-K Hogan was fifteen seconds back of Bikila, still game but in a losing battle.

Bikila went through 35-K in 1:49:01, and soon after passing the checkpoint, Hogan ran off the course, unable to sustain the pace. That put Bikila some three minutes in front of his closest competition.

His pace over the second half of the race slowed considerably, but he maintained his smooth, effortless style.

When he entered the stadium, he was greeted with a frightening din. He was the first man to repeat as Olympic Marathon champion, and he had run 2:12:11.2, the fastest performance for the distance ever!

He immediately pulled into the infield, and as though his run had been nothing, he began a complicated series of calisthenics. Many of the spectators felt that Bikila was flaunting the ease with which he vanquished the world's best, but in fact he had found, from long experience, that if he did not do a strenuous series of stretches and exercises after a long run or race, he stiffened up within a few hours.

While Bikila went through his flexibility exercises, the stands again went crazy, for Kokichi Tsuburaya, although four minutes behind Bikila, had entered the stadium to take second place; the partisan crowd let their Japanese pride swell and they urged him home. But he had no sooner entered the stadium, the crowd sure of his silver medal, than Basil Heatley of Great Britain entered less than a dozen feet behind him. Heatley stayed on Tsuburaya's shoulder until the final turn on the track and then sprinted around him to steal the silver medal. Tsuburaya had nothing left with which to hold off the Englishman. Tsuburaya's accomplishment, however, heralded the beginning of what was to be an impressive onslaught of Japanese performances over the next decade.

The next spring at Boston, Japanese runners would take the top three places, all of them under the course record.

While the top Japanese marathoners were away astounding the rest of the world with their prowess, the Ethiopians invaded the Japanese homeland, Abebe Bikila and Mamo Wolde going to Mainichi for the May 9 race. The day was hot (eighty-three degrees), and Bikila dominated the race from the start. Although Wolde dropped out at 30-K, Bikila went on to win handily at 2:22:55.8, nearly three minutes ahead of the second-place finisher.

A month later, a contingent of Japanese runners would travel to the Polytechnic Marathon (the "Poly") in England, and Morio Shigematsu would run 2:12:00, breaking Bikila's world's best by eleven seconds.

Bikila again went into eclipse for a time. But on July 24, 1966, he resurfaced at Zarauz, in Spain, to complete a very tough marathon in 2:20:28.8, more than five minutes ahead of his nearest competition. He traveled next to Seoul where, on October 30, he ran 2:17:04 for another win.

He chose not to go on to the international marathon at Fukuoka, which that year received sanction from the Japanese Amateur Athletic Federation to become an international open marathon championship, making Fukuoka something of the marathon world championship race on the three out of four years when there were no Olympic Games.

Bikila went through periodic appearances and disappearances. When 1968 came, and the Olympic Games were scheduled for Mexico City, promising warm temperatures at high altitude, interest in Bikila again grew. Would he try to make it three gold medals in a row?

What spectators at Mexico City got on October 26 was an injured Bikila, trying to run despite a painful leg problem. Yet when the leaders went through the 5-K checkpoint in 16:44, Bikila was among the group.

But the injured leg could not stand the competition, and even broke, causing Bikila to retire at 17-K. Ethiopia did manage to win the gold medal for the third consecutive Olympic Games, however, as Bikila's teammate and racing companion, Mamo Wolde, won in 2:20:26.4, more than three minutes ahead of Japan's Kimihara.

Early the next year tragedy struck. Bikila was riding in an automobile when it was involved in an accident. His neck was broken and he became paralyzed from the neck down. He visited England frequently for therapy but could not be helped. Because of his sudden inactivity, he began to gain weight, and the waif of a runner that had once been Bikila became hidden within the tragically immobile man in a wheelchair. He was revered as a national hero within his country, despite the country's penchant for downplaying heroes and heroics and preferring national pride to pride of the individual.

At the 1972 Olympic Games in Munich, he was the guest of honor. As soon as Frank Shorter was presented with his gold medal for winning the marathon, Shorter went directly to Bikila to shake his hand.

A year later, at the age of forty-one, Bikila, the running animal, the image of the perfect marathoner, suffered a stroke which resulted in a brain hemorrhage. He died on October 25, 1973, leaving a wife and four children. And an image of the perfect runner's infinite grace that will never be supplanted.

Derek Clayton of Australia was the first man to put the world record below 2:09.

9.

DEREK CLAYTON:
Mister 2:08

Antwerp, Belgium, May 30, 1969, 7:35 P.M.

"I was feeling absolutely great! I was feeling so good that, in discussions with the promoters, I said, 'I'm going to go for a faster time, and I want to make sure the course is exactly the right length.' I have always been very fussy about the lengths of courses, as marathon courses can quite often be short—and there is nothing worse than having run a marathon and finding out afterward that it was a half-mile short. It then becomes a non-event, and there is nothing worse for an athlete than a non-event, busting your guts and finding out the course is short—because then it is no marathon at all. It's just a waste of time. So I said to the guys over there, 'Look, I'm going for a fast time—I can't promise you a record, but I can promise you one thing. It's going to be fast.'

"So I said, 'I want this course checked out.' I remember speaking to Jim Hogan, a well-known Irish runner of that time, as we were driving to the start. It was a perfect night and the conditions were great. The race was to start at 7:00 P.M. It's no good trying to run a world record in the marathon in seventy, eighty, or ninety degrees—no one is going to handle 2:08 in those conditions. You've got to have a good field, because a high-class field pushes you. You've got to have a lot of enthusiasm there—everything has to be right for it.

"And I felt this night that everything *was* right for me. I was running well, the people were there, the enthusiasm was fantas-

129

tic, and the weather was absolutely right: cold and windless. I said to Jim Hogan driving over in the bus, 'Jim, I think I'm going to crack my 2:09.' He didn't believe me. He said. 'What do you think you can run?' I said, 'I reckon I could run 2:07 or 2:08.' He said, 'I wish you luck.'

"It was one race I really went for. We ran through the first 10,000 meters in 30:6, which is a pretty fast pace. I didn't take the pace. The guy who led the race was a Kenyan who was confident of doing pretty well. He led, and afterwards I said, 'Do you know what your best 10,000 meters was?' He said, 'Well, that's it.' I said, 'Why did you want to run that fast?' And he said, 'You've got to be in it to win it.'

"He wasn't in it long, I can tell you. He didn't finish. But I was happy because he got me motoring, and I think once you get moving like that, at that sort of pace, and you still feel good, you just keep going on. I had the proper splits, so I knew I was running fast. I knew I was on the world-record pace for sure. It was just a matter of how much. So when I crossed the line in 2:08:33, it wasn't a surprise; it was the result of a lot of hard work.

"But the thing I remember most about the 2:08 was two hours later when the elation had worn off. I was urinating quite large clots of blood, and I was vomiting black mucus and had a lot of black diarrhea. What I don't think too many people can understand is what I went through for the next forty-eight hours. I have discussed this with the medical profession, asking them why this should be, and have never received a satisfactory answer. I only know one thing. After that 2:08, I was virtually finished. If anyone ever flattened themselves to run a race, I did on that particular day. I don't think anyone realized just what it took out of my body. When I look back on the week after that race, I wasn't the same person.

"It took me a long, long time to recover—I would say up to six months. It worried me that I was urinating large clots of blood. It's quite normal for an athlete to pass a certain amount of blood in his urine, but that forty-eight hours was unbelievable.

"It made me wonder if anyone would get close to this for quite a while. I knew I had a certain amount of natural ability [for] running marathons because it came pretty easy to me. I've run 2:09, I've run a few 2:11s, I've run 2:10s, but nothing, nothing has come anywhere close to what I went through to win with 2:08. In retrospect, it is no surprise to me that no one has knocked that time off, because training really hasn't advanced that much [Author's note: Clayton's record has been lowered. See p. 133].

"I think I was one of the ones who paved the way for running one hundred forty, one hundred fifty, one hundred sixty miles a week. I don't think anyone has changed that. The top guys still run around those distances, but they're not running any faster than I ran in training. So really, until a guy comes along who is pretty strong, or in fact much stronger, it won't happen."

Derek Clayton's oft-repeated story of what it took to run a marathon in under two hours and nine minutes—a marathon at a pace faster than five minutes per mile—and the whole persona he created for himself may have contributed more to creating the wall between 2:09 and 2:08 in the marathon than did the physiological limitations of the human body.

When he was running competitively, Clayton was not well-liked. Part of his strategy for winning was to intimidate the other runners in the field—usually before the race ever started. He did this with an alarming physical presence and a practiced attitude.

While most marathoners are small and slight of build, Clayton was six feet two inches tall and weighed nearly one hundred and sixty pounds –a giant among pygmies. He trained intensely, on two occasions running two-hundred-mile weeks. Word of his training techniques leaked out to the running world. Rumors augmented his training regimen to herculean proportions. According to them, he regularly ran two-hundred-mile weeks, most of those miles at race pace. Clayton did nothing to dispel the rumors until after his competitive career had come to an end.

During his competitive career, Clayton practiced a form of disdain of other competitors that he developed into an art form. His gaze could virtually stop trains. "I never socialized with a runner I was going to compete against," Clayton says. "Sometimes I never shook hands with them before a race, even if they made the gesture. That's just how it was. I was there to race.

"I certainly wasn't training my guts out just to get knocked over in the race. I was like a child who had been given a present for Christmas and had it taken away. I felt I had the right to win, to take the medal, because I trained so bloody hard. I wanted to keep it. Before the race even started, I felt I deserved to win, so I thought everyone was trying to take it away when it was rightfully mine. I really felt when I started that race I *deserved* to win!"

In an interview less than a year after his 2:08:34, Derek, for whom every second counts dearly, cited the time as 2:08:33, although the International Amateur Athletic Federation rounds the actual time, 2:08:33.6, up to 2:08:34. He also revealed that he loves to have another runner next to him at fifteen miles so he can begin grinding him into the ground.

"I actually did say that," he admits, the corners of his mouth going up in a wide smile. "I'd like to think I was a pretty good competitor. I took up running and competing because I enjoy the competition. I think one of the great things about running is that it's an individual sport. You can play the greatest game of football or basketball in the world, but because it's a team sport, if the rest of the team don't compete as well as you do that night, you can still lose the game."

His grind-the-other-guy-into-the-ground attitude carried over well beyond his competitive career. In February of 1979, while he was in California negotiating a job with *Runner's World Magazine,* Bill Rodgers, America's marathon record holder since 1975, was competing in nearby Oakland. Since Clayton and Rodgers had never met, arrangements were made to get them together in Los Altos Hills. They ran together at a local junior college track in the darkness, chatting for nearly an hour.

Rodgers, at that time America's premier marathoner, would soon become the second man in history to post two sub-2:10 marathons (the first was Clayton). During their casual hour on the track, Rogers recalls, Clayton "spent a lot of time trying to bust my balls. He kept telling me what it took to break 2:09, as though he was trying to convince me that I didn't have what it takes to do it—that nobody had what it takes."

When Clayton powered down below 2:09, he was breaking his own world record of 2:09:36.4, set in Fukuoka, Japan, in December 1967. That performance had bettered the world's best of Morio Shigematsu by almost two-and-a-half minutes, a feat that raised the cry of "short course!" The Antwerp performance in

1969 again raised the cry. The fact that Clayton's record stood for more than a decade, despite better footwear for runners, more scientific training methods, and more high-quality marathon runners raised more cries of "short course!"

Clayton's retort was always that, first, he had insisted both courses be remeasured, and, second, there was still no one else training with his intensity.

"The marathon runner should be a really tough guy," he said in 1979. "If he wants to knock his time way down to a 2:07 mark, I think he'll have to be very, very strong. He doesn't necessarily have to be as tall as I am, but he has to be very rugged, with a lot of power, because you get your important fast miles in around the last six miles—that's what makes the difference in getting down below 2:10." He repeatedly claimed that the strength necessary to power through those last six miles was the secret. "Frank Shorter has been on world-record pace on several occasions up to twenty miles," Clayton said, "but he doesn't have that strength to keep up the pace through those last six miles. It's going to take someone who has a lot of efficiency in style and a lot of strength in reserve if my 2:08 is going to fall."

When Clayton's record finally did fall, in October, 1981, at the New York City Marathon, it was broken by a runner who had impressed Clayton the first time he'd seen him run. "That Salazar is the kind of runner who's built for the marathon," Clayton said after seeing him perform at the 1980 New York City Marathon.

Two months later, when Clayton watched Salazar set a world's best mark for 5 miles on the roads in Los Altos, California, he felt his suspicions had been confirmed. Clayton was in the bed of a pickup truck leading the race field. As Salazar powered away from the rest of the field, his legs shuffling along like pistons, Clayton's eyes didn't leave him. He saw the specter of the future record holder. Clayton continued to mutter to himself during most of the slightly more than twenty-two minutes it took Salazar to cover the five miles. "Look at the way he runs; he's bloody efficient, isn't he? See how he doesn't waste any motion or strength lifting his legs too high? He shuffles along. Very efficient. . . . He's a determined kid, you know? Look at him, he's like a computer. He knows exactly where he's at, he knows exactly what he's doing, he knows what he's here for. . . . He knows how to get past the pain and use it. He's a bloody good runner. Look at how he runs beyond himself. . . ."

When Salazar breached Clayton's record, it forever destroyed the wall Clayton had created between 2:09 and 2:08. Less than two months later, Rob de Castella of Australia also broke Clayton's record—at Fukuoka. In a period of six weeks, Clayton lost his world record and then his Australian record.

His response was philosophical: "A lot of the fuss about my courses being short centered on the fact that no one else had ever come within reach of my record. Alberto Salazar knows what tough training is all about, and I feel that his performance has vindicated my records. He had what it took to break my record! He proved that, with the right training, it can be done. No one before him had been willing to give what it took to break my records. I'm genuinely relieved it's finally happened. Now I don't have to hear this 'short course!' crap anymore."

Clayton's course to immortality in the marathon record books did not come easily. He was born at Barrow-in-Furness in Britain on November 17, 1942. His family moved to Belfast, Ireland, when he was eight, where they lived until 1963. During his period in Ireland, Clayton picked up two loves: potatoes and competitive running.

"I suppose it was my Irish background," he says. "I had a tendency to want potatoes when I was done running. The main part of the Irish diet was potatoes and I just felt when I trained hard that I needed potatoes—I loved to eat potatoes. They're very high in carbohydrates, and I shoveled them in!"

His inspiration for running came from watching runners like Gordon Pirie and Herb Elliott on television.

When he, his mother, and his sister moved to Melbourne, Australia, Clayton decided to become a great miler. He pushed himself through grueling workouts day-in and day-out, a system of training that would become his trademark—and his nemesis. For one year he ran intervals every day: he was experimenting on his body, trying to find its weak points and turn them into strengths, working them over until they succumbed to his will. His amazing singlemindedness led him to a formula of doing long, hard runs. His training was awesome, although he now asserts that the legends of his two-hundred-mile weeks were very much exaggerated. "I only ran two two-hundred-mile weeks in my life," he says, "and I'd never want to do another one again. With the kind of high-quality training I was doing, I'd have killed myself doing two-hundred-mile training weeks. During the weeks before a marathon, I would go up to one hundred forty to one hundred sixty miles a week of good, hard training, but I wouldn't stay there forever. I don't see what good it would do anyone to run two hundred miles a week."

As a youngster in Australia, Clayton found himself just a bit too slow. As he recounts in his autobiography, *Running to the Top,* his transition to marathoning was mostly by accident:

"Australia was a big change for my running. After about a year on this radically different continent, I realized that I lacked the necessary speed to become a great miler. The fastest quarter I was capable of running was 52.8 seconds. Although that was not a bad quarter-mile time, it was clear that I didn't possess the basic speed required of a champion miler.

"That could have been the end of my running. The thought of not being able to duplicate Herb Elliott's fabulous 1500 meter run was a big disappointment. But after I considered the facts, I realized that the 1500-meter race wasn't nearly the grueling competiton that the 5,000 meters was. The 5,000 meters was a longer race; it excited me because it allowed me to withstand suffering for a longer length of time. My rationale was that if I was suffering, so was the other guy. To me, the 5,000 meters was a battle of who could stand it longest.

"I don't think you can become an outstanding runner unless you get a certain amount of enjoyment out of the suffering. You have to enjoy absorbing it, controlling it and—ultimately—overcoming it. When I started running 5,000-meter races, I discovered that I received a certain amount of satisfaction from withstanding punishment. I continued to train hard with a new goal in mind—to become a champion 5,000-meter runner.

"I should also mention—and I do it almost in passing—that I ran my very first marathon about four weeks after arriving in Australia. It wasn't a race that I took seriously. The people in the club I had joined were going to run about half of it for training. Instead of running an isolated training run, we decided to run about half this marathon.

"I had no intention of finishing the race. But when I reached the thirteen-mile point, I saw no sense in stopping. I decided to run to the sixteen-mile point. But when I got there, I figured I might as well try to finish the damn thing. The last few miles were agony; it was all I could do just to keep moving, until a race official started shouting to me that I had one mile to go and could break three hours if I 'started to run.' My racing instincts aroused, I changed the pace from one of gentle aerobics to one of brutal anaerobics. It did no good. I crossed the finish line two seconds after the three-hour time. I was bitterly disappointed that I had not broken three hours.

"I was very tired after that 3:00:02 marathon. I swore to myself after that race that I would someday run another marathon just to break three hours.

"That someday came about two and a half years later. I was training hard in hopes of running in the one or three mile events (some people never give up) in the Commonwealth Games. I was averaging about seventy to eighty miles per week. I did all my speed work in the summer. But like all Australian track runners in those days, I did only cross-country and road races in the winter. That was the time for distance work and after a hard summer, I was ready to leave the track behind anyway.

"I had run a few road and cross-country races when I heard about the Victorian Marathon Club Championships. I thought this would be a good workout for me. I decided to run it hard and see how far under three hours I could go. This was my chance to get back at the marathon distance. It was also a great way to finish off a road season and get back to the track and some serious speed work.

"October second, 1965. In my first serious attempt at the marathon I won the Victorian Marathon Club Championship. Not only did I win it, but I set a new Australian marathon record of 2:22:12. That changed my mind about everything. Almost overnight I quit thinking about trying to be number one in the 5,000 meters. Suddenly I was number one in something I never planned to excel in—the marathon. Suddenly I had proof that I wasn't wasting my time. After years of searching, I had found my distance. I was on my way to the top."

In a 1971 interview, Clayton made a very telling comment that characterizes his attitude toward goals: "I believe in getting from point A to point B as fast as possible. When I drive, my foot's always down on the floorboard—either on the gas pedal or the brake."

The intensity of both his ambition and his training took a profound toll on his body. Patterns in the recoveries from his injuries hinted at training methods he should have been employing in place of his death-march tactics. Moreover, each of his world records came in the wake of recovery from a very serious injury, which indicates that his training methods, if modified to allow for rest-and-recovery periods, might have produced even more incredible results, and likely would have prevented many of his injuries.

In 1967 Clayton's intense training resulted in a ruptured Achilles tendon. He had it operated on, and six months later set the world's best time in Fukuoka. The next year—an Olympic year—he damaged cartilage in the knee, but, instead of backing off and having it taken care of, he opted to continue training so as not to miss the Mexico City Olympics. He placed seventh, a very credible performance considering the altitude, the heat, and the humidity, not to mention his torn cartilage.

He had the knee operated on, and was back in shape for racing in early 1969. The ferocity with which he came back from the forced rest became obvious on May 19 when, in Ankara, Turkey, he ran another marathon at a high altitude, in the heat and humidity. He won in a stunning 2:17:26, nearly five minutes in front of the second-place finisher, a native Turk used to the conditions.

It was eleven days later that he unleashed his 2:08:33.6 at Antwerp.

At that point, Clayton wanted nothing more than to go back to Australia to rest and recuperate from his efforts. Unfortunately, he had committed himself to a European tour. In England and the Continent for the summer, he competed on the track almost every second night in anything from 3,000 to 10,000 meters.

But Clayton had been focusing on Manchester and England's Ron Hill, that country's reigning marathon champion. "I

couldn't wait to get in there to run against him," Clayton says,
his words becoming animated as the memories flowed back.
"You see, I built Ron Hill up into more than he really was. And I
built up the marathon in Manchester to be the big one. So when I
got to England I began training hard right away. What I should
have done was to rest for a week or two. Not a complete rest—I
should have just jogged very slowly to get my strength back. But
I didn't. I tried to run ten miles a day. It was a big effort—a really
big effort—and I should have had more sense. That was one big
mistake I made.

"The tour was three months long. There were many times
when I just wanted to go home. I felt like crying; I also felt like
dying; everything I did on that tour seemed to take more out of
me. I just wanted to go home.

"The English press played the Manchester race up as the big
challenge of the century," he says. "I'd say that in a sense it was
one of the harder races I ever ran in my life. It required a great
deal of effort. It was one hell of a grind. I ran myself into the
ground again. Ron Hill and I led the whole way, battling it out.

"Ron beat me by about two minutes. I came in second in 2:15,
but in the last three miles I was finished. I had a complete layoff
for about four weeks. I couldn't face training. Everything was
drained. I couldn't wait to get home. Even after a month's rest,
just doing a little jogging, I really didn't pick up very quickly. It
was Christmas before I wanted to run again.

"The following year I got injured very quickly. It was two
years before I really ran another marathon. That three-month
tour took more out of me than anyone really realized. The feeling I had after Antwerp, and after Manchester, I would never
want to experience again. On looking back at that period, I will
say that I never did run as well again, ever." He pauses, as
though trying to analyze the whys and wherefores of that period
in his life.

"I don't know why I never ran as well again. It could have
been mental and it could have been physical. It could have been
lack of interest; it could have been a combination of things. I
never felt right after that, though. I tried to come back too
quickly. I think efforts like that take more from your body than
marathoners think. I think a top marathoner could knock off

2:15s and 2:16s. He could handle that, but getting down around 2:10, that takes a lot out of him. It's very easy for someone who runs 2:10 to suddenly think, 'Well, if I can run 2:10, why can't I run 2:07?' It's only natural. But those 2:10s take a lot out of you.

"If I had it to do over, I would plan more carefully. I certainly wouldn't do what I did on that tour. That was reckless, to say the least. Toward the end I retired from racing, not because I was too old; I just felt I'd had enough. It was as simple as that. I wanted the world record and I had it. I dearly wanted a gold medal. I think I wanted a gold medal more than anything.

"The world record can be taken away from me, and I'm the first to realize that. I'm fortunate to have held it as long as I have. But once you have the Olympic gold medal, no one can ever take that away. You've got that to keep.

"One of the reasons I retired from serious racing was because I felt I never had a chance to win a gold medal. I think I had the ability, no question about it, but I could never handle running in hot weather. I don't think a big person can handle running long distances in hot weather as well as someone more lightly built. I have a lot of energy that I have to expend. I don't run smoothly, and my style is rugged, toughish. Consequently, I generate a lot of body heat. When the sun is out, I generate even more heat. In hot weather, I can never expect to do better than a 2:17.

"I tried training in the heat to acclimate my body, but it never worked. I was continually thirsty, and then when I was thirsty I seemed to lose my rhythm. My style of running relies an awful lot on my rhythm, and once I get out of that rhythm, I seem to use three times more energy than I normally would.

"The Olympics are always held in the summer and frequently in a hot country. The chances of me ever getting a cold day to run an Olympic marathon seemed pretty slight.

"When I ran in Mexico City, there was a humidity problem. I have this allergy problem, which I tried to believe wasn't going to affect me, but after being there a while I knew it was going to be a problem, and of course it was. I ran a 2:27 in Mexico for seventh place.

"I went to Munich and the weather was hot and sticky. Even before the gun went off, I was looking for a drink and I drank at every aid station they had.

"When I ran my best times, I never had a drink at any station. To me that is very significant.

"So I thought about that seriously, and asked myself, 'Why go on, why slash myself like I'm doing?' There was no way I could win a gold medal. I was plagued because of the way I trained and I had injury problems. During my career I've had nine surgical operations. I had great difficulty in being able to get a week's training in without something going wrong.

"So, realizing that my chances of winning a gold medal were very slim, and knowing that I was never really interested in winning a silver or bronze medal—that's how I am—I knew I had to quit. Winning was all. I could never go into a race and sit back hoping to come through. There was only one way for me. To run a race, you ran it from the front; not necessarily leading the pack, but right up there. I knew that wasn't going to be possible at the Olympics, so I gave it away. It's as simple as that."

Clayton worked in various jobs in Australia for seventeen years, most of them associated with civil engineering; he also dabbled in real estate, but did not make a go of it. He and his wife emigrated to the United States in 1979 at an opportune time in his life. The change of scenery has brought him—at least job-wise—into the circle of running again. And since moving, he and Jenny have produced two children, the second a boy. Those who know Clayton feel he would not have been happy without a son.

Even now, when his records are gone and he is approaching middle age, Clayton must endure the curse of being asked if his world records were set on short courses. People still approach him at the promotional events he attends to question him. Whether the Antwerp course was short or not may have been a moot point since the day the race was run, according to Dr. Dave Martin, an academician who has devoted his life to studying the marathon. In his authoritative book, *The Marathon Footrace,* he has this to say about the Antwerp race:

"Following the race rumors circulated that the course was short. The Belgian Amateur Athletic Federation did not re-quest a remeasurement of the course, which might have put such rumors to rest, and no further measurements were made. Yet the evidence brought forward by the rumor-mongers has not been sufficient to cause the measured course distance to be seriously questioned. For example, no separate group of people actually surveyed the course and produced clear evidence indicating a distance less than 42.195 km. It is true that the Belgian authorities, on occasion, have been lax with their approval of marathon courses as being bona fide. Examples are the courses at Roulers in 1966 and at Berchem in 1970. But these errors were brought to the public eye for benefit of the followers of the sport. Race conditions were such that performances recorded by most of the top athletes were comparable to what they had achieved or would achieve during the coming months."

Clayton argues that none of the critics who, in the late 1970s and early 1980s, charged that the Antwerp course was short were present at the race. They thus fail to realize that when the racers returned to the stadium before the halfway point, they did laps of the track in order to arrive at the correct distance before leaving for their second half of the double-out-and-back course. The difficulty in determining the length of the course in years following the race came about because the course had meanwhile been demolished by construction projects.

What remains of Derek Clayton today is a proud man attempting to translate the toughness he developed during long, hard weeks of training and racing into his day-to-day job. People who know him on that day-to-day level would be the first to contend that if anyone in the world had been capable of running a sub-2:09 marathon while the rest of the world was running 2:12s, it would have had to have been someone with Clayton's single-mindedness.

Frank Shorter continues to compete—and to win—with hopes for Los Angeles 1984.
(COURTESY THE CHICAGO DISTANCE CLASSIC)

10.

FRANK SHORTER:
Distant Drums

Erich Segal, who had Frank Shorter in one of his classes at Yale, tells stories about Frank's attitude toward marathoners and marathons. Shorter really thought marathons a waste of time and a pointless diversion. On days when Segal was flogging himself at the track in preparation for his annual trek to Boston, Shorter would come out, do a casual workout, make a good-natured snide remark to Segal about his mentality—or lack of it—and jog off, while Segal continued his incessant circling of the track.

Ironically, Segal was serving as commentator for ABC-TV a few years later when Shorter stunned everyone at Munich by breaking away from the world's best marathoners incredibly early in the race and winning the event as though it were an exhibition run. Some observers cite Shorter's accomplishment as one of the major factors in the running boom that swept America and, ultimately, most of the world.

Shorter became the first American to win the Olympic Marathon since Johnny Hayes backed into it in 1908 when Italy's Dorando Pietri was disqualified for being assisted across the finish line by anxious officials. The American public took Shorter to their hearts. There was a certain mastery and magnificence in Shorter's easy win that must somehow have called to their minds the tradition and grace of the classic runner practicing his art.

Shorter's running style is extremely efficient and classically beautiful. To watch him run when he's uninjured and in racing trim is to watch the biomechanically perfect textbook runner. If the runner cannot be separated from the run, Shorter's style cannot be separated from perfection. His Munich win was exciting: an announcement that the Americans were ready to take a place in marathon running. That his teammates, Kenny Moore and Jack Bacheler, finished fourth and ninth further underscored Shorter's dramatic announcement that America was getting serious about distance events.

When Shorter again toed the starting line as an Olympic marathoner in Montreal in 1976, his countrymen were watching with bated breath. Running one of the best races (time-wise) of his life, Shorter took the silver medal, while teammate Don Kardong took fourth—another good showing for the United States in front of a gigantic and appreciative television audience. Shorter became a national symbol for a growing number of Americans who were taking up running, often because they were good at no other sport they'd ever tried. Whether he approved or not, Frank Shorter had been made a national figure, and, as happens under those circumstances, the worshippers were allowed to form their hero into any mold they chose. The fact that Shorter had graduated from Yale and had then studied law made him something of a dilettante in their eyes, and this only added to the aura they created around him. The Shorter performances officially opened road racing to the white-collar American: he legitimized it.

Frank Shorter, the Yalie who had good-naturedly put down the marathon and marathoners to Erich Segal, had become the sport's icon.

The entire concept amuses Shorter.

In reality, he is very much unlike the mold into which Americans have poured him. His importance to the running boom is in the eyes of his beholders, but not in the eyes of Frank Shorter. In a 1982 interview with Amby Burfoot (1968 Boston Marathon winner and East Coast editor of *Runner's World*) at Shorter's Boulder, Colorado, adopted home, there was a telling interchange:

Burfoot: "It's often said that Frank Shorter created or catalyzed the running boom in the U.S."

Shorter: "Oh, I dunno."

Burfoot: "When you look at the numbers, the boom certainly didn't follow on the heels of your marathon victory in Munich."

Shorter: "Sure, it was really after Montreal. There was such a tremendous amount of attention paid to the marathon in Montreal. It was a hell of a race. It must have been exciting to watch. It'd be fun to be able to run a race like that again."

Burfoot: "But what do you think has been your role in the running boom?"

Shorter: "I honestly never have thought about it. I think that internationally there was a big to-do made about it on television. I'm still one of the few Americans to win a medal in a distance event in recent times. . . . But as you know, I'll probably be remembered as the guy from the U.S. who won the Olympic Marathon for the first time in however many years it was."

Burfoot: "Seventy-two minus eight."

Shorter: "And in a way I'm the only American who has won the marathon. [Author's Note: American Johnny Hayes won on a technicality in 1908.] If they suddenly decided to can Cierpinski and make me a double gold-medal winner, I certainly wouldn't hold myself out as that. It's just one of those things. But I don't worry about how people remember me. . . ."

In actuality, if one discounts Johnny Hayes's win, Shorter is one of only two Americans to win the Olympic gold in the marathon. Thomas Hicks won the Olympic Marathon at the St. Louis Olympic Games in 1904, but his win, too, was tainted by controversy. He had been doped with sulphate of strychnine and cognac. In addition, there were fewer foreign runners entered in the marathon than you have fingers on one hand. The fact that no one protested the Hicks win was due to the fact that the St. Louis Olympics were as far from the true spirit of the games as any parody could have been.

Discounting Hayes and Hicks, Frank Shorter has the distinction of being the only American to ever *earn* the marathon gold. His win was very much without controversy—a pure and simple overpowering of the best in the world.

Shorter's Olympic gold came in the city of his birth. Frank was born on October 31, 1947, in Munich, where his father was stationed following World War II. One of ten children, he has six sisters and three brothers. His father is a doctor. The Shorter family grew up in Middletown, New York, which Frank still considers his hometown.

Frank's running career began inauspiciously at the age of fifteen while he was attending prep school at Mt. Hermon in Massachusetts. The school sponsored an annual "Pie Race," in which the winners were given apple pies as their prizes. His first effort netted him a seventh place for the four-and-a-half-mile event. Just for old time's sake, he returned to Mt. Hermon in 1979 and ran again in the fabled Pie Race. He won that time, setting a course record of 20:54.

Perhaps one of the factors that accounts for his success in road racing is that he did not burn himself out as a runner in prep school or later at Yale. In fact, rather than burn himself out, he did just the opposite. Yale has no scholarship program and its track team is very much a volunteer affair. During his time there, Shorter was certainly more likely to be studying, skiing in Vermont, or practicing with the school's choral group than he was to be running.

His coach at Yale, one of the most profound influences on his running career, was Bob Giegengack.

"Each spring vacation we normally spend two weeks down South," Giegengack explains. "Frank didn't go on this trip his first three years because he had other pressing interests. One was singing. His singing group took tours during the same spring recess.

"The other interest was skiing. He skied a great deal. Even during our winter track season, after a meet on Saturday, Frankie would take off to New York or Vermont to ski. I don't know whether it was downhill or cross-country. I can certainly distinguish between the shotput and the high hurdles, but I'm not so sure about that other sport.

"He really enjoyed those activities, and that's the way it has to be with a kid at Yale. If he enjoys those things and wants to do them, you can't tell him nay. I don't have the leverage of a scholarship, and even if I did, I'm not so sure I would want to exert it. I'm certainly not permissive in workouts and so forth. But on the other hand, I have to respect the right of someone else to disagree with me about the importance *for him* of doing this particular thing."

It was Giegengack who told Shorter that he could be the best marathoner ever. This revelation came at the end of Shorter's junior year at Yale, at a crisis point in his life when he was wrestling with the importance of running in his life.

His family had moved from Middletown to Taos, New Mexico, where his father had been given a prestigious appointment at the hospital. It was 1968. Frank packed his bags to head to the Olympic training camp at Lake Tahoe, California, for the summer. The conversation, as Giegengack recreates it, went like this:

Shorter: "I want your honest opinion. What do you think aout my running future?"

Giegengack: "Frank, I think you can go as far as you want to go. I wouldn't put any limit on it."

Shorter: "Including the Olympic team?"

Giegengack: "Certainly including the Olympic team. I wouldn't put *any* limit on it. But it's going to take a lot more dedication than you've given it up till now. You've got to get your mileage up. You'll be at altitude, and you'll run all summer. Maybe take a crack at the marathon for Mexico City [he didn't]. Well, maybe you aren't ready for that yet. Come back here for your senior year and do your distance work in the morning, your quality work in the afternoon. We'll see what happens—how far you can go."

Whereas his first three years at Yale had not produced any outstanding running, in his senior year Shorter was virtually untouchable in cross-country dual meets. He went on to finish nineteenth in the N.C.A.A. cross-country championships despite a bout with the flu. In track that spring, he won the N.C.A.A. 6-mile crown and took second in the 3-mile.

John Parker, a friend of Shorter's from his senior year in college track, and later a teammate on the Florida Track Club, wrote a short biography of Shorter following his victory at Munich. Much of the biography is in Shorter's own words, distilled from a massive amount of correspondence the two kept up during Shorter's nomadic existence following his graduation from Yale.

Frank's life after graduation reflected his restlessness and his searching out a perfect niche for running in his life; meanwhile he was warding off the nagging realities of the world that often beset recent graduates.

His association with Florida (and Parker, and, more significantly, distance star Jack Bacheler) began on the first southern trip Shorter took with the Yale team in the spring of his senior year.

"My first encounter with Shorter was on the track," Parker recounts. "We finished 2–3 behind Alan Robinson of Southern Illinois in a triangular meet mile. An hour later, I sat recovering while Frank was out in the blistering sun in the two-mile. He and Oscar Moore were pushing each other all over the track. I remember thinking, 'That Shorter fellow must be some kind of hard-nose!' He ended up running 8:52 for second (behind Robinson again) after his 4:08 mile earlier.

"I went over and began talking to him, really not knowing what to expect. He turned out to be much more affable off the track, and that evening we went to the 'Gay 90's' which later became Frank's favorite pub when he was in Gainesville.

"Probably the most important thing that happened to Frank that trip was meeting Jack Bacheler. Frank had wanted to run a good time in the open two-mile at the Florida Relays, and wondered if he could talk over the race with Bacheler. A meeting was set up, and they agreed to cooperate. Actually what happened was that Frank helped Jack to a good time and died off to an 8:53. Jack ran 8:35. Frank was more than impressed by Jack's racing as well as training—so much that we began talking about his coming back to Gainesville to train after he graduated in June."

The seed was planted in Frank Shorter's mind: by getting away from the New England weather and into a group that shared the kind of interest in serious distance running that was growing in him, he could improve enormously. And a special bond had developed between Shorter and Bacheler. At the same time, Frank wrote for information about the medical school at the University of Florida at Gainesville, apparently thinking about following his father's footsteps.

With his intense undergraduate study winding down, Frank

started running like a fiend. He began doing double workouts, and in May wrote to Parker that he'd had the most massive weekly dose of running in his career: eighty-five miles. He claimed it was the first time he'd done over fifty, and he reveled in the feeling.

His running was going so well that he decided to head for Europe for the summer to take part in their track season; the results were little more than pedestrian. Upon his return he still faced the dilemma of what to do with the rest of his life. He enrolled in medical school at New Mexico University, almost to kill time. Medicine wasn't for him, however. Besides not being something he particularly enjoyed, medicine took so much time that it almost guaranteed that running would be excluded from his life.

While he wrestled with himself, Shorter traveled everywhere—making Jack Kerouac look like a down-home family man. He drifted between his parents' home in New Mexico, his girl friend Louise Gilliland's place in Boulder, Colorado, and Gainesville, where he liked to sit at the feet of his guru, Jack Bacheler, and focus on his running. All the while he was shifting and drifting and moving, the draft board hung in the background like a bad nightmare. When he'd left New Mexico University, he'd also cut loose from his deferment. Shorter was, if you like, playing Russian roulette in a helicopter: if the shot from the draft didn't get him, he might still crash during one of his endless flights from one place to the other.

He flirted with giving in to the draft board, hoping for a stint on the army track team, but couldn't make up his mind on that, either. He went so far as to head for California to talk it over with some of the doughboy trackmen. While he was there, Parker and Bacheler flew out to join him in Berkeley to take part in the Kennedy Games. Jack and Frank ran in the 3-mile, finishing first and second in 13:13.0 and 13:13.8. Frank was scheduled to be inducted into Uncle Sam's track team three days later.

Parker and Bacheler returned to Gainesville, expecting that the next they'd hear from Shorter would be via a letter from boot camp. Perhaps they'd receive a photo of his freshly shaved head! Instead, they received the following letter:

Well, I didn't join the old army. I spent the week at Ft. MacArthur and decided it wasn't for me. Seeing that no matter what I got in the way of benefits, I'd still be in the military *and* talking with some of the more radical members of the team convinced me I should fight it to the end and go down kicking, screaming, and scratching.

I made the decision to bolt as I was sitting around the induction station all day last Tuesday, watching the poor suckers who had sworn in get on the buses to head off for basic training. I was to be sworn in that afternoon but the Army blew it and said I would have to come back at 6:00 A.M. the next day. That was enough for me. I told the coach and captain in charge to get themselves another horse to do their running for them and went to stay with this track nut who is a big Striders booster. . . .

The draft board kept after him, but with Frank changing addresses more often than T-shirts, their mail was always two states behind him. And Frank had an ace-in-the-hole, so to speak: a fairly troublesome urinary infection he had picked up during his summer racing in Europe in 1969 which had never resolved itself.

While the urinary infection worked within his body to make him unfit for military service, Frank was running like crazy. He ran his first 20-miler and, at the beginning of October 1970, was feeling exhilarated.

For the rest of the year he worried about the draft board and the urinary infection (which might require surgery or already have produced a kidney stone). Apparently the army had better things to do with its time than trace down all the letters sent to Shorter which returned with no forwarding address. They ultimately gave up on him. Before the year was out he and Parker and Bacheler went to Chicago for the A.A.U. Cross-Country Championships, a 10-K affair, where Shorter demolished the field by running 30:10.6. In the process, he managed his first victory over Bacheler, albeit a Bacheler suffering from a cold. It was the physical and psychological breakthrough he desperately needed.

By the beginning of spring, Shorter was enrolled at the University of Florida in law. He found a pleasant house to share with Parker and another law student, a non-runner. After a layoff of nearly two years, he was getting back into the grind gradually. But he continued to train twice a day, with his hard workout coming late in the afternoon. Although they fed off each other, Shorter and Bacheler did not train together frequently, because their interval training techniques were quite different. Shorter ran his workouts extremely hard (quarter-miles of sixty-two or sixty-three seconds) with extremely short (fifty yards) jogs between, while Bacheler's workouts seemed much more leisurely, with more humane intervals between the speed runs. Also, Bacheler started his workouts earlier in the afternoon; because of classes, Shorter didn't do his until after 4:30 P.M.

As soon as exams were over that spring, Frank left for Boulder to see Louise. He had begun thinking about doing the marathon; what he had cooked up was typical Shorter in its intensity.

He traveled to Berkeley for the Kennedy Games again, where he ran a 13:31 3-mile on Saturday, and left immediately afterwards for Eugene, Oregon, to try out for the Pan-Am Marathon team, running his first marathon on Sunday. He ran a 2:17, taking second place behind Kenny Moore. He was on the team. He returned to Colorado for three weeks, then headed for the A.A.U. track championships, where he placed third in the 3-mile and won the 6-mile. Then he was off to Colombia for the Pan-American Games.

Shorter's ability to function smoothly in extreme heat stood him in good stead in Colombia, but typical South American intestinal troubles almost did him in. By five miles into the race, he knew he was going to have to keep a tight hold on his insides; he forged ahead to sixteen miles, he and Kenny Moore keeping company with two Colombian runners. Eventually he had to take a detour off the side of the road, and while he was occupied, one runner passed him. Once out of the ditch and a mite lighter, however, Shorter began opening up the afterburners. He passed the Mexican who'd moved up a place and began closing on the trio in the lead.

Because of his classic biomechanics, Shorter's step is so light that none of the leaders heard him closing on them until he cut in with "yoo hoo, I'm back!" At that point in a marathon, such light-heartedness goes a long way toward freaking out the other competitors! To make sure that he kept his edge, he picked up the pace and urged Moore to come along with him so they could drop the Colombians. Ultimately, Shorter also lost Moore, who dropped out from the heat. Shorter won in 2:22:40, adding that gold to the gold he'd already won in what he described as an uneventful 10,000 meters.

He returned to Gainesville, taking Louise with him, where they housed together with John Parker and his mate. Frank's mind was on three things: his studies, Louise, and making the 1972 Olympic team.

He trained hard and studied hard. He left Florida when school let out and headed for Vail for the summer, hoping that training at high altitude would improve his chances in the Olympic Trials. He was joined by Jack Bacheler and Jeff Galloway; all three worked singlemindedly toward the Olympics. They came down off the mountain to qualify for the team, which Frank did easily in the 10,000 and in the marathon (tying with Kenny Moore). Jack Bacheler rounded out the three-man marathon team, while Jeff Galloway made the 10,000 team.

From there it was on to Munich and history. Frank's marathon effort at Munich made him appear to be in a class by himself.

The night before the Munich race, Frank and Louise went out for a pleasant meal. Frank, who enjoys a good beer (because of its calming effect before an important race and because it provides the runner with needed carbohydrates and fluid), drank between one-and-a-half and two liters of German beer. He slept peacefully and relaxed the next morning, for once not taking a run. As he put it, "You've got plenty of time to limber up, and I figure any steps you take are too many that day if you're not doing it towards the finish line."

He ate a huge breakfast of pancakes and cereal, bread and honey and syrup—as many carbohydrates as he could comfortably hold.

He arrived near the stadium about an hour before the race and sat down to relax. He jogged a mile, went past security, and sat down on the grass inside the stadium, where he engaged in the time-honored ritual of eyeing up the competition for any weak spots in their armor. A lot of looking and looking back went on during the five minutes or so before the race. To psychologically ready himself, Frank worked to convince himself that the other competitors had serious flaws and that he was fit and ready in comparison. The day was hot and muggy; it was his kind of a day. Each of the eighty runners was called by name and placed in his starting position. Shorter was on the outside of the front row. He moved out into the lead on the first of two laps around the stadium, running it in seventy-two seconds; he ran the second lap in an identical seventy-two while another runner pushed to a sixty-eight.

Shorter describes what happened then:

"We left through the tunnel, took a right, went about four hundred yards, crossed a bridge over a four-lane highway, and came to a spot where we left the street to get onto a little path. At this point the camera truck had slowed down and all the runners were accordioned behind it, having to slow down. I tried to go to the right as everyone else was going to the left, because, since they were making a right-hand turn, I figured I'd cut it close and save some distance. Well, the truck decided he'd pull off the road at this point. So here I was running along with the driver pushing me off the road, pinching me between the side of the truck and the crowd.

"I knew I wasn't going to get by, so I pounded on the truck, swore a few times, and then stopped and went around the back. I hit it with my hand, so at that point everyone assumed that I'd been struck. What I wanted to do was to make them think about it a little bit so they'd figure, 'Oh, my, we hit one guy, we'd better not hit another.'

"I lost twenty or thirty yards on that little caper, but I caught up pretty soon. The pace was fairly normal. The first part of a race you try to get settled in, try to get used to the crowd, try to get used to the people you're running with—not to mention the camera truck."

Shorter kept himself comfortably in the lead pack, moving back and forth in the group so as to keep it interesting for himself and to eye up the other runners. He was trying to ascertain which of them would make the break from the pack, to anticipate when the break would come, and to make sure he would be ready to go along.

The pace was in the 5:10-per-mile range, which seemed slow to Shorter. To compound things, he felt a bit sluggish. (It would later become evident to him he felt sluggish because he was capable of running considerably faster, and the slow pace was throwing off his race-pace rhythm.)

At about seven miles, Shorter began to develop blisters, which he attributed to the custom-made Adidas shoes; they were too thin to protect him against the asphalt. He hoped they would not get worse. At 15-K he was faced with a new problem. In their paranoia about the other guy, in anticipating where the break was going to come, the front pack slowed down considerably. This felt very uncomfortable to Shorter, so he allowed his momentum to carry him to the front, and suddenly he found himself squirting out of the pack with a ten-yard lead. He couldn't believe it when no one came after him. Apparently everyone was playing it cautiously, figuring that it was much too early for anyone in his right mind to make a move.

"I just felt good," Shorter says, looking back at the race ten years later. "It's one of those things. You can't verbalize it, but you know it's the right time and you go, and later you realize it was the right choice. I knew I was committed, and I knew I had to get way ahead in case I started to die. But I broke away at Fukuoka [where he won] the December before at the halfway and that showed me I could hang on. And I knew something of the psychology, too. Gieg always said that if you break contact, you can relax while the other guys have to struggle. Out front you can go hard but relaxed. If you're playing catch-up, you're always pressing, always pressing. I like to use the knowledge of the extra effort it will take someone to catch me."

He increased the pace and with it, increased his lead. The rest of the lead pack stayed together, apparently figuring he'd burn himself out. He thinks he went through the next 5-K after the break at a 4:40 pace. By the time he hit 20-K, he had a one-minute lead.

Everyone continued to assume that Shorter would die and eventually come back to them. But on that day, it was not going to happen. He ran smoothly, seemingly effortlessly, consistently increasing his lead until, with six kilometers left, he led by nearly two minutes.

His blisters had matured and become painful, but merely as an annoying gnat that he could keep under control. His concentration was supreme. Looking back on the race, he remembers little of the middle portion: "I don't really remember anything until I got into the English Garden which is the far, long stretch where everyone was worried about the gravel. I never even thought about it. All I was really concentrating on in the English Garden was cutting corners, because the path really weaves. There was a lot of tangent running, trying to cut as straight a line as possible, considering that the side of the path was sloped, so you couldn't really take advantage of the whole path. I think this was one of the reasons the time was a little slow. That must have made the course slower by two minutes."

With six kilometers left, he was on a slight uphill and felt confident that if anyone were going to catch him there, he was really going to have to work for it.

One kilometer from the end, his reaction was a completely human one of "my God, I've really done it."

His entry to the stadium—and to victory—was not to the stupendous ovation he had begun to anticipate within the last kilometer, however. Despite the tight security put into effect by the West Germans (Shorter had to pass through several checkpoints and guards just to get into the stadium to start the marathon), a bogus runner had entered the stadium before him, pretending to be the lead runner. The creaky machinery necessary for live television coverage had already swung into action on the imposter and was having a difficult time swinging back to catch the real winner.

Although he knew as he entered the stadium that the Olympic Marathon record was within his grasp, he maintained his pace, refusing to sprint to the end. "I didn't want to do that," he said. "I figure that's bush league. I've always maintained that anyone who's leading by any significant amount at the end of a marathon who sprints at the end is hot-dogging." And Ivy Leaguers don't hot-dog.

After he entered the stadium to the accompaniment of consid-

erable confusion and crossed the finish line, Shorter waited for
Kenny Moore in order to congratulate him on his fourth-place
finish (Moore had suffered a chronic hamstring cramp) and sat
down in the grass to remove his shoes to inspect his blisters. They
were relatively minor; there was bleeding after he removed the
tape, but blood had not seeped through enough to soil his too-
thin shoes.

Although he doesn't admit it, part of Shorter's reason for not
rushing for the record may have been because of the Olympic
record holder. Abebe Bikila was present in the stadium as a special guest; wheelchair-ridden as the result of his automobile accident, Bikila watched Shorter enter the stadium and circle the
track to victory. Immediately after he received the gold medal,
Shorter made a beeline for Bikila to shake the hand of the only
double Olympic Marathon winner. There are many forms of respect one human being can extend to another; Shorter's would
have been understood by any other marathoner in Munich.

After his escape from the excitement at the stadium, he made
his way to his room, drew a hot bath, and, while he soaked,
drank three gins. Later that night he and Erich Segal and their
ladies went to dinner, where they laid heavily into the cham-
pagne.

Then Frank Shorter began methodically to plan out how he
was *not* going to react to the aftermath of his gold medal:

"After the race, I guess the normal thing to go through is the
'Big Letdown' where you start to ask yourself where your life
goes from there. But I was ready for it this time. I had won big
races before and knew what was in store. I figured that I would
sit there and let whatever happened to me happen for about
three days until we came home. It was a kind of minute-to-min-
ute thing. I wasn't going to worry about what happened then or
in the future. I just gave it a few days and drifted along.

"I didn't want to sit around pondering on how the race was in-
dicative of how my life was going to change.

"Okay, you do some television interviews and that's fine. Flying back on the plane, the pilot lets you come up and look out the
front window, that's okay too. You get home, my old hometown
in New York gives me a big reception and a key to the city. A lot

of people were very happy. You don't want to play dilettante and go into seclusion."

But in that sense, Frank was very much mistaken. Although he had control over his side of his life, once you become a celebrity, your real life and your celebrity life often part ways. Frank Shorter went merrily away marching to his own drummer, but the public who saw him as a symbol pursued the ghost of Frank Shorter entering the Munich Olympic stadium. And the public marched to seventy-six trombones.

It is certain that Shorter was aware of his celebrity: it was thrown at him everywhere he went. (It is no wonder he enjoys solitary runs in the mountains above his home in Boulder; one needs some time with one's self.) But it is doubtful if Shorter, even today, realizes the impact he had upon the running boom.

As he stated, there was no real boom after his Munich victory. But then, no one moves that quickly from being a confirmed sedentary to being a fifty-mile-per-week runner training for the marathon. What Frank Shorter did was create in the subconscious of a large portion of the American male public the idea that it was all right to take up running, to go daily onto America's roads, to sweat, to pursue something at your own speed—without needing the support of other members of a team.

Although there had been occasional college men such as Johnny Kelley who moved up to the marathon before Shorter, road racing in America had long been considered a blue-collar sport. Track racing was for the college-bred, the gentlemen. Trackmen looked down on road racers, and road racers mistrusted college-bred runners moving into their ranks. Even today there is a sort of resentment when a good 10,000-meter man moves over to road racing. Shorter forever changed the distinctions between road racers and trackmen; he erased the wide gray line.

He was a college graduate—an Ivy Leaguer at that—and to make it even more impressive, he'd gone out and won the Olympic gold medal away from the whole world, making it look easy in the process.

The recent standard-issue college graduate, who often as not was suffering an identity crisis while being ground up in the white-collar world, suddenly had a sport, a brazen idol, of his own. He couldn't identify much with the two-hundred-and-seventy-six pound middle linebacker who had never taken regular courses while in college, and he had little in common with the javelin thrower, but with Frank Shorter he could identify. And Frank studying to be a lawyer, yet!

Had Shorter had time to analyze while it was happening, he would easily have seen that, demographically, the growing number of men who came up to gaze wonderingly at him or, following his appearance in a 10-K race, to ask his advice, were not—by and large—stonemasons or carpenters or hospital orderlies or garbage collectors. They were accountants, engineers, lawyers, doctors, and teachers.

Although between 1972 and 1976 Shorter ran well, he ran as a celebrity; and when he wasn't running, he retreated back into his own private world. This served only to heighten the reverence with which he was regarded by growing throngs of runners. His classic style, his appearances in television advertising, his appearance as a TV sports commentator, and the seeming ease with which he qualified for the 1976 U.S. marathon team—all contributed to his celebrity status.

People were happy to ignore his increasing radicalism about runners' rights; most of that was behind the scenes, and people wanted to know about Shorter the runner, not Shorter the reformer.

He ran the marathon in Montreal, one of the best marathons of his life, and was beaten by East Germany's Waldemar Cierpinski, who used an incredible 2:09:55 to get the job done. Shorter's silver medal did not diminish his luster in the eyes of the American public, however. To most of the American runners who had taken up the sport, and to those who took to the streets and roads following his silver in 1976, Shorter had been "cheated" out of the gold by an East German factory runner who had the support of an entire country's resources behind him.

And then Shorter developed a foot injury. And Bill Rodgers, who'd surprised himself perhaps more than anyone else by setting an American marathon record of 2:09:55 at Boston in 1975, began skipping almost flippantly to the forefront of American road racing while Shorter mended, raced, reinjured himself, and went back to mending.

There can be only one King of the Roads reigning at a time, and while Shorter mended, Rodgers went on a running binge that at times astonished everyone. In possession of a seemingly "spaced out," effervescent, almost childlike attitude toward running, runners, and the public in general, Rodgers resembled the kid next door, but a kid who made it all seem easy—and fun besides.

Despite his injuries, Shorter occasionally descended from the mountain fastnesses of Boulder to do battle, frequently giving a good accounting of himself. He spent a good deal of his time working behind the scenes trying to hammer into shape a thing called TACTRUST, a trust-fund arrangement into which the winnings of runners could be placed, the savings to be used for their living and training. Shorter's hope is to rid the sport of both "shamateurism" and professionalism of the crass, purely money-oriented type. (Shamateurs plead amateurism while taking the money under the table; the pros take the money out in the open in the face of rules against it.) Today Shorter is proud of his work on TACTRUST, perhaps almost as proud as he is of his medals. "The important point [of TACTRUST]," he says, "is that it will encourage athletes in this country's talent-pool. We have to develop athletic talent in a manner that doesn't require the athletes to sacrifice their professions and potential earnings. Also, an American athlete has to be able to toe the Olympic starting line and look to the left and right and not feel that he or she has been at a disadvantage getting there."

While the TACTRUST percolates, Shorter is building his training for a comeback that he feels will impress many and once again put to rest the feeling that he is done, finished, over the hill.

While he was on the descent and Bill Rodgers was on the ascent during the late 1970s and early 1980s, the two engaged in some duels that are still talked about. Rodgers came out the victor in most of them. But in return engagements in the spring of 1982, Shorter had the upper hand. Frequently their hard-fought battles were at the expense of some of the young lions who were expected to show their heels to the aging duo (both were thirty-four in the summer of 1982), but who instead were given an education by two of America's greatest road racers in action.

No one who has followed Shorter's career and his periodic comebacks will be surprised if he lines up at the 1984 U.S. Olympic Marathon trials; many won't be surprised if he is one of the three runners to make the team. From there on, Frank Shorter is in his own element: in Olympic competition, with Los Angeles guaranteeing a hot temperature and first-class competition.

Bill Rodgers was King of the Roads during the height of the
American running boom.
(COURTESY BOB SACCHETTI)

11.

BILL RODGERS:
Everybody's Brother

On March 7, 1982, Herb Lindsay proved that he doesn't understand Bill Rodgers.

Herb Lindsay is an incredibly effective running machine who lives and trains in Boulder, Colorado (via Michigan, where he was one tough college runner), but who does not fit the long-distance-running mold. Instead of being built like a waif, he's built like a Sicilian bodyguard, who works out with two-hundred pound barbells before and after each meal—the meals consisting of raw meat. He is strong and he is fast. And he sometimes gets angry.

He became incensed when he learned that Peter McLaughlin, a Boulder attorney in charge of the McLaughlin & Company Symphony Run, had spent his seven-thousand-dollar budget—intended to bring in name runners to help promote the event—by blowing it all on Bill Rodgers, who lived all the way back east in Boston, for God's sake, while the Boulder runners were completely ignored.

The Symphony Run was scheduled as a 7.63-mile event. The distance was measured to equal that used in the San Francisco Bay-to-Breakers race, an event that in 1982 would draw 55,000 so-called runners, many of whom never run another race throughout the year. The Symphony Run was set up to benefit the Denver Symphony, and, like the Bay-to-Breakers, was destined to get everyone and anyone who could run even a few steps to enter, to take part, and benefit the charity.

Which is why McLaughlin hired Rodgers. Rodgers (along with Frank Shorter) is the biggest draw at a race. Runners who train seventy miles a week will turn out to see Rodgers and/or Shorter and to run in a race with them. And people who don't even run will turn out to see them run. If you want a successful running event, your first thoughts are of Bill Rodgers and Frank Shorter. And, more recently, Alberto Salazar.

Lindsay took it upon himself to point out to McLaughlin that local runners should not be overlooked. He sent in his entry form. It was returned automatically, with a request for the eight-dollar entry fee. He was also informed that the charity organization, the Denver Symphony, was willing to pay the fee in exchange for using his name in race promotion. To settle it, McLaughlin paid Lindsay's entry fee out of his own pocket.

Lindsay arrived sniffing for blood.

When the race started, he went out fast and stayed fast. He quickly opened a lead and held it. Sixty yards from the finish line, he stopped, turned and waited for Rodgers, bowed, came to attention, walked backwards across the finish line, and bolted.

The gesture was profoundly confounding to McLaughlin and Rodgers, especially since Lindsay—despite his formidable appearance and his oft-proven prowess on the roads—is normally extremely reticent and unassuming.

Lindsay claims that his was a spontaneous gesture. "I was frustrated over the fact that it could have been a better event," he says, citing problems during the race with the press truck being too close to him, spectators and bicyclists getting in his way, and his inability to locate mile markers as factors which had increased his sense of frustration. Following the incident—the race, by the way, raised some eighty-five thousand dollars for the Denver Symphony—the three principals settled their differences.

It is not difficult to understand Lindsay's state of mind. His frustration must be a cumulative one shared by many of America's top road racers who see Rodgers (and Shorter) pulling down large appearance fees whenever they want to. Lindsay has very fine credentials, and he has frequently beaten Rodgers within the last few years, even wresting from him the title King of the Roads in recent years. Other top runners like Thom Hunt, Kirk Pfeffer, Craig Virgin, Greg Meyer, and Randy Thomas are treated as though they are on a different—and very much lower—level than Rodgers.

What is overlooked is the fact that Bill Rodgers, the fair-haired boy, is more than a runner—he's an institution in American road racing.

There can only be one King of the Roads at a time, and in the early 1970s, it was Olympic gold medalist Frank Shorter, who reigned supreme and reigned well, but who was at the same time something of the man in the high castle: Ivy League, private, idolized from afar. When, through injuries and overracing, he allowed a breach in his fortress walls, Bill Rodgers rushed in to take over. Bill Rodgers is always the first to point out that he was in the right place at the right time. He had been pounding on the Shorter stronghold for some time. The two of them waged some classic duels between 1975 and 1979. Rodgers scored higher than Shorter in twenty events to Shorter's fourteen during that period, for those who like to keep score. The press tended to play up every race they entered as a duel between them, as though there were no other runners in the field. During the period they had one intentional tie—at the 1975 Virginia 10-Miler at Lynchburg, Virginia (which officials broke up and eventually awarded to Rodgers). They did not meet in 1980, and in 1981, each scored once against the other.

Rodgers rose to the top in the late 1970s while Shorter nursed chronic injuries. And Rodgers was exactly what the running movement needed at that time. Whereas Shorter was Elvis Presley, Bill Rodgers was Bruce Springsteen. Rodgers was accessible, gregarious, resembling the kid next door. He reveled in running—and in winning. He'd stick around after a race and sign autographs for hours, rerunning the race with one average runner after the other, while his wife, Ellen, attempted to pull him away so he could stretch, wind down, and get to his next scheduled appointment.

He raced frequently and well, almost never suffered injury, was always good for a quote. His consistency became legend. While Shorter worked behind the scenes for changes, Rodgers worked as a front man, speaking out against the state of affairs in which runners were urged to accept under-the-table payments while other professional athletes could sign huge contracts (and, according to Rodgers, they didn't usually work as hard or as often as he and other top runners).

When plans for attending the 1980 Olympic Games went sour for the United States, Rodgers began to see the writing on the wall and was outspoken as usual. Other people in the U.S. Olympic movement were saying it too, but he said it more dramatically:

> I wouldn't go over and compete if I thought there was really an issue. If there was a law revoking tourist visas, I wouldn't go. If seventy-five percent of the American people thought it would hurt the interests of the United States— participating in the Olympics—I wouldn't go. I'm not insane.
>
> But I feel what I'm saying is right. I think the issues are totally clouded. The more you confuse them and put them together, the more you cloud the picture. I think the way to solve a diplomatic problem is through diplomacy.
>
> Do we want an end to the Olympics? I am speaking, deep down, from my own experiences. I've been to an Olympics. I know how a lot of athletes feel about them. I'm a romantic. I believe the Olympics is worldwide. I'm speaking as an American who has represented America for six years [in international competition], and there were times when I had to take time off from my job [as a teacher] without pay.
>
> Patriotism is not an issue. I see a lot of hypocrisy lurking out there. My political opinions are no more potent than a lot of people expressed after Watergate. Anyone who denies that the C.I.A. is any different from the Russian K.G.B. is living in fairyland.
>
> I read an article that said I make important money out of the Olympics. I make good money out of my business. I'm entitled to it. I'm as good at what I do as any pro athlete in this country is at what he does. How about boycotting pro football in the United States, saving all that money and donating it to orphans who were attacked in Afghanistan?
>
> As far as my participating in the Olympics, I don't even know if I'll make the U.S. team. I'd like to go back to the Olympics, but I'm not guaranteed I'll make the team. Even if I did, the only way I could benefit financially would be if I

won a gold medal. I view my chances of getting a gold as minimal.

When the boycott became a reality, Rodgers passed up the U.S. Olympic Marathon trials race.

Despite his outspoken views, or perhaps because of them, Bill Rodgers has over the years become an institution in American running. On the international scene, he turns down more invitations than he accepts. The invitations come from every continent in the world, for it's Shorter and Rodgers that the rest of the running world wants to see. They want Rodgers in Japan and in Manila, in Stockholm and in London. It's easy to understand Lindsay's frustrations; they didn't even want him in his adopted hometown.

Bill Rodgers is perhaps one of the least likely people to become a household word among the country's thirty million joggers and runners.

He was born the second of four children in Hartford, Connecticut. His older brother (by one year), Charlie, manages Bill's Cleveland Circle store in Boston. "Our mother was a practicing Catholic," Charlie says. "She didn't let too much time elapse between having kids. I came along in December of 1946, Billy in December of '47, and Martha came along thirteen months after Billy. Then she stopped until '56 when Linda came along."

Although born in Hartford, the Rodgers kids grew up in Newington, Connecticut. Both Charlie and Bill ran in high school on a rutted dirt track around a football field. Training in high school was very rigid. There were extensive calisthenics followed by interval workouts every afternoon, which the distance men were expected to run just as quickly as the sprinters. There was no overdistance work; any additional training had to come from within the runner himself.

Charlie tells the story of how he and the rest of the cross-country team used to go to a girl friend's to talk, drink Cokes, and relax when they were supposed to be out on workouts. Bill was the only one conscientious enough to do the entire workout without stopping for a rest or a snack. In his senior year in high school, Bill astounded the rest of his team one day during roadwork. Spotting a sign for the next town six miles away, he headed off on a whim to visit it. Having reached it, he turned around and came back.

Bill put in extra mileage simply because he liked to run, not because he was intelligent enough about running to know that overdistance was needed. He became state champion in cross-country, frequently competing against and beating Amby Burfoot's younger brother.

Rodgers's cross-country accomplishments brought scholarship offers. Among the colleges he checked out was Wesleyan. While visiting the school, he met Amby, who was a student there. Burfoot was a sophomore, while future Olympian Jeff Galloway was a junior. Rodgers liked the fact that the runners he talked to enjoyed running, instead of seeing it as a chore.

"When Billy came to Wesleyan, he was pretty uptight about his training," Burfoot recalls. "He had a tight, regimented background in high school. His coach was very strict. Billy couldn't conceive of doing a workout without checking with the coach first. For Billy, the coach was the fountain to whom every runner went for inspiration."

That attitude didn't last long. "Amby taught me to relax more and enjoy runing. Jeff went so far as to offer to help me with homework, if I got behind, and I took him up on it several times," Rodgers remembers.

While Rodgers and Burfoot roomed together, they concentrated on achieving goals in running that reflected the divergence in their styles.

For Rodgers, the goal was a sub-9:00 2-mile. In his senior year he accomplished his goal. For Burfoot, the goal was to win the Boston, which he did in 1968.

"It seemed to me that after he'd reached that goal, he just gave up running," Amby recalls. Rodgers claims that he gave up running because there were more important things to worry about. It was the year of the national college strikes against Vietnam, and Rodgers didn't bother showing up for spring track practice.

Both Billy and Charlie received conscientious-objector deferment. Charlie speaks of his alternative service at an alcoholic detox hospital with fondness. Bill's was a less positive experience. He worked as an orderly, wheeling dead and dying patients around Peter Bent Brigham Hospital in Boston, living meanwhile in Jamaica Plain. Eventually he was fired from the job for trying to organize the workers into a union.

By this time, Bill had met Ellen LaLone in a bar. Both were working drudge jobs in hospitals and each was smoking a pack of cigarettes a day. Bill was only running sporadically at a small indoor track at the local YMCA. Although he had given up serious running, there was apparently still a flicker of interest remaining.

Ellen's reaction to Bill's first trip to the YMCA to run was not exactly a positive one. "I thought, 'What is this? He wants to go running more than he wants to see me?' I eventually changed my perspective on his priorities," she says.

One day Bill and Ellen loaded all their worldly belongings into their battered Dodge van and headed for the West Coast, hoping to change their luck. Once there, however, they felt displaced and homesick, and returned to Boston. "I'm not exactly sure why we came back," Bill says. "I guess it was a combination of things. We weren't doing very well in Boston. We were pretty close to broke and I guess we believed all the press California had gotten as the state of opportunity. When we got there, though, we checked out Marin County and saw how expensive everything was. I'd hoped to find the ideal place to run in California, but we soon saw that we couldn't afford to stay there. We began driving south, counting the two hundred dollars we had left. We turned east at San Jose."

"I remember one day at a race in Wesleyan," Amby Burfoot recalls. "As I topped a hill at the three-mile mark, I saw this pale-looking guy with blond hair down to his shoulders in a fatigue jacket standing along the side of the road. I did about sixteen double-takes as I went by. It was Billy. He apparently was still interested in running, but was watching from the sidelines."

Burfoot remembers an incident a few years later. It was February of 1973 and there was a 30-K race from Hopkinton, along the Boston Marathon course, as a warm-up for Boston. "I saw Bill jogging around Hopkinton in a pair of grungy, torn sweatpants and a torn sweatshirt," Burfoot says. "I embraced him warmly. I hadn't seen him in several years. I thought to myself, 'Gee, it's great that Billy is at least getting back into jogging a bit. Running used to mean so much to him.' Jogging, huh? When I reached the ten-mile mark in 49:49 and he was still at my shoulder, I knew he wasn't merely jogging, but was making a comeback. He eventually fell back a little and took third place. I won that one, but it was one of the last times I'd ever beat Billy. He was serious about coming back. He'd been training seriously for nine months. He'd once again gotten his life under control."

March of 1975 was a turning point in Rodgers's life. He made the American team going to the World Cross-Country Championships in Morocco. He took third place and, although that gave him no status in American racing, it gave him a niche among international runners.

A month later, inspired by Amby Burfoot, Bill entered the Boston Marathon for the third time. "I was finding my distances," he says, "and the road races were the kind of running I was really feeling comfortable with. Amby had tried to talk me into doing some road racing in college but I resisted. As it turns out, he was right. I was wasting my time at the 2-mile and other shorter distances." He proceeded to set the American marathon record at Boston with a blistering 2:09:55, during a race in which he made three drink-stops and one stop to tie his shoe.

The rest is history familiar to every observer of the marathon scene.

He went on to amass a twenty-two race winning streak on the roads in 1978. The following April, winning his third (of four) Boston Marathons, Rodgers knocked twenty-eight seconds off his American marathon record (which he would ultimately lose to Alberto Salazar, a kid who used to be a sort of mascot to the Greater Boston Track Club when Rodgers was the reigning stud). In all, he won four New York City Marathons in a row (1976–79), set a world record on the track at 25-K at West Valley College in Saratoga, California, and started a line of running clothing that became extremely popular.

He wrote a book (with *Boston Globe* sportswriter Joe Concannon) on running in general and his career in particular.

He continued to race thirty to thirty-five times a year, pulling in appearance money, much of which he poured back into his running stores and clothing company and other enterprises.

He won eighteen of the twenty-nine marathons he entered, and ran nineteen sub-2:20 marathons.

He and Ellen built a dream house in fashionable Sherborn on ten acres of land.

But things began to unravel.

In October of 1980 he went into the New York City Marathon in less-than-perfect-condition and, running in the huge lead pack at about the halfway mark, was tripped up and went down with three other runners. The mishap put him out of the competition (he finished fifth). He lost other races, some of them because he was racing too frequently, and others because, although his times would improve, the times of some of the young lions coming up (like Lindsay) were just a bit better.

Nineteen-eighty was a frustrating year in general. He had tried to keep himself psyched for his tremendously heavy training and racing schedule through 1979 by keeping the carrot of the Olympic Games in front of his eyes—even training well in the heat—always his nemesis—which he knew he would face in Moscow in 1980. He won the 1979 New York City Marathon in heat that would have stifled him the year before. Then, the political troubles in Afghanistan put an end to America's planned involvement in the games and, seeing the writing on the wall, he didn't bother entering the U.S. Olympic Trials Marathon in May, 1980.

At the same time, his marriage was coming undone. He and Ellen, who'd sustained and supported him through the meager times, had grown farther and farther apart. Ellen, somewhat retiring and shy, was forced by A.A.U. rules to act as Bill's agent (runners were not allowed to use professional agents, so spouses often acted in that capacity), a role that in no way suited her. She was required to assume the role of the "bad guy" in dealing with the business side of Bill's running, often having to untangle Bill's good-natured promises to people to race. She began viewing her role as Bill's mother—a role he was happy to have her accept, because it allowed him freedom to do what he wanted to do: run and be a nice guy to one and all.

"I just got tired of that side of it," Ellen said after their separation. "Bill enjoyed people enjoying him and his success. He loves to run but he doesn't like to deal with the hassles that go along with it these days. Not that I blame him. His job was to run, and I was supposed to take care of him, I guess. I kind of gravitated to the role after sort of subtly being pushed into it. After a

while it really began to get to me, though. He'd come off as the
nice guy and I'd come off as the heavy, because I was the one
who had to say no to people, who had to come and drag him
away from people so he'd get in his run that afternoon. That
wasn't really me and I didn't like it one bit. It would have been a
lot easier on all of us if the A.A.U. hadn't been so old-fashioned
and hypocritical"—she smiled and shrugged her shoulders—
"and a few other things that shouldn't be put into print. But what
can you do? People change, and they change so quietly that you
wake up one day and they aren't the people you thought they
were at all."

Bill's comments about the problems were quite simple: "We're
in the process of getting a divorce. It is true that Ellen is better in
business negotiations than me. How this divorce will affect my
future is hard to say. The only thing I can say about my personal
situation is that it's the hardest thing that has ever happened to
me. It's sad and hard for both of us right now, but ultimately I
think it's best."

Meanwhile the A.A.U. (by then called The Athletic Congress
after the A.A.U. had to divest itself—technically—of all but one
of its sports because of its position as a sport monopoly) softened
its stand on agents, and Bill engaged people other than Ellen to
direct his career. Pressed by the needs of his businesses (which
neither he nor Ellen own outright), he kept his racing schedule
heavy through 1981. In January 1982, attempting an experiment
that failed utterly, he raced two marathons on consecutive weekends. After that debacle, he worked diligently toward a good comeback at Boston, but temperatures in the seventies and a spirited
duel between Alberto Salazar and Dick Beardsley—one of the
other three runners who had taken the fall with him at New York
in 1980—conspired to keep him from a fifth victory in that race.

What remains is the same agreeable, popular, next-door-
neighbor kind of presence Bill Rodgers had always exuded, but
with a bit more maturity around the edges—and a growing list of
worries, not the least of which are the young lions snapping more
viciously at his heels (Rodgers is now in his mid-thirties). There
is also the pressure of businesses which started in the hopes they
would free him to concentrate on his running, the pressure of
having more and more people depending on him as his business

empire becomes more complex and takes on more and more personnel.

And behind it all is still the guy who, for years after he and Ellen could afford something better, stayed in a second-story one-bedroom apartment in Melrose, drove a VW Beetle in need of a good rest, and frequently preferred to eat bell-pepper-and-anchovy pizzas with a small group of friends rather than go to a good restaurant. Occasionally, Rodgers would vanish for hours with a pocketful of quarters to play Asteroids and Space Invaders at a local video arcade.

Rodgers has been and remains the Luke Skywalker of the running movement—the child warrior going out to conquer, and, in conquering, making it look like fun. Rodgers and Shorter have done more to put road racing on the map than all other people in the running movement combined. Certainly they made their contributions in different ways and at different levels, but between them, they defined the sport for the 1980s. And they continue to do so.

On March 8, 1982, at the Azalea Trail Run in Mobile, Alabama, Benji Durden (one of the three Americans to qualify for the 1980 U.S. Olympic Marathon team) and Robbie Perkins took the field out quite fast; it was a rather warm day. "At one point I was certain it would be either Perkins or me," Durden stated. "But at four, four-and-a-half miles, Perkins kept looking back and I realized someone must be getting close. It turned out to be Rodgers." Bill caught Perkins at five-and-a-half miles and Durden at six miles, and the three of them waged a terrific duel over the final two-tenths of a mile. Rodgers won the 10-kilometer race in 29:00; Perkins trailed by one second, and Durden was one second farther back. The winning time was the best ever by a runner thirty-four years old.

Two weeks later, Rodgers and Shorter met at the Florida Derby Festival 10-kilometer (Rodgers had competed in the Leprechaun 10,000 Meter Road Race in Dublin, Georgia, the day before, taking second place with a 29:30). Tony Sandoval, another of the trio of qualifiers for the U.S. Olympic Marathon team in 1980, tried to stay with them. "It was like watching two legends," Sandoval says. "It would have been nice to hang around them for a while. I ran side by side the first mile with Bill, but when it was time to go off and run with Frank, it just wasn't there." It was exceptionally hot, and although the two battled back and forth for the lead, Shorter won in 29:11, setting a course record. Rodgers finished a few seconds later. Sandoval finished in third, with 31:06.

It's the magic that Sandoval understood and Lindsay didn't. And the fact that there's only so much room at the top: the top in running that Shorter and Rodgers will likely dominate until they retire or change their names.

Rodgers seems intent on a comeback. On Oct. 16, 1982, at the Big M Marathon in Melbourne, Australia, on a very difficult course, he won in 2:11:08, setting a world marathon record for thirty-four-year-olds.

Waldemar Cierpinski became the second man in history to win two Olympic marathon golds.
(COURTESY ALLSPORT PHOTOGRAPHIC, SURREY)

12.

WALDEMAR CIERPINSKI:
The Shadow Mask

In 1964 Abebe Bikila ran himself into the history books by winning the Olympic gold medal in the marathon for the second time. It was the first time a runner had repeated as marathon winner at the Olympic Games. The accomplishment put the graceful African runner on a mountain peak that would have remained inaccessible to him had he won a dozen Boston Marathons and a half-dozen Fukuokas.

In 1976, Frank Shorter went to the Montreal Olympic Games to defend his 1972 marathon gold medal. He was clearly the favorite to win and become the second man in history to reach the rarefied air on that mountain peak. Although he ran one of the best races of his career, he took second place to East Germany's only entry in the marathon, Waldemar Cierpinski, who ran a 2:09:55, stunning the sports world. Cierpinski was virtually unknown outside his own country.

In 1980, Waldemar Cierpinski traveled to Moscow for the Olympic Games and once again won the gold medal, this time with a 2:11:03. He ascended to the mountaintop, but his niche there was a few steps down from Abebe Bikila, due to the boycott of the Moscow games that kept the formidable American and Japanese marathon teams from competing.

Boycott or not, though, Cierpinski's accomplishment placed a spotlight of curiosity on the East Germans and their sports-hero factories.

To get a clear picture of Cierpinski, it is necessary to have a working knowledge of the system that produced him.

When critics refer to the East German system of producing athletes, they often cynically refer to it as the development of factory runners, not too unlike the references applied to an auto manufacturer's factory-backed team of racing cars competing at LeMans: the image is of a brooding Teutonic castle, with a storm brewing behind it. A garage door opens and light spills forth; four sleek, identical Porsche prototypes, endurance racing cars, descend to flaunt their prowess through the countryside of LeMans. The rest of the world plays catch-up.

In the case of Cierpinski (and teammates Baumgartl, Lesse, Truppel, Arnhold, and others), the factory is on the east side of the Berlin Wall. The castle is perhaps more brooding. The impact on the running world was more profound because of its unexpectedness.

The reference to factory runners in East Germany may be made cynically, but it is quite accurate. Under the East German structure, the athletic programs that produce athletes for the Olympic Games and other major competitions throughout the world come from sports clubs financed by specific industries; and the national sports program in East Germany is supported by a law that earmarks six to eight percent of a company's annual profits for that use. Additionally, every worker in the country is required to donate one day's wages to the country's sports effort.

The sports program in East Germany is a thing of national pride and is firmly ingrained in the daily life of all inhabitants.

There is a movement in East Germany to raise the health of its people as a whole. In that regard, Berlin Wall or not, there are great similarities with other countries. The East German government is concerned about the amount of heart disease among the adult population, and there is an excessive amount of cigarette smoking. In order to combat these problems, incentive programs have been set up to involve all the people in some sort of physical activity.

There is a "Mile Running Movement," backed by an ambitious public-relations campaign. Citizens who participate in the program receive certificates for each "mile" completed; after collecting thirty certificates, a citizen receives an award. In 1977, anyone who completed one hundred "mile" runs (the miles are actually metric runs that equal the number of meters in the current year; in 1983, 1983 meters equals a "mile") was given a trip to the Spartakiad '77 in Leipzig.

There are also "trimming courses" available, which are very popular, similar to our Parcourse or Game Field courses.

East Germany is committed to the health and fitness of its citizens, and its involvement with sports is so much a priority that it is even written into the country's constitution. Also, the performance of an East German athlete in international competition is a powerful propaganda weapon for their system, and the state is very aggressive in encouraging youngsters to pursue a career in sport.

An East German athlete enjoys fairly extensive travel, including trips to countries in the West. When the outstanding athlete retires, there are coaching jobs available, and, later, state pensions. While the athlete is competing, his or her club provides free room and board in the club dorm or in an apartment. Vacations are given for rest and recuperation, and the athlete's name is placed high on the waiting-list for an automobile. The athlete can just about write his or her own ticket for higher education, and the parents of outstanding athletes are given better jobs. The athlete is given the opportunity to purchase electrical equipment and clothing before other citizens, is given tickets to special events, and spends part of each year training in ideal locations. There is financial security and social recognition, some of which comes from the fact that under East German law, twenty percent of all television air time must be devoted to sport. Distance-running events are covered thoroughly; when Waldemar Cierpinski was winning in Montreal in 1976, East Germans were watching him while clustered around their television sets.

The search for good athletes begins very early. Youngsters are required to participate in sports and physical education classes from the time they enter school at the age of six. Distance running is stressed as one of the endurance activities. Each school year features three sports highlights:

1. A national cross-country championship is held at various sites around the country. Known as the Youth Cross, the annual event draws more than a million participants.

2. Twice a year, there is a cross-Berlin relay road race, sponsored by a newspaper in which school teams participate.
3. The Spartakiad is an annual age-group competition that begins at the local level and progresses to a national meet in which the country's finest young athletes compete to see who are East Germany's best.

Naturally, sports experts and coaches are watching such competitions with the proverbial eagle eye, because in East Germany, an athlete's coach is given as much recognition for a job well done as is the athlete.

At the age of eight, if a student shows particular promise in sport, he or she is offered the chance to attend special sports schools. If the coaches or sports managers see a gifted child and want to send him or her to a special sports school some distance from home, they often make arrangements to move the child's family, also. Although it is not an across-the-board reaction, most East German parents are honored to have their children picked for accelerated sports education.

Youngsters in such sports schools must maintain high academic standards, but their academic work is scheduled around their physical development. Frequently, a factory-based sports club is located near these schools, and the schools often draw from the club's expertise in coaching and also use its medical facilities.

Naturally, each child is given certain goals to strive for if he or she is to stay in the special sports school. Students who consistently fail to attain the expected goals are transferred to regular schools.

The system does not work perfectly, of course. Some of the selected students never develop into outstanding athletes, and some who were not picked are late-bloomers and end up with the ability to run circles around the specially trained. There are incentive and bonus plans in effect for coaches or teachers who discover highly talented youngsters in the regular schools who were originally overlooked.

Despite all of the attention given to sports—and especially to running—the results and times achieved by the youngsters at the annual Spartakiad are not superior to top performances by United States school children of comparable age. The difference comes in the sports opportunities given the East German children once they exhibit the talent. They are freed up to pursue and develop that talent without having to worry about the work-a-day world.

As the young athlete progresses, he or she is given individual attention by a coach who has been specially trained in that sport, and who has earned a four-year degree in that specialty at the Sports Research Institute (DHfK) in Leipzig. In East Germany, coaching is a profession, not an avocation. The coaches are well-paid, usually by a sports club that hires them to recruit for the club and to train recruits to bring glory to the club.

The clubs are sophisticated institutions. They have dorms, training areas, tracks, coaches, doctors, dieticians, and masseurs. Their support program is extensive and all-inclusive.

They constitute the backbone of the East German athletic system.

For distance runners, the clubs provide a stress-free environment in which to run eighty to one hundred twenty miles per week. And in addition, it also allows them two hours per day for weight and flexibility training, an hour a day for massage (something American marathoners such as Bill Rodgers and Alberto Salazar are only now enjoying regularly), a precise diet formulated to their specific needs, personal coaching, and plenty of all-important sleep. Alcohol is strictly forbidden.

The club athletes and their coaches can also tap into the massive sports computer at the DHfK in Leipzig. Each athlete's vital information is amassed daily and fed to the computer in an attempt to gain that valuable bit of information that will give the East German athletes the edge in important competitions. A staff of fifty researchers at the institute have read and analyzed seventy-five thousand volumes on athletics, and each month information from one hundred sixty periodicals and journals around the world is fed into the computer.

The athletes are constantly tested and their coaches fed the information so as to head off potential problems in the training routines, and in hopes of finding scientific answers to the question of why certain athletes turn in peak performances frequently and others do not.

The computer also analyzes film footage of world-class athletes from other countries to learn what works or does not work for them from a biomechanic and style standpoint. The same footage reveals weaknesses in athletes from other countries that can be exploited when the East Germans meet them in international competition. This use of film is not unlike that made by professional football teams when they analyze game films to find weaknesses in the other team's defenses.

Coaches and trainers have been able to evaluate mathematically what the most effective pace in a particular race will be for a particular athlete at a certain point in his training; the formula works on blood lactic-acid levels determined from samples taken after training sessions and races. The scientists also keep track of urea and phosphokinase levels in the blood so that they can ease an athlete's intensive training if his muscle tissue begins to break down. For each athlete, the maximum period between complete checkups is six weeks; six weeks has been determined to be the ideal period for sustaining one training format before a runner becomes stale. The computer, through logic, has reached the conclusion most distance runners have come to on their own: in any one week, the perfect training regimen includes three days of endurance (longer distance) work and two days of strength (or speed) work. Stretching and flexibility exercises are heavily stressed.

By taking small blood samples at the end of a workout, the coach can have the results on his desk the next morning and can have his athletes work that day accordingly. It is therefore possible to set up the day's workout to conform ideally to an athlete's capacities, thereby making maximum use of the training sessions and avoiding injury by not training the athlete to the point of exhaustion or physical breakdown.

There are arguments against putting so much science into sport, of course; but on the other hand, as the East Germans argue, it is certainly inhumane to allow an athlete to train hard on a day when he is physically and chemically incapable of doing the workout without risking injury.

There is, moreover, a great effort made in East Germany to avoid exhausting the runner psychologically. Great pains are taken to keep the workouts from being monotonous. In order to keep their routines interesting, groups of athletes are periodically taken to locations such as Algeria, Scandinavia, and the Bulgarian mountains for altitude and hillwork sessions.

The system is not, however, perfect.

Waldemar Cierpinski was twelve years old when his athletic talent was spotted. He was running cross-country in school and found that he enjoyed it very much. "I began to develop an interest in athletics," he says, "and I made up my mind to give running a try."

He was taken in by the Aufbau Nienburg, a factory sports club, where he was given intensive coaching. At the age of sixteen he was entered in the annual Spartakiad, in the 1,500-meter steeplechase and the 7.5-kilometer road race. "I was so overpowered by the unusual, overwhelming atmosphere that prevailed—it involved ten thousand boys and girls—and by the milling crowd," he recalls, "that I erroneously went to the wrong stadium when I had to compete in the steeplechase. I hastened to the right stadium, just to arrive at the last moment, dripping with sweat. I quickly changed and had to rush to the start. I clocked a new personal best in the heats and made up my mind to try to win a medal in the final. But inexperienced as I was, I fell at the start of the final. I got up quickly and continued, but the fall had cost me too much strength. I finished fifth and was a little disappointed because I knew I could've done better. I learned my lesson to avoid rash and unsurveyable situations and took home the silver medal in the road race."

The mistake the East German system had made was to have put him in training—for seven years—in the steeplechase, which was definitely not his event. Why didn't it work for him?

"Apart from all other reasons, the tempo over the 3,000-meter distance was simply too fast for me," he says. "Training for it certainly promoted the development of my basic speed, but the marathon distance was more my cup of tea."

He came upon the marathon almost by accident.

"In 1974 I was vacationing in Czechoslovakia," he recalls, "and feeling in good humor, so I decided to try a marathon in Kosice. I came in third with a 2:20:20. In 1975, I ran Kosice again and came in seventh with 2:17:30. My first serious marathon was at Karl-Marx-Stadt in 1976, which I won with 2:13:57. Six weeks later, I won our Olympic trials."

His training at that time (he had moved to a sports club in Halle, the industrial town where he lives) consisted primarily of running, with soccer and cycling mixed in. Over the winter he did no intense training—merely long runs to maintain endurance, usually between fifteen and thirty kilometers a day, with an occasional sixty kilometer (about 37 miles) training run thrown in, something American marathons rarely if ever do. To increase his leg speed, he occasionally threw in a 5,000-meter run on the track.

The races that Cierpinski and his fellow athletes enter are purely at the discretion of the sports czars. In picking their team for the 1976 Montreal Olympics, their decisions confounded everyone.

After Waldemar Cierpinski won the Karl-Marx-Stadt Marathon in the middle of April, he entered the East German Olympic Marathon Trial at Wittenberg, where he lowered his best time to 2:12:21.2, the second-best time ever run by an East German. The East German record was held by Eckhard Lesse, who ran fourth in the trials. Truppel took second with a 2:13:44 and Bernd Arnhold third with 2:14:53.6. The East Germans did not feel their other marathoners were ripe for Montreal, so they sent only one man: Cierpinski.

In fact, the East Germans held back most of their running talent, causing observers to theorize that they were preparing for the 1980 Olympic Games in Moscow, when they would blitz even their Russian hosts with their prowess.

Frank Baumgartl and Cierpinski were sent to Montreal; Baumgartl won a bronze medal in the steeplechase, Cierpinski's former specialty.

In the thirteen weeks leading up to Montreal Cierpinski ran the third and fourth marathons of his career. At Montreal, Cierpinski toed the mark with absolutely no outside pressure on him: no one even knew who he was, much less gave him a ghost of a chance to show in the medals. The East Germans had gone through a great deal of paperwork to have Waldemar wear an all-white uniform instead of the traditional East German uniform everyone else on the team wore. Their scientists had concluded that light fabric colors reflected the sun, thereby keeping a marathoner's body temperature lower during a warm marathon. They wanted to give him every advantage possible. As it turned out, Montreal's marathon was run under overcast and drizzly skies, so the experiment was moot, although their theories were quite correct.

The going-away favorite for joining Abebe Bikila as a two-time gold-medal winner was Frank Shorter. The American marathoning movement was growing, and the United States was finally becoming a force in the event, with Shorter the pioneer.

There were sixty-seven starters, and Bill Rodgers took the field out at an awesome pace. Rodgers had ulterior motives: Finland's Lasse Viren, who had, for the second straight Olympics, won the gold medal in the 5,000- and 10,000-meter events, had announced, almost casually, that he would run the marathon, going for the distance triple as Emil Zatopek had twenty-four years before. Rodgers was insulted. It seemed a slap in the face to runners who specialized in the marathon that Viren should regard the event with such a cavalier attitude. So Rodgers decided to burn Viren out, a very foolish move on his part considering that Bill had not yet recovered from a foot injury (which he had received sometime after the U.S. Olympic Trials marathon).

They went through the first 5-K in 15:19, and through 10-K in 30:48. Rodgers had two runners for company, Göran Bengtsson of Sweden (who was running only his second career marathon) and Anacleto Pinto of Portugal. The big pack of runners stayed in the background, allowing the trio in front to do the work of setting the pace.

Rain started to fall, and Frank Shorter began to see his chances for a gold medal slipping as though through a self-fulfilling prophecy: he had confided to Erich Segal the day before the race that if it rained, he'd not win. The first casualty was not Shorter, however, but one of the other pre-race favorites: Giuseppe Cindolo was hurting and would leave the race before the 15-K mark. Cindolo was a favorite as the result of an impressive 2:11:50.6 marathon performance on April 25 which had put him in an exalted position with Shorter.

As the lead group passed 15-K, Rodgers had already begun to drop back (he would ultimately finish fortieth in 2:25:14.8), and

Shorter took command. The leaders went through 15-K in forty-six minutes flat. Over the next five kilometers, Shorter threw in surges to test his opposition, but the bursts only dropped the lead pack from an even dozen to eight: it did not break the pack as in 1972. Among the lead group were Shorter and Rodgers, Karel Lismont of Belgium, Jerome Drayton of Canada, Lasse Viren, and Waldemar Cierpinski.

Shorter continued to throw in surges, each surge shaking up the lead pack a bit. By 25-K, Lismont had fallen out of the lead pack and was a minute behind. Shorter threw in another surge and opened up a thirty-meter lead, but the white-clad Cierpinski, thinking Shorter was weakening, threw in his own surge around the 30-K point (which they reached in 1:32:08). Shorter did not respond.

"Shorter ran with surges, which is what we expected," Cierpinski said in reviewing the race a year later. "His first surge came at 23-K. It was hard to catch up at that point because it was unexpected and Shorter did it with such great strength. In fact, it broke the field. I had enjoyed good training with no injuries so I made the decision to catch up with him. I had been told to stick with the leaders and I had this in mind, since Shorter was the favorite. My only fear was that by catching him, I would ruin my own pace.

"Each surge he made had less distance and was done with less strength. They became easier to make up. As the race went on, I started to gain confidence."

It was at the 30-K point that Cierpinski knew he could win. "I decided to challenge for the lead because I felt Shorter was fading, and I had all the reserves I needed. So at about 32- to 33-K, I went right past him after his final surge. It was very emotional for me. Earlier, everything had been in Frank's favor, and then it became man-to-man."

By the 35-K point, Cierpinski had a thirteen-second lead over Shorter. The pack was broken. Drayton, Viren, and Lismont were about fifty seconds behind Shorter, and Don Kardong, using the same even-paced tactics he had used to make the U.S. team at the trials, was moving up through the pack; he was now in sixth.

By the 40-K point, with only two kilometers left in the race,

Cierpinski was thirty-two seconds in front of Shorter and Kardong had moved into third, with Kismont hanging on his shoulder. Viren and Drayton battled for fifth.

Kardong, however, was starting to cramp in the legs and he would be unable to hold off an inside-the-stadium charge from Lismont.

Four years before in Munich there had been confusion for Shorter when a prankster, posing as the marathon leader, entered the stadium to steal Frank's ovation. Now, in Montreal, Cierpinski was confused as he entered the stadium: he wasn't sure of the number of laps he had to go around the track to officially reach the finish line.

Ironically, as he entered the stadium, the band was playing the East German national anthem—not for him, as it turned out, but for the East German women's relay team, which had just won. "I couldn't hear the anthem at all because everyone was shouting as I approached the stadium," Cierpinski said. "I was overcome by the event, and I had an indescribable feeling that made me dizzy."

Explaining his confusion, Cierpinski says: "I was mixed up at the finish because an official told me to stay in lane three. I saw the 'one lap to go' sign but it didn't register. Also, two kilometers from the finish, I looked back and saw Shorter just behind, so I wanted to make certain of the win and sprint home with a fast final one hundred meters if necessary. I was concentrating so hard that I didn't react to the one lap sign. Also, it was raining and I couldn't see it clearly. Then I came around and saw the 'one lap to go' sign so I went around again. When I finished, it still said I had one lap to go. [Author's Note: The "one lap to go" sign Cierpinski saw on his second lap was being displayed for Shorter, who had entered the stadium.] I was furious with myself because I could've done a faster time if I had known the sign meant just one lap to go on the track. I could've become the fourth fastest marathoner ever in the world."

Between 1976 and 1980, Cierpinski was hobbled with one set of injuries after the other, and observers of the marathon began to write him off as a flash-in-the-pan. They'd done much the same with Finland's Lasse Viren after his 1972 Olympic 5,000- and 10,000-meter double gold, because outside of Olympic competition he seemed consistently inconsistent in his performances.

Cierpinski's best performance between the Olympic Games of 1976 and 1980 was a disappointing fourth-place finish in the 1978 European Championships Marathon. But when East Germany came to choose its marathoner of the hour in May, 1980, Cierpinski, like the supreme peaker he is, rose to the occasion and ran his second-best race (2:11:17), guaranteeing his trip to Moscow.

At the beginning of the 1980 Olympic Marathon race, Vladimir Kotov, the reigning Soviet ace (national record of 2:10:58 in May of 1980), took the field of seventy-one starters out of the stadium and along the Moscow River; he held the lead through 20-K. At that point, Lasse Viren made a move to come up with the leaders, but he dropped back quickly.

At 30-K, Mexico's Rodolfo Gomez took the lead and moved out by two hundred meters, followed by Cierpinski, Gerard Nijboer of Holland (2:09:01 in April 1980), and Leonid Moiseyev and Satymkul Dzumanazarov of the USSR. As the leaders headed back toward the stadium, Nijboer, noted for his speed in the closing miles, moved into the lead, but Cierpinski was ready, and, as he'd done with Shorter in Montreal, so he did with Nijboer. He moved up with him, then past him, and salted the race away. He clocked 2:11:02.4, the second-best time of his career, surpassed only by his 1976 Olympic time. Nijboer was second. The Soviets filled out the third through fifth positions.

Some marathon experts argue that Cierpinski's 1980 victory was a hollow one because of the boycotted Olympic Games. Others argue that he is more a robot than a human being.

On the first matter, it is true that the race would have been a different matter had the Americans and Japanese been entered; but it is not certain that Cierpinski would not have vanquished the rest as he did Nijboer. And as for Cierpinski being an East German robot, it is odd that, with the priority placed on sports in his country, there have not been other robots of his caliber. Besides, his injuries made him only too human. And there is the fact that East Germans, when it comes to their sports and their sports heroes, aren't much different from American football fans.

"Since my victory at Montreal, I have been under much stress," Cierpinski said in an interview in 1977. "I have many things to do and so many friends and people who are now interested in me. I have a busload of letters that all must be answered. I was surprised to become a hero to the people and find that they had voted me German Democratic Republic Sportsman of the Year. I've received so many letters from all strata of the population saying that when they saw me push ahead on television, it was one of the biggest moments of their lives."

Heavy is the head that wears the crown; it doesn't matter if the country is communist, totalitarian, democratic, or a monarchy.

When there are six miles left in the marathon, the masks fall, the runners move out of the shadows, and it's man-to-man.

Toshihiko Seko is a man driven by his mentor and his love of his country, Japan.

(COURTESY MATTHEW M. DELANEY III)

13.

TOSHIHIKO SEKO:
Ninji Runner

A duel is fermenting that will make every Kung Fu movie and every Western epic pale by comparison. The duel, when the two men line up against each other, will be a battle of Eastern culture against Western. It will also be a battle of styles and strategies.

The battleground will likely not be the New York City Marathon. More likely it will be one of the traditional races where internationalists battle to vanquish each other: either Fukuoka, in one contender's homeland, or Boston, in the other's.

Or perhaps it will be the neutral lotus land of Los Angeles in 1984.

The two big guns who will create the ultimate distance-racing duel, acknowledged by most as the world's best marathoners, are Alberto Salazar of the United States and Toshihiko Seko of Japan.

Both exhibit a fervent, intense approach to their training, and both foray into marathons with a tremendous amount of track training behind them. But in strategies they are decidedly different. Where Salazar runs at the front, trying to control the pace to his own advantage, Seko runs with the front-runners, relaxing on their shoulders, and then uses his speed to burn his competition in the critical 10-K that comes after twenty miles are gone.

There is also another curious difference, and that concerns the relationship of each to his coach. Alberto Salazar has always had a tendency to overtrain, so when he met his coach, Bill Dellinger, one of Dellinger's greatest challenges was to mellow the intensity

191

of Salazar's prodigious capacity for training. In direct contrast, Toshihiko Seko admits to having been rather lazy before meeting Kiyoshi Nakamura, his coach and ultimately his *sensei,* or master. It was his coach/*sensei* who whipped Seko to the intensity needed to become one of the world's best and most consistent marathoners.

As a child, Toshihiko Seko had a dream of becoming famous at something, as children often do. With baseball being as much a mania in Japan as in the United States—perhaps more so— Seko's first thoughts were to become a household name in Japan by becoming a baseball star.

But as a high school junior, Seko set his feet on a different path. He became the Japanese national champion in the 800 and 1,500 meters, and he repeated the feat in his senior year. The die had been cast; he was the best in his country and, because it came so easily, he became somewhat lax and overconfident. There had certainly been no intense training involved in becoming Japan's best. When he graduated from Kuwana High School, he was the typical high school grad, and, like many recent graduates, not quite ready to find his place in life. Although Toshihiko's parents urged him to train harder, he wasn't really interested. After all, they were talking to the national champion—two years running—weren't they? Didn't he know what was best?

Besides, he had college to look forward to, where he'd have time in which he could decide important things, such as what to do with the rest of his life.

But then Toshihiko took the entrance exam for Waseda University in Tokyo and failed. His parents urged him to go to the United States, thinking that some American experience would both perk up his studies and perhaps motivate him to train to improve his running. Seko went to the University of Southern California along with two other Japanese students who were on special scholarships.

"From an academic standpoint," he said in a 1982 interview with American journalist Hanns Maier, "I didn't learn that much about running. I wasn't dedicated enough. I went with two other Japanese runners . . . and we played around too much. We spent all our time stuffing ourselves with hamburgers and junk food. I came back to Japan twenty pounds overweight."

Despite his excesses, Toshihiko may have learned some things in America from televison or by osmosis, because when he returned, he retook the entrance exam and was admitted to Waseda University. "That's been the greatest thrill of my life," he says. "Even greater than winning Fukuoka three times."

At Waseda, Seko came under the profound influence of Nakamura, an outstanding runner in his own time who had set the Japanese record at 1,500 meters with a 3:56.8—a record that stood unscathed for some sixteen years.

Nakamura had made several fortunes in business after World War II and had then retired to study a variety of world religions (chiefly Christianity and Buddhism), living off his considerable resources. After an absence of fifteen years he had returned to the university to coach, for which he was paid a nominal one hundred and fifty dollars a year. His love of running was enough—his love of running, access to upcoming runners with whom he could work to develop his unique approach to running, and winning. This interest in sport was integrated with his studies of religion, natural sciences, and philosophies, all of which emphasized functioning within the world by functioning in concert with it.

When Nakamura saw young Seko, he had an inspiration. He was impressed by Seko's flowing style of running and immediately told the impressionable Seko to move up in distances—a suggestion which both Seko and his parents felt was madness, considering his high school successes at the 800 and 1,500 meters. But even then, there was something that Nakamura exuded that convinced Seko to give it a try. He upped his mileage under Nakamura's guidance, and the bonbon pounds melted away, his style became even more fluid, and he began to show decided improvement.

Nakamura promised Seko that he could make him one of the greatest marathoners in the world if he would put his fate into his sixty-seven-year-old hands. "God gave Seko to me and I want to thank God by making Seko the best," Nakamura says.

And when he says that God gave Seko to him, Nakamura means it literally. Nakamura demands that his charges give themselves over to him totally.

Nakamura has put together a running club of young men who

are willing to give one hundred percent of themselves to him and to his teachings. There are ninety such young men in his club, which is very much like a martial arts school—or a school for kamikaze pilots. He demands everything of them: total loyalty. His methods have been criticized in Japan because they rely very much on a certain fanaticism of which the Japanese are capable.

Nakamura spends about fifteen thousand dollars a year of his own money feeding his runners steaks and other foods highly prized but certainly financially out of reach of most young runners in Japan. His club members hold some nine Japanese records, from the 200 meters to the 25-K, and Seko is very much on the mark for gathering in the marathon record.

Other coaches in Japan are very critical of Nakamura's methods, but Nakamura and his charges dismiss such criticism as stemming from jealousy. Some of the bad feeling comes from the fact that, until a few years ago, Nakamura used to upbraid his runners by beating them until they did what he wanted. He has changed his methods, however, using his teachings in place of beatings. "I gave up hitting my runners when I discovered that words were more effective," Nakamura says.

Of himself, he puts it quite simply: "There will never be a second Nakamura. When I read to my runners the stories of Jesus, the disciples, and the other great religious leaders, they believe the stories because they see me and the kind of life I am leading, and they know people like that can really exist."

Indeed, Nakamura lives the life he espouses. He and his wife live simply, and for many years they had Seko live with them so that he could reap the benefits of Nakamura's teachings and philosophies twenty-four hours a day. This practice is catching on somewhat, for the Soh twins—Shigeru, current Japanese marathon record holder, and Takeshi—live with Hiroshima, their coach. Nakamura's methods are also creeping into the training that other coaches are using. Success has a way of making its own point about methods.

Today, Seko sleeps in a small apartment connected to the Nakamura residence and spends his waking hours with Nakamura. "It was important to have Seko live with me so I could prepare him mentally," Nakamura states. "Physical training is only ten percent of the total preparation; the other ninety is mental. We have to do things like this so we can overcome the bigger, stronger foreign competitors." Both Seko and Nakamura contend that if Western runners trained like Seko, they would be unbeatable.

The feeling that physical preparation is only ten percent of the picture is a rather radical view of running; a few years ago it was revolutionary in the Western world to hear that *fifty* percent was physical and fifty percent mental. The dedication to the mental aspect harkens back to what some call brainwashing, but it more closely approximates the great traditional Japanese disciplines of the Samauri and the Ninji. Anything that does not lead them in a direct line to their goal is abstained from. This attitude has precedents in many societies in many ages.

At one point early in their relationship, Seko attempted to break away from Nakamura's influence. He fled Nakamura and returned home to his parents, but they would not take him back, because they felt that what Nakamura was doing for him was what he needed. While Seko tried to regain admittance to his parents' house, they called Nakamura: "Do whatever you must with him; he's yours."

Nakamura took Seko back and began spending hours each night teaching Seko the words of the Bible and of Buddhism. The most oft-repeated teachings came from Daruma-taishi, a Buddhist monk: "Welcome the hardships when they come. Be patient and work through the burdens. Only then can you overcome them and grow stronger."

Now that he is finished with college, Seko works four hours each morning at SB Foods, Japan's premier spice company. When he races, he wears the singlet of SB, and because of the close loyalty of Japanese workers to their places of employment, he keeps the medal from his victory at the 1981 Boston Marathon at the factory.

For a month each year, Nakamura takes Seko and several of his other runners to New Zealand for training in more open countryside, with more hills. Nakamura enjoys the trip, too, because it allows him to indulge in his other passion, hunting.

Nakamura's coaching and teachings have had a profound effect on Seko's career. He holds various Japanese records, including the 10-kilometer record of 27:43.5, which accounts for his devastating kick at the end of a marathon performance. The marathon is where both he and Nakamura see his future—and his performances would seem to argue in that direction. He won Fukuoka three years in a row (1978–80). He and Nakamura decided to sit it out in 1981 and not attempt to match Frank Shorter's spree of four Fukuoka Marathon wins in a row. As it turned out, Australia's Rob de Castella ran the world's second-fastest marathon in winning the 1981 Fukuoka race (less than two months after Alberto Salazar had broken Derek Clayton's long-standing world record). Seko accepted those circumstances philosophically. He does not regret missing Fukuoka, even with de Castella's outstanding performance. "No one knows what would have happened if I had run," he says. "Since I didn't, it is no use speculating about it."

Nakamura and Seko do not make the Western racing scene frequently. Some of it is the politics of the Japanese running world. Seko says he would never run in the New York City Marathon because of its obvious commercialism; such media attention would aggravate the tensions between Nakamura and his methods and personal accomplishments with runners on the one hand, and the Japanese Amateur Athletic Federation and its nationalistic efforts on the other. The federation believes there is no need to rock the boat. They, too, have great nationalistic spirit— they merely wish to raise the glory of Japan through their own special methods.

Because of its traditional amateur status and because of its favored status with Japanese runners for decades, the Boston Marathon has been a different matter. No one gets paid to come to Boston and no one earns a cent under the table; it has always been a truly amateur event to which runners came because of the power and the glory of the tradition—and because it was frequently the scene of extremely high-level competition. And also because, before the rise of the New York City Marathon, it was the one road-racing event in America that received significant worthy media coverage. At least in the Japanese press.

Nakamura brought Seko to Boston in 1979, where he finished a strong second to Bill Rodgers. Seko was undone by the hills of Boston (Japanese marathon courses and other road races are almost perfectly flat). It was on the Newton Hills that Rodgers broke away from Seko and went on to win. Seko hung in for second place, running an incredible 2:10:12, while Rodgers set a new American record, bettering his 1975 effort on the same course. That 1975 win was the only other Boston win that Seko's second-place time wouldn't have bettered.

Seko vowed to come back and have another go at Boston. In fact, after winning the 1980 Fukuoka Marathon in 2:09:45, nearly a Japanese record (Shigeru Soh holds the Japanese record of 2:09:06), Seko had only one thought on his mind. Within an hour after his seemingly easy win, he encountered an American journalist who had interviewed him before the race. He smiled and said one word: "Boston."

Seko came to the Boston loaded for bear. His month of training in the Cashmire hills near Christchurch in New Zealand had gone so well that Seko decided to take a fitness test on the track there. Although he won't admit it, the entire thing may have been an attempt to psych out Bill Rodgers. On March 22, Seko went after the 30-kilometer track world record; he broke it handily with a 1:29:18.8, and on the way to it, went through 25-K in 1:13:55.8, breaking Bill Rodgers's world mark of 1:14:11.8 at that distance. Although usually more than modest, Seko returned to Japan and announced that he was fit enough to go after Derek Clayton's world record when he traveled to Boston.

Talk of the world record was everywhere. Seko was obviously ready, and Rodgers felt that he was in pretty good shape, too, despite having had to cut back his training for three weeks due to a cold.

When the race at Boston started, Gary Fanelli, figuring to help the pace along to the expected world record, went out very, very fast—but no one went with him. Fanelli went through the 6.75-mile checkpoint in Framingham at 31:54, and went through the 10.37-mile point (checkpoints at Boston are traditonal landmarks and therefore are not located at regular five-mile or five-kilometer intervals), in 50:00. He reached the approximate halfway point in Wellesley at 1:04:50, but then he began to fade.

By the time Fanelli reached Lower Newton Falls, he was being closed on and passed by Greg Meyer, Rodgers, Seko, Craig Virgin, Dave Chettle (of Australia), and Kirk Pfeffer.

Once into the hills, however, the race came down to a duel be-

tween Virgin (one of America's premier 10,000-meter trackmen)
and Seko. "I could see Virgin and Seko get into a duel," Bill
Rodgers said later, "and I sort of knew Seko would wait until
twenty-three miles or so to make his move, and that would be it.
I wish I could have gone with them, but I was just holding on."

Virgin and Seko went through the Newton Hills together and
then came down out of them. This year, Seko was ready. Seko
made his move going into Cleveland Circle, in plain view of the
Bill Rodgers Running Center. He threw in a surge and opened a
thirty-yard lead. He continued to accelerate, going though the
twenty-third mile in 4:33. He completed the final 4.7-mile check-
point-to-checkpoint in a record 22:43, giving further credence to
his late-race kick. He had come back two years later to avenge
his defeat by Bill Rodgers and had taken away Rodgers's course
record—by a mere one second. It was the fastest marathon ever
run in America and Seko's fifth performance under 2:10:36. He
became the first Japanese runner to win Boston since 1969.

Seko's goal now is the 1984 Olympic Games. He was very disappointed when, because of Japan's support of the United States
boycott of Russia, he was not able to go to Moscow. It was especially galling to him when Moscow winner Waldemar Cierpinski
came to the 1980 Fukuoka race and was quoted by newspapers
as saying that he'd have won in Moscow even if the formidable
Japanese team had been present. "That increased my appetite to
win even more," Seko declares.

To Seko, as to most world-class runners, the Olympic gold
medal is *the* award, the pinnacle. "I would be very honored if I
could win the gold medal," he said in a 1981 inverview, "but I
don't train solely for the Olympics, like Cierpinski. In communist countries, the athletes place so much emphasis on the Olympics because they know if they do well, they will move up to a
higher social status. That's not necessarily true in Japan or
America."

Seko has much racing to do between now and the Olympic
Games, and he seems to look forward most to racing against the
American runners. He feels that Fukuoka is the greatest race in
the world next to the Olympic Marathon and is somewhat disappointed that top American marathoners have not been running it
during the last few years (there is no money associated with Fu-

kuoka). He very much wants to run against Americans—especially before the 1984 Olympic Games. Unless he runs against them, he cannot know them, and in accordance with the training philosophy he and Nakamura use, Seko strives to be the best Seko can be, but in addition also studies the other top marathoners and attempts to adapt some of their good qualities to his own training and racing. And unless he can have the opportunity to race against them in person, it is more difficult to develop those qualities—a film of Alberto Salazar is not the same as running on his shoulder at twenty-three miles and seeing what he would do if you threw in a surge.

Seko is a dedicated runner; some say he is a fanatical robot. As 1984 approaches, he shows evidence of becoming more and more a slave to his *sensei*.

In Hanns Maier's interview with Seko in the May/June 1982 issue of *Running,* there is a telling point in the introductory remarks:

"Maier found Nakamura's influence on the runner so great that sometimes Seko would ask his coach to answer the questions. Maier had to ask the same question two or three times—when the coach was present and not—to be sure he was hearing Seko's real answer."

When Seko lines up in Los Angeles to gun it out with the rest of the world's greatest marathoners, it will be almost impossible to tell if it is Toshihiko Seko or merely the Ninji runner of coach Kiyoshi Nakamura. If he wins and travels back to Japan with the gold medal, the discussion may be rather moot. But marathoners the world over may have seen the first Olympic gold medal for the marathon won by two men instead of one.

Grete Waitz has been largely responsible for bringing recognition to female runners.

14.

GRETE WAITZ:
The Reluctant Mother

On Sunday, June 6, 1982, Lorraine Moller easily dominated a field of over six hundred to win the fifth annual Avon International Women's Marathon on a very hilly course in San Francisco. Wearing a lavender running outfit with a matching scarf tied in her hair, the New Zealander covered the course in 2:36:13. The time was not as fast as her win in the London edition of the Avon race two years before and well off her countrywoman Allison Roe's world record of 2:25:28.8, set in New York in October of the previous year. Nancy Conz, the defending Avon champion, did not race although she, like Roe, was in town; Conz was feeling ill, while Roe was suffering injuries that had plagued her for months.

The race was somehow uninspired, somehow anticlimactic, despite the fact that it was run through America's most fascinating city on a beautiful day. "Everyone," a spectator said, "seems to be marking time until 1984."

The point was astute.

The two best female marathoners in the world—Roe and Norway's Grete Waitz—did not line up for the Avon International Women's Marathon. Neither of them had ever run the Avon race. The race did feature women from twenty-five countries, however, a statistic which made its own point. But the point had been made before 1982; the powers that be had taken notice, one of the reasons being Grete Waitz, the reluctant heroine of women's long-distance running—and, so to speak, mother of the 1984 Olympic Women's Marathon.

Women had fought for years to be allowed to compete in the same races as men. In very small numbers, and then in a growing wave, women took up road running and ultimately road racing. Kathrine Switzer, the director of the Avon sports program, had made headlines at the men-only Boston Marathon in 1967 by applying for an official number using her initials, "K.V. Switzer," in her application. She received the number (women had run Boston without numbers the previous year). Early in the race, after B.A.A. officials on the press bus spotted her and slowed the bus, Will Cloney and Jock Semple went after her. Jock outsprinted Will and attempted to wrest the number from her, but her boyfriend, running next to her, threw a bodyblock into Jock. The entire sequence was captured by an alert photographer, and the next day the Boston Marathon got more publicity around the world than it had ever received before. Unfortunately, it wasn't the kind the promoters would have liked.

The incident brought to the public eye the ongoing struggle of a few women to gain the right to run road races as official entrants instead of as bandits.

At the first Olympic Marathon in 1896 there was a woman runner, Melpomene, who completed the course in about four-and-a-half hours. In 1918 a woman finished thirty-eighth in a French marathon. In 1923 a South African woman ran in, and completed, the extremely tough fifty-four-mile Comrades Marathon in her home country. Three years later Violet Piercy ran in the famed "Poly" Marathon in England, handily breaking four hours. In 1928, Olympic officials allowed the 800-meter track race for women to be included in the games; although three of the women broke the existing world record in the event, several of the competitors collapsed following the effort due to insufficient training, and the horrified officials revoked the event; it would be 1960 before it was reinstated. In 1959 Arlene Pieper completed the grueling Pike's Peak Marathon, a race up Pike's Peak and then back down. Two years later, Julia Chase and two other young women braved official censure and entered the Manchester, Connecticut, 5-mile Thanksgiving Day road race.

In 1966 Roberta Gibb ran the Boston Marathon without a number, completing the course in 3:20 after jumping out of the bushes at the starting area.

Although the scattered efforts of women to take part in men's road racing raised a bit of interest, they never were much more than a curiosity until Switzer's act made the issue political. Most of the women who had taken part in breaching the barriers had been very apolitical. They merely liked to run, and decided to enter the only available races, which happened to be men's races. In most instances, they were welcomed and encouraged by the men with whom they were running. The trouble usually came from stubborn officials who either feared to break with the time-honored tradition of "men-only," or who believed that women could be very severely injured by taking part in distance events, or that women who ran too far would be rendered incapable of having babies. (Much of this information was dispensed by female physical-education experts.) The controversy was further fanned by the media who, in general, studiously ignored coverage of road races, but who were quick to jump on a quirk in the boring and harmless activity.

The Switzer incident received so much publicity that it galvanized the topic of women's distance running. In the minds of some women it planted the idea of running distances; in the minds of others, the idea of using running to make a point about women's rights and liberation. It forced into the open an issue that many withered track-and-road-racing officials had never even considered, because, first of all, women didn't run races—it just wasn't done—and, secondly, they never realized there were so many women out there who didn't realize that it just wasn't done.

The entire subject escalated over the years until more and more women became interested in participating in road races, and women felt that there should be more Olympic events to accommodate them—to make them equal to men. As they mobilized to assure women's divisions in road racing events, they also mobilized to attempt to add women's running events to the Olympic Games over and above the 1,500 meters, which was the longest event allowed. The men had the 5,000 meters, the 10,000 meters, and the marathon. The women found, soon enough, that it is no quick and easy matter to add a new event to the Olympic Games. There are committees and more committees, and there are sluggish rules and institutions that must be shifted gradually to make way for such changes.

As more and more women began taking part in road races—began taking up running in general—and undergoing more strenuous training, their times in the marathon, the event always used for argumentative purposes because of its extreme challenge, began dropping gradually.

In an effort to bring attention to the women's running movement, various interested parties, in order to make a point, instigated reverse discrimination in the form of races for women only.

Under the auspices of Dr. Ernst Van Aaken in West Germany, a staunch supporter of women's running, the first Women's International Marathon Championship was held in Waldniel in October 1974. Forty women took part and the winning time was 2:50:31; the field was drawn from seven countries. The event followed shortly the establishment first by West Germany and then the United States of women's national marathon championships. Women were allowed to enter Boston officially as of 1972.

Two years later, the next women's international championship was held, again in Waldniel, with forty-five finishers from nine countries. In 1977 the women's record was lowered twice, to 2:34:47.5 by the end of the year, the record-holder being Germany's Christa Vahlensieck.

The following March, Avon sponsored the first Avon International Women's Marathon in Atlanta. Built on the framework that worked in Waldniel, the race featured women from nine countries. Also, both the Bonne Bell Cosmetics Company and L'eggs, the stocking people, set up either individual races or race series for women only at shorter distances. Behind the scenes, women and men worked on trying to convince the International Olympic Committee that longer events for women should be scheduled for the Olympic Games. Under the Olympic rules, the host country is allowed to add one new event; it was assumed that the USSR would not add the 5,000 or 10,000 meters or the marathon for women in 1980. The rules further stipulate that, in order to be fair to all countries taking part in the Olympic Games, it must be proven that a considerable number of countries are interested in the event and that its addition to the schedule will not benefit the few to the exclusion of the many. The hope of the women behind the movement was that they could convince the organizing committee of the Los Angeles Olympic Games for 1984 that a marathon for women should be included. To convince the committee, what was needed was a mountain of evidence indicating that many countries were interested in a Women's Olympic Marathon and, to convince the old-liners, evidence that women have proven they are capable of running the race competitively and safely.

October 1978. New York City. There were 1,134 female starters in the race. And one of them, running her first-ever marathon (in fact, her first run over eighteen miles), would do more in two hours, thirty-two minutes, and thirty seconds than all the agitating and political maneuvering had done up to that moment.

Grete Waitz's strategy for her first New York City Marathon was characteristic of the track runner she is: to go out cautiously, since it was a new event for her, and stick behind the best runner—in this case, world record holder Christa Vahlensieck—with the hopes of out-sprinting her at the end. Because of the crowds (something that was then and is now a wonder to the five-feet, seven-inch Norwegian) and the conservative pace of the other women, Grete found herself alone in the lead. She was running in the midst of the men and feeling tired and sore. Her husband Jack, an accountant for *Aftenposten,* the largest newspaper in Norway, and his wife's training partner, was leapfrogging along the course, attempting to keep her abreast of her position and offer encouragement.

When Grete Waitz entered Central Park and crossed the finish line in front of Tavern on the Green Restaurant, her stunning 2:32:30 was a new world's record by two minutes and eighteen seconds. The excitement that a world record performance generates buzzed through the spectators like wildfire, passing from one to the next until runners still on the course began overhearing the buzz and some of the details while they continued their own race toward the finish line. The word was, a Norwegian

school teacher and track runner had won the women's division
and she'd really put a stranglehold on the record. Then came the
logical questions, among them: What's her name? And amidst
the excitement—especially among women runners, who (correctly) saw Grete's time as a significant addition to their solid ar-
gument for women's ability to run the marathon comfortably—
the pronunciations of her name were as varied as the colorful fall
leaves.

The pronunciation is the easy part: Waitz as in "whites." The
difficult thing for the press then and now was to extract information from Grete, a woman who is warm but cautious, careful of
her privacy, and mistrusting of her celebrity status. Pulling
quotes from Grete Waitz is as difficult as pulling teeth and just as
unpleasant for her. The matter is further complicated by the fact
that Grete feels she has nothing significant to say. Following the
1978 New York City Marathon and over Christmas and New
Year's, when she and Jack returned to the United States so she
could run the *Runner's World* 5-Mile Invitational Race in Los
Altos, California, on New Year's Eve (where she set a world's
best of 25:28 for five miles on the roads), Grete spent much of the
time during interviews insisting that she was not a road racer but
a track racer.

She was reluctant to talk about road racing because in those
days to her it was not really a form of racing. Racing was something done on the track, on that mathematically perfect oval
where one tests oneself against the clock, the distance, and other
real runners. Grete, competing in a world far removed from road
racing, considered her runs at New York and in Los Altos as
larks, things of little consequence. She not only downplayed
them, she had very little to say about them.

All the attention was disconcerting to someone who traditionally goes to bed at 9:00 P.M. and who avoids the bright lights and
parties. She was gracious but reserved, wanting to please but
wanting to make certain that people knew she was a track racer
and not a road racer. Road races, after all, were not properly
races at all since the varying conditions, terrain, and distances
made them impossible to classify in terms of the precise divisions
of the International Amateur Athletic Federation. And for

Grete, if it didn't fall under the sanction of the I.A.A.F., it didn't really count.

Grete began running—and running well—at a very young age. She is one of three children in a family loyal to the Norwegian ideal of sport. Her father is a pharmacist and her mother worked in a grocery store. When she was eleven, a neighbor, Terje Pedersen, a former world record holder in the javelin, lured her onto his track team. In a year she was Norway's best track runner. She started out as a sprinter but then moved up to the longer distances to take advantage of her tremendous endurance. Grete eventually found herself stalled at 1,500 meters, the longest distance women were allowed to run at the Olympic Games (in which she represented Norway in 1972 and 1976). She knew that she would be a superior 5,000-meter runner, but the event was not contested; at 10,000 meters, she would be even better, but again, there was no 10,000 meters for women. And for the track runner the Olympic Games—and the gold medal—are the ultimate goal.

Road racing has always been for her a diversion, a lark, something much less than serious.

It is not difficult for one to appreciate Grete Waitz's astonishment at what happened to her and her life once she ran the New York City Marathon. It is not difficult to understand the frustration of the media when they naively pushed a microphone in front of her and inquired: "That was a brilliant peformance— what other marathons have you won in Europe?"

She would cock her head just a bit almost as though she wasn't sure she'd heard what they said, smile nervously just at the corners of her mouth, and give them her answer: "I do not run races on the road. I have not run a road race before. I am a track runner." She would turn to the ever-present and ever-patient Jack, signaling him imploringly to confirm what she said, afraid that her quite-good English was failing her. "Grete is not a road racer," Jack would confirm. "She runs 1,500 meters—on the track."

If it was frustrating for Grete to get across that she was not a road racer, it was more frustrating for the leaders of the women's running movement, who swarmed over Grete every time she returned to the United States (and she did return frequently, always leaving afterwards as a winner and the possessor of another world record), hoping to find her the symbol, the spokeswoman they needed to take a giant step toward their goal of getting the women's distance events into the Olympic Games. Grete Waitz did not see herself as a savior come to raise the women's running movement to its goal by virtue of her miraculous running ability. She was polite but adamant about her position.

In sum, there was nothing she could do to prevent other women from pointing to her as an example of what women were capable of if given the opportunity, but she would not actively take part in such things.

Over the next two years Grete became almost a legend. She returned to the United States to race in Central Park in the L'eggs Mini-Marathon, the New York City Marathon, the *Runner's World* 5-Mile Invitational, and the Falmouth Road Race. The closest she came to defeat (or actually, the closest anyone came to staying with her) was at the 1980 Falmouth Road Race in Massachusetts, a 7.1-mile course on Cape Cod. America's Jan Merrill came within forty-four seconds of Grete while she was breaking the course record by sixty-three seconds—it was during a week when she was suffering a very sore Achilles tendon. She also managed to win the World Cross-Country Championships for three years in a row, 1978–80, always by thirty seconds or more over the very short distance of 5,000 meters.

Grete's only competition was herself—and her records. She came back to New York City in October of 1979 and claimed that she'd done no special training for the race; she was coming off a very busy—and tiring—schedule of forty-one races in nine months. Yet she ran the race in what can only be described as a meticulous manner. She covered the first 13.1 miles in 1:14:51 and then picked up the pace, covering the second half in 1:12:42, for a 2:27:33, bettering her own record by four minutes and fifty-seven seconds.

And there was another subtle difference: she was slightly less uncomfortable with the media and her growing public. She was getting used to the public side of her running if not actually becoming comfortable with it. Her answers were still short and to the point, and she still jealously guarded the fortress walls around her vulnerability and her private life. But she smiled more, and she felt more comfortable using her English in America. She was slowly allowing the fact that she had become the queen of road racing to sink in and have an effect. Her incredible domination in the road-racing arena—even if she still stubbornly refused to admit that she was, indeed, a road racer—was welcome to her, for it softened somewhat the years of struggle she'd gone through trying to carry her success as an outstanding track star in her own country into international competition.

Back in 1972, Grete Waitz (then Grete Andersen) had gone to the Munich Olympics as a nineteen-year-old physical-education student and something of a wunderkind. She had gone to the games lightheartedly. It was like entering a fairyland, with the world's best athletes everywhere, a fantastic city to explore, and, in the Olympic Village, all the food you could eat—at any time you wanted it. The rigors of training were successfully met and annihilated. She was running in the 1,500 meters. In her heat she ran 4:16, a personal best for her by a full second. She returned to Oslo six pounds heavier and with happy memories of the experience. But it was childhood's end.

Grete improved steadily while attending school. In 1975 she graduated and then headed off to the summer track season. At the Bislett Games in hometown Oslo, she ran the 3,000 meters in 8:46.6, setting her first world record. A few days later she got married. Soon after she began her teaching career. The Montreal Olympic Games were on the horizon, so she upped her once-a-day training to twice a day. She ran every day, even when she was sick. Looking back at it, she admits that she must have been killing herself.

Her efforts, however, defined her character. Grete is single-minded in what she does, and, in her training, she has learned to understand and accept personal discomfort. There is time later to allow the pain and emotional release to come out—away from the public eye, away from almost everyone.

Her double workouts preparing for Montreal and the 1,500 meters were not unlike the method used by most male track and distance runners the world over. A morning run of five or six miles, usually taken very easily, serves as a wake-up call for their bodies; then they do a quality workout in the afternoon. Grete modified that regimen somewhat. She and Jack rose at 5:30 A.M. and ran twelve to fourteen kilometers near their apartment, in the hills, at about a six-minute-per-mile pace. In the afternoons, Grete would do her speedwork.

In early 1976 the team from Norway traveled to Spain to train. Her mileage jumped to 125 miles a week. Her afternoon workouts were intense. She would frequently run forty repeats of two hundred meters with a mere ten-second rest between. Johan Kaggestad, who was in Spain with Grete (he was training for the 5,000 meters), recalls the evenings when Grete's eyes would fill with tears she could no longer hold back, tears due to the tremendous pressure of training. "Later, when the Russians began breaking four minutes while she wasn't improving, she fell apart," Kaggestad says. "She was mentally defeated."

In Montreal, Grete failed tactically. In her semifinal, she allowed herself to get boxed in, and Jan Merrill of the United States scooted around her to run 4:02.62, an American record for the 1,500 meters, while she finished in sixth with a 4:04.6, and thus out of the running for the finals. Her Olympic experience for 1976 ended on a note exactly opposite that of 1972.

Fortunately, by then the 3,000 meters had been added to international competition for women. Grete gave up the 1,500 meters, after having spent 1976 learning that, although she had the will, she did not have the physical speed to be competitive at that distance. She felt, however, that her tremendous capacity for building endurance would give her an advantage in the 3,000 meters. She occasionally still ran a 1,500 meter race, but now more as a sharpening experience, as part of her training. She prepared herself arduously for her first international 3,000 meters at the World Cup Games in Dusseldorf in September of 1977. She knew that, tactically, she'd have to dominate the race from the start in hopes of burning out the people with the tremendous kicks before they had a chance to use them against her.

She went out in the lead at Dusseldorf, settled into what she felt was a comfortable but fast pace—only to have Jan Merrill go around her. Instead of retaking the lead, she settled in behind Merrill. "We were all together," she says. "I could hear the other girls breathing hard, getting tired. I was still feeling so strong.

For the first time I was enjoying a track competition. I wasn't fighting at the front, I wasn't forcing the pace, I wasn't running alone against the clock. It's so much fun to run to attack instead of at the front to prove you are the best. I kept feeling very comfortable." On the side of the track, Jack was feeling very *un*comfortable. He kept urging her to pick it up, afraid she'd lost her grip on the race. But she was in complete control. As the race came down to the end, as the rest of the women were beginning to fag out, she opened up a sprint that astonished everyone. She won handily in 8:43.5.

Grete entered 1978 from a position of strength. She went to Glasgow, Scotland, in March and won the World Cross-Country Championships in very adverse, muddy conditions; her nearest competition came from Romania's Natalia Maracescu, who was thirty seconds behind her.

She went into the summer looking forward to the 3,000 meters in the European Championships at Prague. In quality of track competition, the European Championships are second only to the Olympic Games. She had managed to bring her 3,000 time down to 8:32.1, but she was honest enough with herself to realize that she was not going to Prague as a guaranteed winner.

The race was a bitter reversal of the European Championships in 1974, when she had been pleased to win the bronze. She went out hard, hoping to burn off Maracescu with the pace, but it didn't work. Maracescu (who later admitted that she almost dropped back at two thousand meters because of the fast pace) clung desperately to Grete, and, as they battled each other at the end, they were both stunned by a finishing kick from the Russian Svyetlana Ulmasova, who overcame a fifty-meter deficit in the final lap to take the gold. Maracescu edged Grete for the silver.

Grete was stunned. Jack was outraged, claiming that the Russian had used steroids, and that Maracescu probably had, also.

Grete was not the only Norwegian stunned, however. Knut Kvalheim, the Norwegian record holder for the mile, 3,000 meters, and 5,000 meters, had run a Norwegian national record in the 10,000 meters that afternoon, and although the day before his 27:41.3 would have been the eighth-fastest time in history, on that day he had placed ninth.

Kvalheim joined the Waitzes for a walk through Prague that evening, in the course of which they all shook their heads in disbelief. Now, however, the marathon comes into the story.

Kvalheim had started the New York City Marathon in 1976, the first year it had been run through all five boroughs (the six previous years it had been confined to Central Park). He had gone out with the leaders, but the pace had been too much for him, and he'd dropped out after ten miles. Now, being in excellent shape, with the New York City Marathon a mere six weeks away, he decided to enter that race, thinking he could do fairly well. Besides, Kvalheim would have a goal and could take his mind off his ninth-place finish that day. He hoped that the officials in New York would invite him back.

He told Grete that if she were interested in running the marathon, she could probably get an invitation. Kvalheim was surprised to see that she showed some interest. Grete wondered out loud how she would do at the longer distances, since her training runs were never over twenty kilometers (about twelve-and-a-half miles).

While Grete concentrated on her track running and the women against whom she would compete, Jack read voraciously every running magazine he could find, especially material about marathoning and its tremendous growth in the United States. He soon knew as much about the female marathoners as he did about Grete's competition in track events. He began working on Grete's apparently casual interest in running New York City. "I had to work very hard at it. I told her that her training was as good as or better than the other girls'. I was pretty sure she could beat them," Jack said.

Grete's decision to go had to do with the plane tickets for herself and Jack. If nothing else, she figured, it would be a terrific opportunity to see New York City. She was approaching the New York race in the same way she'd approached Munich in 1972—thinking like a tourist as much as like a competitor. She felt it would perhaps be the only chance she'd ever have to visit New York, so they wrote to friends at Finnair to see about such a possibility. "I would not go alone, a single girl, to New York," Grete said firmly.

Fred Lebow remembers the late night he was at the New York City Road Runners' Club (all of those nights were late nights in preparation for the world's largest marathon). Pat Greene was gathering the day's reports to run them past Fred. Pat rattled off rejections and acceptances. Then came: "I rejected the girl who wants expenses for her husband."

"Wait a minute. Who's that?"

"Let's see. . . . Uh, I don't remember her name. I got her letter from Finnair. I think she's a cross-country runner from Norway, but she's never even run a marathon. She's not worth it."

"What's her name? Take a look, will you?"

"OK. Here it is. It's Grete Waitz."

Fred Lebow's mind went into overdrive. He knew Grete's name and her performances for the year. The thing that impressed him was her cross-country win. After all, Bill Rodgers's American record in 1975 had come on the heels of his third-place finish in the World Cross-Country Championships. And Lebow had ulterior motives. He felt that, although track runners tended to blow a marathon by going out too fast, having Grete Waitz would be terrific, because it might pull world record holder Vahlensieck to a new record—something that never looked bad on a marathon's record books.

The idea of a world record on his course fascinated Lebow, especially considering the criticism of the rough surfaces and the turns in the course. Lebow told Greene to have the tickets taken care of. Fred rubbed his hands together. Word had come to him that California's Marty Cooksey was going for the record or die. Now, with track rabbit Waitz to take them out even faster, a record could be in the making.

Grete and Jack arrived two days before the marathon and had a wonderful time being tourists, a privileged time in New York they would never enjoy again. Grete was not invited to press conferences because Fred Lebow was sure she'd drop out around the ten-mile mark.

Instead of going out as a rabbit on the day of the race, however, she decided to go with experience, so she dropped in behind Vahlensieck and Julie Brown. Unseen by the women, Marty Cooksey had gone out like a jet and was far ahead of them. Grete hung with Vahlensieck and Brown and went through the half-way point in—for her—a pedestrian 1:18:30. She was elated because she felt fine and she knew that if she could keep going she would run the fastest first-time marathon ever by a woman.

By the time she came off the Queensboro Bridge, Grete, bored by the pace, had already left Vahlensieck and Brown behind; Jack was waiting there and called to her that Cooksey was only one hundred meters ahead. Grete had thought that she herself was in the lead. She began searching ahead for Cooksey, spotted her, and went after her. She moved up with Cooksey, who tried to fight her off with a surge, but Grete moved around her comfortably.

At about twenty-two miles Grete began to learn about the uniqueness of the marathon. "My thighs were getting so sore," she said, "and I got a stitch in my side. I almost stopped to walk—I wanted to walk so bad—but I thought I might not start up again if I did. I was sore all over, but I kept going to get it over as fast as possible."

As Grete worked her way through her discomfort, all of those years of pushing herself beyond the zones of comfort on the track and in practice came back to pay her dividends. She pushed into pain that women marathoners had until then avoided; she moved steadily toward the finish, on automatic pilot. Jack waited at the twenty-four-mile mark and yelled to her that she was under the world record, but in the noise and confusion she could not make out his words, although his presence further reassured her she could make it to the end.

Grete worked her way through Central Park, where she and Jack had walked so serenely for the past several days. Now, however, the park was bedlam. She remembers very little of it in detail: merely the rows of people and the mile markers—and the knowledge that the longer she could hold her pace, the sooner the torture would be over.

She ran through the finish line amidst groups of men, a slim, tired figure who would never again be able to run anywhere anonymously. She was surrounded by reporters, all trying to piece together a bit of additional information that would tell them who this mystery woman was, who the new world record holder was. They wanted to know why she was not smiling, why she was not happy about the new record, and in a few terse sentences Grete Waitz set what would become the Grete Waitz credo: "Maybe I am too tired. The race was very hard. We Norwegians are not as emotional as you. Maybe it is our long, dark winter. And I do not consider this a new world record. Only track races can be official records."

The distant, almost cold personality. And the contention that road racing wasn't really racing, that it didn't really count because the I.A.A.F. didn't accept it.

Grete had unwittingly pushed the women's running movement a huge step forward toward the 1984 Olympic Women's Marathon they wanted, but it would have been the last thing in the world she'd have considered. During that first marathon experience, Grete was supremely naive.

But time has a way of subtly changing people. For the Christmas holidays, *Runner's World* brought Grete and other members of her family to National Running Week, a week-long conglomeration of races, clinics, running-equipment shows, banquets, running-film festivals, relay runs, etc. Jack came across as the outgoing, the social one, while Grete stayed cautiously in the background, polite but reserved. She ran the *Runner's World* 5-Mile Invitational through a Los Altos lined with Christmas lights and won with ease; she and Jack had jogged the course the day before so she could get a feel for what would be needed to win.

The number of trips to the United States increased, and although their personal life did not change significantly (invitations to American races did make it possible for her to give up her teaching job), subtle changes did occur. Each visit to America saw a new record fall and her number of admirers rise. And each visit saw Grete smiling a bit more and becoming less defensive about the celebrity status that she was beginning to accept as part of her career—like her afternoon speedwork-sessions.

What she accomplished by breaking the world's best marathon mark for women three years in a row was more far-reaching than the changes it brought to her own life. Examining her training methods, other women runners saw what was needed to run truly world-class times. Waitz completely redefined the parameters for women runners; because of her, now a woman can run the marathon competitively. And in the same manner, but more subtly, she reaffirmed the right of women to attempt longer distances. It became increasingly difficult to argue against women running the marathon as she brought the record from 2:32:30 to 2:27:33 to 2:25:41.

Although Jack and Grete have taken pains to maintain the same kind of life they led before her accomplishments, it is difficult. As 1979 ended, a major newspaper poll in Norway declared her the name of the decade. She has been besieged with offers for endorsements but summarily turns down most of them. She refuses to cash in on her success. Her attitude frustrates Hans Skaset, the president of the Norwegian Amateur Athletic Federation, because under the Norwegian amateur rules, the N.A.A.F. would act as her agent, or go-between, and thereby gain some money for its coffers—money it could very well use. But Grete has her standards, and Skaset respects that. He respects what Grete has done so much, in fact, that he has become an advocate of making the women's marathon as widely accepted as the 1,500 meters. The major track championships now feature the women's marathon, and Skaset and others have finally prevailed at the Olympic level. "Grete has done the marathon in a way every man must accept," Skaset says. "She has done it the man's way. They have to shut up about a 2:25. There is nothing more to say."

Obviously, interest has been growing in the women's marathon. The fact that women from some twenty-five countries were competing in the Avon International Women's Marathon weighed heavily in favor of the decision to include it in the 1984 Olympic games. Hitherto, there being no I.A.A.F. sanction and no chance to win Olympic gold in the event, the Eastern European countries have ignored the women's marathon. Now that there is gold at stake, the Russian and Romanian and East German women runners will become a factor—at the moment they are very much an X-factor. Therefore no one—especially Grete—is making predictions for 1984. In naively demolishing the barriers against the marathon for women, Grete may have opened for herself a Pandora's box.

While the clock ticks toward the Los Angeles Olympic Games, Grete's career has undergone some changes. Following the 1980 New York City Marathon, she began taking additional coaching from someone other than her husband, namely, from Edvard Stolba, a refugee from Czechoslovakia. He radically changed her arm carriage and arm swing and intensified her speed workouts. She arrived in New York for the 1981 marathon with a new style (with which, at the January 4, 1981, running of the *Runner's World* 5-Mile Invitational, she set a new world record of 25.21.4). She also arrived with an injury. She had developed severe shin-splints and came to New York hoping for the best but expecting the worst.

"We talked it over," Jack says, "and it was entirely her decision to start the race. But I wanted her to drop out if it became too painful, and she agreed."

In the race, Julie Brown of California went out at a blistering pace and Grete ran with Allison Roe of New Zealand as they methodically reeled Julie in. But at the fifteen-mile mark, Grete knew it was not going to work. Just before the Queensboro Bridge Grete told Allison that the pain was too great and that she was going to drop out. Roe went on to break Grete's record by 12.2 seconds. Buoyed by her success, Roe began to race too frequently and raced herself into injuries that have hobbled her ever since.

Meanwhile, Grete worked to come back through her injuries and set her sights on the 1982 Boston Marathon, which she felt confident would allow her to recapture the world record.

At Boston, she went out at a five-and-a-half-minutes-per-mile pace, shooting for a 2:24. She was running comfortably through the first half of the race, despite heat that was wilting many of the competitors. She reached twenty miles in 1:50:30 and continued pounding up the hills. But her thighs were bothering her. She had never run the course before and had never run a course with downhills like Boston's. As she topped Heartbreak Hill, still well in the lead, still more than a minute under the world record, her thighs began to spasm with the beating they were taking from the pronounced downhills. At twenty-three miles she walked off the course, unable to continue. The next day she was hobbling around the Sheraton Hotel lobby as she and Jack prepared to take a flight to New York, and from there to Oslo.

"I never train running *downhill,*" she said. "No one I know trains to race *downhill.* We only train uphill." It is as though she is saying that running downhill isn't working hard enough and therefore should not be considered real training. "But," she said, smiling, "now I know that it can be as hard to run downhill as uphill. And next year when I come back to Boston, I will be ready."

Grete now goes so far as to admit that perhaps she is very good at road racing, and perhaps, yes, there is something to it. And perhaps, yes, she is a road racer, too; but first she is a track racer. Jack has given up his job as an accountant and works for Adidas, the German running-shoe company that Grete has been associated with for many years. His job forces him to travel quite a bit. "It is a good job," he admits. "But the travel. . . . I do not get as much time to spend with Grete as I would like. In that way it is hard."

She returned to New York in 1982 to run a winning time of 2:27:14, effectively announcing an end to her injuries. Their battle against the encroaching world continues, but it seems as though they will always keep the upper hand. The celebrity the world wants to force upon Grete will not overcome her aversion to going out in public, her penchant for the quiet life, and her habit of going to bed at 9:00 P.M. She and Jack are not likely to embrace the jet-setter's existence.

And in the meantime, the women's running movement coasts along without Grete standing at their fore like a Joan of Arc. She is used and referred to, and she supports the idea of women being able to run the 5,000, 10,000, and the marathon. But although she smiles more frequently now, travels more frequently, and continues to improve between injuries, Grete has not become a feminist firebrand. She has not been coaxed into the all-women marathons that Avon has promoted, and she likely will not be. When she lines up at the start of the women's Olympic Marathon in Los Angeles in the summer of 1984, she will be thirty years old, the age many experts regard as the ideal age, when a blend of talent, speed, endurance, and "smarts" comes together. Whether she will be able to bring it all together on that specific day against what will certainly be the most formidable field she has ever faced, remains to be seen. It is something the women's running movement has eagerly anticipated for years; it is something Grete Waitz never expected in 1978 when she asked for a plane ticket to bring her husband along to New York so they could see The Big Apple once in their lives.

Outstanding as a runner for Oregon, Alberto Salazar seemed a natural marathon champ.

(COURTESY WARREN MORGAN PHOTOGRAPHY)

15.

ALBERTO SALAZAR:
The Eternal Rookie

On October 25, 1981, at the seventeenth mile of the New York City Marathon, Alberto Salazar, running in his second marathon, threw in a 4:33 mile on a slight downhill in an attempt to break any remaining contact with Jose Gomez of Mexico, the last of the runners who'd composed the lead group. The large group of runners had dropped off one by one, dwindling under a ferocious pace on a course that was said to be too atrocious to allow a world record. The road over which the marathon wound featured potholes and sewer covers, ripples in the asphalt and awful grating over bridges, and the sharp turns that slow runners. But Alberto Salazar of Eugene, Oregon, by way of New England by way of Havana, Cuba, was proving the experts wrong. He was on a pace to break the twelve-year-old world record set by Australia's Derek Clayton.

Characteristically, his eyes were half-closed in relaxed concentration, his stride low to the ground and shuffling, the kind of ground-eating style that Clayton had. Alberto Salazar's style was being pasted together by dogged determination. As he ran through Central Park, it was easy to see the weariness and the pain—and the determination.

Following two disastrous years of live coverage of the marathon by independent television producers, the 1981 running of the then-largest marathon in the world was being covered live by ABC-TV, on a grand scale. The media hype in New York City that weekend was thick enough to stop a runaway tractor trailer.

It was the first time a non-Olympic marathon was being covered live by American network television. Now, besides the more than a million people who lined the course, eleven million people across the country were getting an even better view of the proceedings as Salazar methodically ran down the miles toward the finish line on the southwest corner of Central Park, in front of Tavern on the Green Restaurant.

The year before, Alberto Salazar had entered the New York City Marathon as his first-ever marathon. On his entry form he had put a "2:10" in the space for his estimated finishing time. If he ran a 2:10, it would be the fastest debut marathon ever. But those who knew Salazar had always predicted that the marathon would be his event, and it was a belief he'd harbored himself for many years. So when he ran a 2:09:41, breaking Bill Rodgers's string of four straight New York City Marathon wins, there was a close knot of people (including his former and current coaches) who were almost smugly happy, and certainly not very surprised.

When 1981 rolled around, and it was again time to fill out the application, Alberto Salazar confided to a friend that he'd run conservatively the year before and that he was now in better shape. He figured he could run one minute and forty seconds faster. That would make a 2:08:01, well under Derek Clayton's almost venerable world record.

Alberto Salazar had indeed improved during the previous year. He had blitzed the January running of the *Runner's World* 5-Mile Invitation road race in Los Altos, California. After predicting that he'd break twenty-two minutes, he came very close with a 22:04. Then in late summer he'd gone to Falmouth on Cape Cod (where he'd come close to death in 1978 by running himself into heat prostration and a 106-degree body temperature) and created a new course record, completely dominating the event. He'd also set a new indoor American 5,000-meter record and won the Athletic Congress (T.A.C.) 10,000-meter race, and then had run a personal best in the 10,000-meter at the World Cup by unleashing a 27:40.

Moreover, several weeks before the New York City Marathon, he'd completely destroyed his personal record on a course back in Eugene that he used as a test meter for his conditioning, so the prediction was further validated in his mind when he lined up with 14,495 other runners on the Staten Island side of the Verazzano-Narrows Bridge.

As he came out of Central Park and up Central Park South, on his way to the little turn that would take him back into the park for the final quarter-mile of the race, Salazar's body reflected his effort to push himself along at a pace that would bring him in under Clayton's 2:08:34.

His legs were tightening up and his shoulders had turned inward just a mite more than usual; he was using his arms more, and his brow was furrowed. It was a portion of the race Salazar relishes: after the competiton has been vanquished and he's in territory only he dares to enter.

He had, in a mere two marathons, carved a place for himself at the very front of the world's massive marathoning ranks. The event had gone from being regarded as a freak show to the premier event in a running movement that showed every sign of steadily growing into a world mania. People were running the roads and identifying with the heroes who were running the roads the best.

And Salazar was proving that he was absolutely, positively, indubitably the best in the world. "My training has never been geared specifically to the marathon because I really don't see much difference between training for 10,000 meters and the marathon," he explains. "I'll continue to train more for the track than the road because I don't want to be just a road runner. I believe that if you train for the track you can always run the roads at a fairly high level, but I don't think you can train exclusively for the roads and do well on the track. I could easily just train for the roads and be the top-ranked guy, but that's not what I want. I want to become an overall runner who can run any distance and run it well."

On this day in October, with the autumn leaves turned bright colors and on their way to brown, Alberto Salazar was, whether he knew it or not, whether he liked it or not, burying his considerable track accomplishments. More people were watching him along the New York City Marathon route than had watched him in person in every track event he'd run in the last five years combined. His name on that day was becoming a household word to the average runner.

And his prediction of his performance? What of that?

It marked a departure from the demeanor of the road racers who'd gone before him. Take Bill Rodgers. His shy, stumbling attitude to questions of how he expected to do in a race had always been somewhat self-effacing: "I'll be there, that's for sure. I hope to run with the leaders and then we'll have to see how it goes around the twenty-mile point." Right.

In the running world, Alberto Salazar's self-confidence most resembled Derek Clayton's. But Clayton, when he told promoters before Antwerp that he felt he was going to unleash a record performance, hadn't predicted it months in advance. Alberto Salazar was taking Derek Clayton one step further in more than his marathon speed per mile. It was not surprising, then, that his brazen attitude was compared to the young Cassius Clay's. A prediction based upon extreme self-confidence is the end result of a certain amount of training mixed with a certain amount of talent, the effort being expended to get a predictable result. It is not unlike a recipe that consistently creates grandma's prize-winning chocolate-chip cookies. If I do this and this and this, and my times are these and these and these, it seems only logical to me that my time will be . . . a world record.

The result was almost as Alberto had predicted. He was a little off, as he had been in January in Los Altos. Less than one-tenth of one percent one way or the other can be overlooked, however, especially when you break the world record by a good twenty-one seconds. Alberto crossed the finish line in Central Park in 2:08:13 and rewrote the road-racing record books. He also created for himself a not necesarily enviable persona as the guy who told you so.

To many who had run the distance before him, his supreme confidence in himself came across as supreme cockiness, a cockiness the more infuriating because, by doing what he'd done after having predicting it, he'd made himself seemingly invincible in the marathon—a person, perhaps the first in history, to approach the distance without fear or respect. In doing that, he raised himself—perhaps in reality, perhaps only through his own well-planned marketing of the image (marketing was his major in college)—to a level well beyond anyone else in the world.

In an interview with Salazar following the race, Frank Shorter had this exchange with him:

Shorter: "After your really fast stretch, from fifteen to nineteen, you settled down with a 5:02 mile. I think that's really significant because it means your anaerobic threshold is way below five minutes. You were *recovering* at five-minute pace at that point, right?"

Salazar: "Yeah, it felt easy."

He studiously made feints after the race to avoid the press, to avoid publicity: as though to pull a Greta Garbo, to add to his persona, to place himself beyond anyone else. Whereas Bill Rodgers after finishing a marathon stood around talking for hours with reporters and fans, Salazar made serious moves to avoid talking to anyone.

He didn't want to be bothered with *that*. He made himself come across as a very intense, private person who wanted to be left alone, someone who ran world records, setting the marathoning scene on its ear, just because he loved to run against himself to see how well he could compete with his idea of himself.

Was he predicting his times to give himself a person worthy of competing with him?

There was a certain duplicity or duality in Salazar, however.

If he merely wanted to run the best he could (which was obviously the best in the world) and didn't want any of the attendant hoopla, why didn't he stay home in Eugene and run in the Nike/O.T.C. (Oregon Track Club) Marathon in September? The course was much better, it was the Olympic trials course for 1972 and 1976 in fact, and the place was a lot more sane and serene than New York City. There were at least a hundred marathons with better courses than New York. If you're trying to avoid the press, the people, and all the attendant nonsense, why run in a race with 13,360 finishers, a television audience of nearly twelve million people, and somewhere between one and two million people along the route?

And about his predictions and his seeming attitude problem: where did the cockiness begin and the self-assurance and the pride in himself start? And where did it end?

Who, in fact, was Alberto Salazar? And just how untouchable was he, anyway?

To begin to learn about Alberto, one must go back a generation to Jose. Or, if one is to believe Jose, one must go back many generations, because what Alberto is, what Alberto has done, is a combination of his genes, his upbringing, and God's will.

Jose Salazar lived in Cuba. He went to college with Fidel Castro and he got on well with the charismatic law student. Young Salazar and young Castro were activists while they were in college in the 1950s; they spoke out and rallied against Fulgencio Batista, the reigning dictator. When the revolution came in the late 1950s, Salazar senior was in the thick of it.

When the Castro forces managed to overthrow Batista in 1959, Jose was put in charge of reviewing Cuba's agreements with other nations. Salazar wanted France to pay Cuba the several million dollars it owed, but Che Guevara was getting arms from France and didn't want that arrangement messed up by a gung-ho patriot. The two had it out.

To avoid revolution within the revolution, Castro moved Jose Salazar to a new job in charge of construction projects aimed at building the tourist trade. In an interview with Marta Salazar, Jose's wife and Alberto's mother, Kenny Moore of *Sports Illustrated* learned that the period was a blissful one. "Jose was so happy then," she said, "doing his dream, working for the government with all the help and money he needed; he was having a grand time."

But the revolution was taking turns that its backers had not expected. "The rest of·us looked around at the way things were going," Mrs. Salazar continued. "Parents were to have no say in their children's education. It was to be government indoctrination. Castro expelled the priests and nuns who had educated generations of Cubans."

Jose's realization of the changes that were going on within the government came to a head while he was building a community housing development. He wanted to build a church, as was traditional in a village, but Che Guevara wanted the village built without a church. Jose was incensed and let it be known. A serious mistake: in a state sliding inexorably toward Marxist dictatorship, a buttoned lip is the first step to survival.

The word was instantly out that Jose Salazar was unhappy with the way things were going, and within two hours the police were knocking on his door. Luckily, his friends had more sense than Jose had, and they'd already spirited him away. He was already on the way to Miami.

He immediately began working on getting Marta and the children out. She managed to leave with her four children after a heartstopping pass through the police at the airport; Jose moved the family to Connecticut following the diastrous Bay of Pigs.

At the time of the flight from Cuba, Alberto was two years old. As a result, much of what his family had gone through was lost on him. He was a kid growing up in Connecticut and later in Wayland, Massachusetts, and his father's rantings and ravings about Cuba seemed to have little to do with him. There were more important things for a young guy with his whole life ahead of him.

Alberto had two older brothers, Richard and Jose. The eldest child was a girl, Maria Cristina, and there is a younger brother, Fernando, who was born in the United States.

As a youngster, Alberto was noted for his tendency toward rages and revenge. His mother claims it comes from her side of the family, which is of Basque descent; at a young age she, too, was inclined to rage.

From his father's side of the family, Alberto inherited the Salazar pride.

Several of the boys developed a love of running on their own. Richard was quite good at it, and constantly challenged Alberto, who was four years younger, to compete with him on the same level. Richard obviously had the advantage, but Alberto was tenacious enough to want to challenge him occasionally, which may account for his rapid development as a runner. He simply loved running. Because of his inherent talent, and because of the challenges his older brother constantly threw at him, Alberto was far superior as a runner to kids his own age. His talent stuck out like a sore thumb. In order to play tag with him, the other kids had to rely on relay teams.

Richard continued to be an influence through high school, where he ran extremely well. Richard eventually went on to the Naval Academy (where he ran a 4:06 mile) and from there to the cockpit of an F-14. It was Richard who relayed to Alberto tales of the fabled land of Track Town, USA—Eugene, Oregon. Alberto sat on the edge of his chair as Richard told him stories of the University of Oregon runners, of Hayward Field, of coaches Bill Bowerman and Bill Dellinger, and of the performances of superstar Steve Prefontaine.

Alberto's determination to be as good or better than his brother, and his pride to make himself better each day than he'd been the day before, had its effect. His high school coach, who was very sensitive to his talent, wrote a few of the chapters in Alberto's future by allowing him to train with the big guys. In this case, the big guys were members of the then potent Greater Boston Track Club, under the direction of the enigmatic Billy Squires.

Don Benedetti, his high school coach, and Bill Squires, his after-school coach, together instilled in Alberto the philosophy that a runner is a piece of work that should function and grow over a long period of time. Instead of egging him on to burn out for the greater glory of the high school, they urged him to take the long-range approach to his running, a philosophy common in England (which accounts for runners like Seb Coe reaching their peak when they are mature enough to make maximum use of it) but sadly lacking in the United States school systems. Alberto Salazar still talks in terms of his long-range goals and is extremely patient with himself in that regard—an apparent paradox, considering his sometimes fiery temperament.

When he trained with the G.B.T.C., he had the advantages of training with the likes of Bill Rodgers and Dick Mahoney. The young Alberto was all arms and legs, much like a young colt, but when he got everything rolling together, things worked pretty well. The older guys began calling him "the rookie," a name that sticks with him even today, although others who've seen him train have at various times called him either "the horse" or "the mule" because of his tremendous capacity for hard work and for racking up mileage.

Fortunately, Squires and, later, University of Oregon coach Bill Dellinger worked steadily to keep Alberto's mileage within a reasonable and humane range. If it were up to Alberto, he'd be out running two-hundred-mile weeks and would end up running himself into the ground—both because he loves to run and because he is always looking for that little edge over "the big guys."

When it came time to go to college, Alberto had his choice. He had been an excellent student through high school, and therefore academically secure. But he wanted to build on the accomplishments he'd already made in running (he'd run 14:04 for 5,000 meters and had made the U.S. International Cross-Country Junior Team), so he chose Bill Dellinger and Oregon.

It is extremely fortunate that Bill Dellinger was the coach at Oregon, because Alberto's early collegiate career on the track and cross-country courses there were less than his high school performances had promised. Dellinger knew Alberto's time would come, once everything was put properly into place. The disappointments were dulled somewhat by Alberto's relationship with his roommate, Rudy Chapa, an extremely talented runner. In some ways they had much in common and in other ways, little in common; they seemed to get along beautifully.

Both possessed fiery temperaments and tended toward noisy displays to make their point. But when they ran together, they were like day and night. Chapa was smooth and his running seemingly effortless; he was compact, a running artist. Salazar, on the other hand, was an awkward-seeming runner who appeared to run more on willpower than on style. Chapa was fast and smooth and, at the shorter of the long distances, he was exquisite (in 1979 he would set the American record of 7:37.7 for 3,000 meters). He was also relaxed about his running and took it as a blessing instead of a sacred crusade. Alberto on the other hand was intense about his running, almost obsessed by it. His tenacity seemed to make him perfectly suited for the longer events. Everyone who was close to him knew that the marathon, the final test of tenacity, would ultimately be Alberto's distance. In their freshman year in college, Salazar informed Chapa that someday he'd hold the world record in the marathon. Both Billy Squires and Bill Dellinger believed that Alberto's accomplishments were merely stepping stones to the marathon.

Alberto's career with coaches has been a constant give-and-take: the coaches trying to convince him to change this or that in

order to improve, Salazar resisting, then accepting, and finally
making the change with an almost frightening determination and
obsession.

Bill Dellinger says: "One of the problems with coaching Al
then was convincing him he didn't have to run five hundred
miles per week."

The relationship that developed between Dellinger and Salazar over their years together smoothed out much of the resis-
tance—primarily because behind all his fire and emotion, Alberto
is the calculating, careful, intelligent captain of his own career,
and he's seen that Dellinger's advice produces the desired results.

In 1977 Alberto and the Oregon cross-country team won the
1977 N.C.A.A. championships, but his ninth-place finish was
personally disappointing to him.

Two years later Salazar and Chapa headed a cross-country
team that they thought would sweep all before them when they
went to the N.C.A.A. races. What actually happened, however,
was that it provided an opportunity for the omnipresent Jose Salazar to teach his son—and the rest of the team—a valuable lesson. The championships were held at Lehigh University in Bethlehem, Pennsylvania. Jose drove a group of the Salazars down
from Massachusetts to see his son perform. There was a point to
be made by the Oregon team: the team of the University of Texas
at El Paso featured a brace of foreign runners, and Oregon was
eager to best them and thereby make a statement that a championship between American colleges and universities should feature only American runners competing against American runners.

The team was confident of making its point quite well. Alberto
had won the individual title in 1978, and now he had a personal
battle within the race: he wanted to make a point by beating
Henry Rono of Kenya, who was running for Washington State
University. There was a great deal of emotion and pride rolled
up into the race.

But after a hard-fought battle, Alberto finished second to
Rono, and the team finished second overall. They had failed to
make their point, and they had just plain . . . failed. They hung
their heads, picked up their equipment, and headed back to their
hotel. The last place in the world they wanted to be was at the

awards ceremony that would be taking place in an hour. But they hadn't counted on Jose Salazar. *He* was at the ceremony, waiting to see his son receive his second-place award.

"My father had been waiting around for the trophy presentation," Alberto remembers, "until it occurred to him we were back at the hotel. He drove back there and began ranting and raving about how we owed it to ourselves to be champions and accept whatever we had coming to us—even if it was second place. Some of the guys on the team were thinking, 'Who *is* this guy?' because he really was furious at our attitude. We had gotten beat by a better team, but we weren't willing to accept it. He felt we had an obligation to accept the trophy and that everyone on the team had reason to hold his head up like a champion. I didn't see his point at the time, but of course he was right."

As the years progressed, Alberto's view of life has come around more and more to his father's. His perspective merely needed some chance to develop and mature on its own and then needed Jose's remarkable kind of encouragement.

In 1980, Alberto concentrated much of his energies on training for the Olympic Trials—but the trials didn't lead to Moscow. He didn't let all of that high-quality training go to waste, of course. Instead he took it to New York in October. He and Bill Dellinger felt it was time for him to step up to the marathon. Alberto considered the event to be just another race, a race that he was physically and emotionally built for. He approached the marathon as though he owned it but had been too busy to claim it already.

The fact that he won his first-ever marathon in a record time for a debut at that distance speaks for itself. It is a moot point as to whether or not he'd have been given more competition in the final miles had Bill Rodgers and Dick Beardsley not fallen in a tangle of arms and legs at the fourteen-mile point. As it was, Beardsley, once he was on his feet again, worked his way up to the leaders and ultimately finished in ninth place, while Rodgers finished in fifth. These circumstances do not at all change the fact that Alberto Salazar had already announced that he was ready to claim his throne as king of the marathon. The day before the race he was asked at the press conference about his claim that he'd run the race in 2:09 (this was subsequent to his writing "2:10" on the entry form). "A lot of people have been playing up

my supposedly saying I could run 2:09," he said. "I'd like to rec-
tify that. All I want is to be competitve and to win. Whatever
time I run will be fine." He elaborated on it a few minutes later:
"If someone else runs 2:10 tomorrow, I think I will, too." Of
course, he did break 2:10.

His program for 1981 was much more ambitious, and he
seemed to be right on target for following Bill Dellinger's plan,
which called for him never to lose a marathon.

His application for New York went in with "2:08" on it, and
he managed to further stir up controversy by being so brash as to
announce his intentions. He later stated that he wasn't sure he
should have made his prediction, especially since it put added
pressure on him. He ran 2:08:13, breaking the twelve-year-old
record of Derek Clayton, and seemed to place himself on a level
over and above other marathoners. "When someone asks Alberto something, he can only give an honest answer," Bill Dellinger has said. "I know it might sound at times like he's brag-
ging, but he's not. Really, he's one of the most modest athletes
I've ever been associated with. The problem is that his honesty
sometimes overshadows his modesty."

In the minds of many, Alberto Salazar was the next genetic
step in marathoning, and all that was left now was to fight it out
to see who would take second place when he announced he
would enter a race.

After his New York hat trick, Alberto made a feint of not
wanting to be interviewed. He returned to Oregon. Then, on November 5, an interview was set up between Alberto and Derek
Clayton and Bob Anderson, editor and publisher of *Runner's
World.*

Much of the interview centered on the strategy and effort of
the world-record performance and his training leading up to that
effort. One question, however, concerned Boston:

Runner's World: "Do you have plans to run Boston?"

Alberto Salazar: "At some time. I'm not sure about this year.
Now that I have the record I just don't see the need to have to
run another one. It's not going to matter when I peak around
twenty-eight whether or not I ran Boston this year or not. But it
may matter if every year I start running too many marathons and
I start neglecting my track speed. I think just one or two a year

and concentrate on my track [and] then ultimately I'm going to run my best marathon."

In December Alberto married Molly Morton, a former Oregon distance runner. They vacationed in the Bahamas.

With spring, the running world's attention turned to the Boston Marathon, as it always does, and, despite his indication that Boston was something that could, and probably should, wait, Alberto Salazar's name began popping up in connection with it. It seemed impossible, a month in advance, to get the field pinned down—much less to get Alberto pinned down. The word was that he was bored and that he had decided to run Boston. And word filtered out of Eugene that he was in the best shape of his life.

Following New York, speculation was rife that if he would run the same effort in Boston that he ran in New York, he'd blow the marathon record down into the low 2:07 range; the experts believe that Boston is about ninety seconds faster than New York.

As the Boston Marathon grew closer, Alberto characteristically kept a very low profile, and, although people knew he was in town, they were sure no one would know whether or not he was running until he lined up. The talk was already circulating that if he lined up, everyone else had better move his expectations down one big notch, because first place was already spoken for.

But not everyone was accepting Alberto Salazar as the undisputed king of the hill. There was a revolution brewing. Ironically, Billy Squires, who had coached Salazar while he was still in high school, had changed camps. He was now coach of the New Balance Track Club, a group of athletes who marketed New Balance running shoes by wearing them in races and giving them exposure by winning. When Squires had been lured over to their side, he'd taken some of his Greater Boston Track Club talent with him and had gotten other promising runners from outside the club besides. Among the talented runners in the group was Dick Beardsley, one of America's foremost marathoners, a man who ran class marathons as often and easily as some people eat ice-cream cones. In mid-1981 his performance of 2:09:36 in the Grandma's Marathon put him second on America's list of top marathoners.

Hailing from the cold fastness of Minneapolis, Beardsley is the opposite of Salazar. Whereas it is all a reporter can do to search Salazar out before—or after—a race in hopes of getting a quote, Beardsley is glib, quotable, seemingly light-hearted, and cooperative. Whereas Alberto runs America's largest marathon and expects to dictate when and if anyone will talk to him about it, Dick Beardsley seems genuinely surprised that someone wants to talk with him.

To prepare for Boston, Beardsley—anticipating the worst, i.e., a hot day in New England—had left Minnesota months before to train in Atlanta so as to get acclimated to the heat. He'd spent the week leading up to the marathon with Bill Squires discussing strategy for the race—how to run the course, how to handle the heat, and a thousand and one details.

For inexplicable reasons, when the marathon came, it was as though it were a duel between Salazar and Beardsley. The press was quoting odds that Beardsley and Rodgers were the only ones who would be factors *if* Alberto Salazar ran the race; but no one had known for sure that Alberto would run until a few days before—and then it was not entirely certain. This fact negated statements that Beardsley had been training for months specifically to beat Alberto. If no one knew for sure that Alberto would run, it would have been impossible—and in any case unwise—for Beardsley to customize his training specifically to counter Alberto's presence.

The entire scene leading up to the marathon was a rumormonger's playground, made even more appetizing by all the rumors about what was going to happen to the Boston Marathon now that seventy-seven-year-old Will Cloney had reputedly lost touch with reality. After years of resisting change in the hallowed traditions of Boston, Cloney had tried to push the event into the modern era and in the process had let himself be bilked by an allegedly crooked lawyer into signing over the marathon rights lock, stock, and porkbarrel. Would the Boston Marathon be catapulted into crass commercialism? The Prudential Center, a low-key sponsor for seventeen years, was pulling out for 1982 and wouldn't even allow the race to finish in front of their landmark building in downtown Boston. The new "owners" of the marathon didn't care. They claimed they could get mega-sponsors. Anyway, they wanted to change the time-honored course and to hold the race on Sunday for ease of network TV broadcasting instead of on the traditional Patriot's Day Monday (which put local churches into a furor).

The weekend leading up to the race was a witches' brew of slander, insinuation, hand-wringing, protests—and heat.

The word was that Alberto Salazar *was* running, and that he *was* planning to cash in on that ninety-second advantage that the Boston course had over New York to break his own record and knock it down into the 2:07 range. But the heat, the heat! Less than two weeks before, there'd been a traffic-stopping snowstorm, and now the day of the race dawned with heat, and plenty of it. Ideas of records went up like so much hot air as all of the rumors festered in the seventy-degree temperatures and high humidity. The race promised to be a race of attrition, instead of competition, as the high-noon shoot-out approached.

When the shot was fired in Hopkinton (replete with signs of WE WANT BOSTON '83 TO START HERE!), the rumors took a backseat to the runners.

Salazar had entered a 10-K track race in Eugene nine days before Boston so he could test himself. There he had run an excellent 27:30, losing by less than a single full step to Henry Rono. He was obviously in shape for his third marathon and his first Boston.

The 1982 race was also Beardsley's first Boston. He had won the London Marathon and his 2:09 at the Grandma's Marathon indicated to him that he was ready for the Big Race. Moreover, a hip injury, the result of an attack by a pack of dogs, had healed nicely. And Beardsley had gotten in two months' good training in Atlanta.

The leaders sprinted out of Hopkinton to get away from the masses of runners behind them. The lead pack stuck together tenaciously over the first few miles as the heat and the pace both increased.

Going into the race, Salazar had a knotted hamstring. He had had it worked on some days before by Bill Rodgers's masseuse. The hamstring worried him; there was the constant threat that it might weaken, but it held up throughout the race.

Salazar later complained about the tactics used by several of the runners in the early miles. "During the first ten miles, Ron Tabb and this Dean Matthews guy were constantly pushing the pace," he claims. "When it comes to running marathons, they're the biggest bunch of jerks I've seen. They were surging, but they were stupid because they accomplished absolutely nothing except they destroyed their own rhythm."

This annoyance vanished past the halfway point, however, as the pace took its toll. The leaders passed the midway point in 1:03:57. The lead group had come down to Salazar, Beardsley, Ed Mendoza, and Bill Rodgers. Past the halfway mark, it was fairly plain that Salazar and Beardsley were working on each other.

Salazar had run repeat miles in training with Bill Rodgers while Rodgers had trained for the 1975 Boston Marathon, in which he set a new American record of 2:09:55. Now it was Salazar, the kid grown into manhood, who took command of the session. Salazar and Beardsley eventually dropped the competition (Rodgers fell off the pace at sixteen miles and Mendoza eventually dropped out), and the race came down to the expected duel.

The heat was making a shambles of the rest of the field. Up front, Beardsley was taking sips of water everywhere he could, sipping and dumping the rest of it over his head to keep himself cooled. Alberto, on the other hand, was taking drinks of water sparingly, trying to keep his concentration riveted on the race. By the twenty-mile mark, their pace was almost suicidal. They continued to exchange the lead. There were more than one million people along the route enjoying the warm weather, rubbing suntan lotion on themselves and drinking copious amounts of beer.

Salazar and Beardsley were so evenly matched that neither could make an effective break from the other. They went through Kenmore Square and had less than a mile to go, but now the complexion of the race changed. Although Salazar's hamstring knot was ever-present, it had not acted up; Beardsley, on the other hand, developed a hamstring cramp, and it proved enough of a sudden impediment to allow Salazar to take advantage and move ahead. As they headed toward the right turn onto Hereford Street, however, the winter that had ravaged the

Northeast came to Beardsley's aid: he stepped into a pothole, and the change of his legs' attack on the road surface pulled out the cramp, just enough to let him accelerate again and begin closing on Salazar.

As Salazar went up Hereford Street, he took furtive glances over his shoulder to see where Beardsley was. Beardsley was, in fact, making up ground very rapidly. He had almost closed on Salazar as they took the left turn onto the road fronting the Prudential Center, where a motorcycle policeman escorting Alberto forced Beardsley to the outside. He cleared the policeman and tried to sprint after Salazar but Salazar, his distress mounting, saw it coming. Tired and extremely dehydrated, Alberto exhibited the tenaciousness and pride that has allowed him to fight his way to his exalted level. Uncharacteristically, he picked up his knees and surged toward the finish line. Beardsley did not have the speed to catch him.

Salazar fell forward across the finish line, to be caught and surrounded by officials and police, while Beardsley ran through the line a mere two seconds behind him, his momentum carrying him past Salazar and through the dense crowd.

Salazar was rushed into the underground garage area of the Pru, where each year the emergency medical units are set up like a field hospital. He was extremely dehydrated and was immediately covered so as to bring his body temperature up from its eighty-eight-degree level; he also received two simultaneous intravenous infusions to replace the more than one gallon of body fluids he had lost. He was kept on the cot for nearly an hour. According to his wife Molly, Salazar said to her that he'd never run a marathon again. "But, of course," she adds, "he always says that right after he finishes." His father Jose tries to put the entire experience into perspective: "People must realize that when you get to the top, there's a great price you must pay."

While Alberto recovered, Dick Beardsley was upstairs in the press room giving a conference that lasted nearly an hour and a half, characterized by good humor and high spirits. Yes, he was very disappointed to have lost, especially by only two seconds. "What does it take to win around here?" he asked good-naturedly.

Despite the unfavorable conditions, both Salazar and Beardsley had gone under 2:09, the first time in history two finishers had broken 2:09 in the same marathon. Alberto's time was 2:08:51, Beardsley's 2:08:53. Rodgers finished fourth in the race he'd won four times.

"Dick Beardsley is one of the toughest runners I've ever competed against," Salazar admitted. "He really made me hurt."

Some days later, in a post-race interview conducted with the two runners independently, Alberto was his usual confident self. He was recovered from the experience, he was training with the sprinters at the University of Oregon in an attempt to gain more legspeed so that when the 10-K (or, God forbid, the marathon!) comes down to the final steps, he'll be ready to turn on the afterburners.

"I feel I put a greater effort into Boston than into my world record," he said. "Mentally, I gained more from running Boston than New York because there I've always been by myself at the end. Here, Beardsley pushed me the whole way and that's good for me, because when I run the Olympics, somebody is going to be with me the entire way. It was good to get that experience of going to the wire with somebody. If Beardsley hadn't pushed me, I think I would have won in 2:10. I hope Beardsley does run New York again. I'm going to teach him a lesson. I don't just want to beat him; I want to make him die with six miles to go."

The fact that Dick Beardsley not only stayed with Alberto Salazar at Boston but in fact almost took him, removed some of the mystique from Alberto's carefully planned scheme to move to the top spot in long-distance running and stay there, on a level occupied only by himself. Boston even went so far as to persuade Alberto that the marathon may be a unique event after all and not just another race, as he'd considered it all these years. Faced with the knot in his hamstring at the starting line, he was conscious of it all the way. When the race started, he became aware that it might turn out to be his Achilles heel. "The only thing I can remember thinking about during the first few miles was something Rodgers had said," he indicated after the race. "I always say that the marathon is just another race to me—and it is—but Billy insists that someday the marathon will humble me.

I thought about that in the first four miles: 'Could this be the race that gets me?' I could feel the knot in my hamstring and I started to think, 'Gee, this must be what Rodgers is talking about.' Here my leg was hurting and I still had twenty-two miles to go."

(Author's note: Alberto Salazar returned to New York in October 1982 to win with a 2:09:29. He had effectively run each and every of his four marathons under 2:10, a record that is unique.)

Postscript

Bill Rodgers dropped out of the 1977 Boston Marathon at the eighteen-mile point. It was a hot day and a fast pace. "The marathon," he wrote shortly afterwards, "can humble you." More than one hundred thousand marathon veterans know what he means. Every weekend, other marathoners are learning what he means. Everyone ultimately learns.

Suggestions for Further Reading

A book as specialized as this offers the author an opportunity to go on a research binge that turns the spare bedroom into a seeming confusion of books, tapes, articles, notes, and discarded drafts. In the end, it means gathering together between two covers an awesome mass of information. It also offers a pleasurable education in what has gone before. I'd like to share with readers some sources that will provide interesting reading should they wish to pursue further the subject of marathon running and marathoners.

On the subject of the Olympic Games, three excellent books are the entertaining *History of the Olympics* (Alfred A. Knopf, 1975) by Dick Schaap, *The Olympic Games* (Collier Books) edited by Lord Killanin and John Rodda, and John Lucas's *The Modern Olympic Games*.

Also of interest, and interesting reading, are *On the Road: The Marathon* (Crown, 1978) by Jim Shapiro, *The Complete Marathoner* (Runner's World Books, 1982 edition), *Challenge of the Marathon* (Stanley Paul, London, 1981) by Cliff Temple, *The Marathoners* (Putnam, 1980) by Hal Higdon, *Marathoning* (Simon and Schuster, 1980, 1982) by Bill Rodgers, *Running to the Top* (Anderson World) by Derek Clayton, *Marathon* (The New England Press, 1981) by Clarence DeMar, *Boston: America's Oldest Marathon* (Anderson World, 1980) edited by Ray Hosler, *The Boston Marathon* (Macmillan, 1977) by Joe Falls, *Just Call Me Jock* (Waterford, 1982) by Jock Semple with John J. Kelley and Tom Murphy, and the ultimate marathon fan's book, *The Marathon Footrace* (Charles C. Thomas, 1979) by David E. Martin and Roger W.H. Gynn. An excellent article is "The Frank Shorter Story" (*Runner's World Magazine,* 1972) by John Parker, whose running novel—*Once a Runner*—perhaps better than any other details the dedication needed to be a national- and world-class athlete.

Then, too, it is special fun to read research that is especially well written, and running is blessed with four outstanding writers who regularly chronicle the sport: Amby Burfoot and Bob Wischnia of *Runner's World* and Kenny Moore of *Sports Illustrated,* and Hal Higdom.

I wish to thank two very special men who, through conversations and correspondence, shared their memories of those days when marathoning was much simpler: Johnny "Jock" Semple and John Kelley the Elder, Mr. Boston Marathon.

And finally, to Marty Post, who reviewed and kept the manuscript on track from the statistical standpoint, a special thanks.

Richard Benyo went to a high school that was too small to support a track team, then ran on a Pennsylvania college cross-country team that functioned on a travel budget of less than five hundred dollars a season. He abandoned his running career when he began his journalistic one, at age twenty-two, on a small-town evening newspaper. From there Benyo moved to Alexandria, Virginia, to become editor of *Stock Car Racing* magazine, where he won prizes for his writing and earned a reputation for keeping up with the big guys when it came to eating Southern style. He reached his thirtieth birthday weighing 207 pounds.

The death of a close friend from a heart attack shook him up enough to make him change his life: he became managing editor of *Runner's World* magazine, and adopted a running program to bring his weight under control. Benyo completed his first marathon just nine months after starting running again. In 1978 alone, he ran seven marathons and competed in three 50-mile events. He's run more than twenty marathons since, breaking three hours several times. He continues to fight the battle of the bulge, trying to bring his weight down to under 160 pounds for his next marathon while still consuming his share of pizza, pastries, and beer.

Benyo is the author of several books, including *Superspeedway* (1977), considered the definitive work on Southern stock car racing, and *Return to Running* (1978), the way back as he experienced it.

He lives in Palo Alto, California, with his collection of rock 'n' roll oldies and three pythons.